The Meaning
of the Book of Job
and
Other Biblical Studies

Essays on the Literature and Religion
of the Hebrew Bible

The Meaning
of the Book of Job
and
Other Biblical Studies

*Essays on the Literature and Religion
of the Hebrew Bible*

by
Matitiahu Tsevat

Ktav Publishing House, Inc.
New York

Institute for Jewish Studies
Dallas, Texas

Library of Congress Cataloging in Publication Data

Tsevat, Matitiahu.
  The meaning of the Book of Job and other Biblical
studies.

  Includes bibliographical references and index.
    1. Bible. O. T.—Criticism, interpretation, etc.—
Collected works. I. Title.
BS1171.2.T78   221.6   80—18801
ISBN 0—87068—714—X

MANUFACTURED IN THE UNITED STATES OF AMERICA

Contents

Prefatory Note

Nine articles of this collection were previously published in scholarly journals and jubilee volumes, seven in English and two in Hebrew. Two others appear here for the first time. All present their arguments in a way accessible to the general reader; technical details are contained in the notes. All have been brought up to date in various degrees regarding research and bibliography; some have been reworked extensively. The Hebrew articles have been much expanded in the process of translation and constitute virtually new essays.

I am deeply grateful to my friends Rabbi Herbert C. Brichto and Rabbi Jack Bemporad. The former read most of the studies and made uncounted inestimable suggestions concerning substance and expression. The latter first suggested the publication of this volume and edited it and saw it through publication, all the while giving valuable advice and taking meticulous care of the script.

It is a great pleasure to offer sincere thanks to the publishers and editors of the journals and books where these articles appeared first for their permission to republish them. The sources are mentioned on p. 205. I am much gratified by their generosity and cooperation.

M.T.

*This book is affectionately dedicated
to the loving memory of*

ABE P. HOROWITZ

*Husband, Father, Grandfather
Jew and Humanitarian*

The Meaning of the Book of Job

The opening of the Book of Job is a case of the rule that a great author can be recognized by the way he fashions the opening of his work.[1] As the prologue (chs. 1 f.) tells the events on earth and in heaven, it provides the reader with the factual background of what is to come and introduces him with equal clarity to the problem of the book.[2] The poetic part (3:1—42:6) may appear to modern readers overly

[1] Special abbreviations used in this essay are: Kuhl 1953 and Kuhl 1954 = C. Kuhl, *ThR*, N. F. 21 (1953), pp. 163—205, 257—317; and *ThR*, N. F. 22 (1954), 261—316, respectively. Rowley = H. H. Rowley, *From Moses to Qumran* (1963), pp. 141—83. "Com." following the name of an author refers to his commentary; when it follows Tur Sinai, his 1954 Hebrew commentary is intended.

Views widely held and readily available in the scholarly literature are not identified or specifically referred to, nor are the arguments adduced for them. A balanced view, supported by detailed exegesis and a discussion of differing opinions is found in G. Fohrer, *Das Buch Hiob* (1963), 565 pages. The reader who prefers an English book is referred to S. R. Driver and G. B. Gray, *The Book of Job* (1921, and reprints) LXXVIII+376+360 pages. A detailed and excellent survey on Job research between *ca.* 1921 and 1953 is given by Kuhl 1953 and Kuhl 1954. It is supplemented by the more recent article of Rowley, first published in *BJRL* 41 (1958 f.), pp. 167—207; re-edited and brought up-to-date in his *From Moses to Qumran*. Reference to these articles is primarily to the literature which Kuhl and Rowley survey and only infrequently to their own opinions.

An extensive, if overextended bibliography is found in J. Lévêque, *Job et son Dieu* (1970), pp. 693—757. The reader who is interested in the history of the interpretation of the book or in an assortment of modern approaches is refered to P. S. Saunders, ed., *The Twentieth Century Interpretations of the Book of Job* (1968); and N. N. Glatzer, *The Dimension of Job* (1969).

[2] There are three critical views as regards the relation of the prose frame, comprising the prologue (chs. 1 f.) and the epilogue (42:7—17), to the poetic colloquy it encloses. (1) The author of the poetic part (i.e., the author of the book, since there are almost forty chapters of poetry to two-and-a-half of prose; the reduction of the number of forty to about thirty for critical reasons, such as the excision of the Elihu section [chs. 32—37; cf. n. 17], does not affect the point I wish to make) used and possibly adapted an older prose story, enclosing in it his own larger work. (2) The author wrote the prose as well as the poetry. (3) A later editor provided the narrative frame for the poet. Cf. Kuhl 1953, pp.

long and, in places, wordy and confused (responsibility for which may be assigned, on the one hand, to an abundance of additions by later hands, textual confusion, and an exceptionally difficult language and, on the other, perhaps to the intention of the author to show by the growing repetitiveness of the *dramatis personae* that they have exhausted their arguments); the 35 verses of the narrative introduction are concise and pithy and yet contain everything the reader has to know.

There is Job, the pious man, on whom God's blessing rests. But this idyl of piety and prosperity is introduced only to be immediately menaced by the accuser, Satan, as he presents himself at the heavenly council and demands: "Is it for nought that Job is pious?" (1:9). He questions not Job's deeds but his motivation. Nor is this an act of viciousness on his part; God Himself has provoked him to probe and shake the foundations of the beautiful edifice of righteousness, serentiy, and happiness and finally wreck it completely. For God has asked him: "Have you considered My servant Job, that there is no one on earth as blameless and upright as he?" (1:8). Job is the pious man, if there is one. The problem is: is there one? Which is secondary to the main problem: is there piety? Which is, as the accuser insists: is there disinterested piety? He claims that Job behaves according to standards of religion only as long as he finds it useful, whereas piety begins where usefulness ends. God accepts the challenge as proposed by the accuser and on his terms, and this acceptance determines the meaning of piety for the rest of the book. From now on, he who performs an action in expectation of material reward is not to be credited with religious or moral behavior. Different and less pure concepts of piety which find their way into the speeches of the friends later on (8:5—7, 20—22; 11:13—19; 22:21—28) are thus invalid and implicitly rejected *a limine*.

We now know what piety is; this is a question *quid iuris* in Kant's terminology. What we do not know is the answer to the first question: is

---

185—205; Rowley, pp. 151—56, 159. I hold with the great majority of students in favoring the first or the second view. A choice between them is of little consequence for the issue at hand, the question of the author's having composed the frame or appropriated an existing one is one of literary prehistory; in either case the resulting book is his creation, and the object of our concern is this book.

there piety? This is a question *quid facti*. While we do not learn the answer at this early stage of the book, we have a preliminary indication that it is likely to be in the affirmative, that there is piety in the world, for it is God Who is the proponent of this view (2:3).

Amplifying what was touched upon before, the narrative content of the prologue and its thought content are not dissociated, but rather the two, plot and ideas, are intimately wedded, and this union now constitutes more than merely the sum of its two components. The prologue informs the reader of the cause of Job's suffering, information which Job himself cannot and must not have. We know more than the hero does. But the hero, precisely because of his ignorance, will experience problems and gain insights before which our superior knowledge pales. It is not the spectator's knowledge of the drama but rather Job's problem that matters. The prologue *qua* prologue is a work of genius.

At the beginning of the poetic part we find ourselves in a different world, not only as regards the plot—if we may so refer to the regular change of speakers and their ever-increasing animosity—but also as regards the ideas. The latter, while not unrelated to the ideas of the prologue, assume very different forms, and it is only towards the end of the book that we recognize them in their earlier formulation. In our treatment the three friends and their philosophies will not be differentiated from one another but be seen as one group with one position, over against which will stand Job's philosophy.

One of the friends speaks up in response to Job's initial lament (of ch. 3). His purport, in which the others join him later: Job should behave himself, live up to the very convictions which he formerly preached to others, and rely on God because afflictions are God's chastisements (chs. 4 f.). As Job finds this counsel cold comfort, the friends become ever more adamant and finally quite aggressive as they develop their theology. Their view, they claim, is based on both tradition and observed reality. A web of causality is spun over the world. Man's fate is in his hand; what he gets depends on what he does. The just man is rewarded, the sinner punished. This cause-and-effect relation, widely accepted in the ancient Near East, is also reversible: distress and tribulation are punishment meted out for sin. The inescapable conclusion is that Job, distressed and afflicted, is a sinner. His sins may be unknown to him, but they are no less real. Causality in the realm of morality is guaranteed by God; this is the meaning of the sentence "God is just." As for Job, let him search out his sins and repent, and the happiness of his former status will be restored to him.

The friends came to comfort (2:11), but their philosophy will afford a grievously harrowed man no consolation. Yet the literary device that spurs the action and aggravates the situation is the ever-increasing vehemence of the friends, their self-righteousness and unqualified condemnation of their disputant, all of which not only fails to console or at least convince Job but increasingly makes a true conversation impossible. There is no meeting of minds. Repeatedly Job says: "If you only would listen to my words" (13:5 f.; 21:2 f.). But they launch a massive assault, attacking him from all sides with such force and viciousness that one might expect his backbone to be broken and his personality, the pivot of the drama, extinguished. We must remind ourselves how hard it was for an ancient Israelite, grounded himself in tradition, to withstand the logic of the friends.

Job's backbone is not broken. Up to the last verses of the book he not only stands upright but actually grows in strength, and as the disputation continues we see the development and integration of his personality. He undertakes to demolish some of the friends' arguments and to reject others. Reality, he contends, does not accord with their theory. The world is not governed by the principle of measure for measure. Almost everywhere the wicked prosper. Against these incontrovertible facts, tradition and authority, to which the friends appeal, are without validity; wisdom is not necessarily found with the elders (12:12)[3]—a shocking pronouncement in those days. So clear is the discrepancy between theory and reality that the theory can only be saved by distortion of observation and misrepresentation of reality, in short by a lie. "You whitewash with lies [the dark side of life]," is the accusation Job hurls at the friends (13:4). A few verses later he demands: "Will you speak falsely for God, speak deceitfully for Him?" (13:7—11). This is probably the first time in history that pious fraud is clearly recognized and denounced for what it is: a contradiction in terms. Fraud is never pious, it is always impious.

But Job does not stop with presenting his own, very different view of

---

[3] The verse presents a rhetorical question the answer to which is no. Cf. Tur Sinai, com.

the world. Decisive is his rejection of the principle which underlies the argument of the friends: the inference from observed reality to the causation of that reality, and this rejection is independent of the accuracy or inaccuracy of the observation. His misery is not evidence for sin on his part because he did not sin. Neither logic nor clever dispositions of commonly held opinions nor glib talk can produce what does not exist: his iniquity. To be precise, Job does not deny absolutely that he has sinned. He grants the possibility of minor transgressions. (7:21; 13:26). But what he denies categorically is sins of such weight as to warrant their being related to his lot as cause to effect. The friends' argument rests on a doctrine; his argument is grounded in his life, his experience, his person. And since he knows himself, and since the course of his life lies open before everyone, he is compelled to affirm that the cause of the terrible atrocities that God has unleashed against him lies not in him but in God. God wants to torment him, torment him without reason, because God is cruel. From the lack of rational reason in a person's behavior we take a clue to his character. God's outstanding characteristic appears therefore to be a demoniac ruthlessness. In ever-repeated and diverse ways Job accuses God of wanton cruelty. God's eyes are on man (and on Job as the representative of mankind) not, as the Bible frequently asserts and as the friends faithfully echo, to guard and protect him but to watch and destroy him. Would that He leave man alone to finish out his days in quiet; but no, He searches him out for horror and doom. The friends speak of God's might and wisdom. Surely, says Job, He is mighty and wise, but might is brute force, and wisdom is craftiness seeing that they serve God's caprice and outrage justice. No wonder that omnipotence and omniscience, ordinarily epithets of praise of God, turn in Job's mouth to expressions of blame.

Yet Job does not limit himself to such statements of facts, as he sees the divine facts. He describes them so keenly because they concern his own person. He is the target. Thus description becomes accusation. Job, the accuser, wants to bring God, the defendant, to court. Nor is this all. Job craving judgment, objective, rational judgment, knows that there is no judge but God. It is in the rational milieu of the tribunal that God will shed his demoniac features, and Job's troubles will be over. Again and again he wants the encounter, longs to see God. For it is his innermost and strongest hope, implicit for the most part but sometimes pronounced,

that God also longs for him, His creature, the work of His hands. This
hope upholds Job in the hours of his greatest despair. Besides this all else
pales. Progressively his dispute with the friends loses in importance as his
address to God—accusation, challenge, prayer, and prediction—gains in
importance. In his final long speech (chs.26 f.; 29—31) the presence of the
friends gradually becomes dim, in its last three chapters they are not
mentioned at all. The only protagonists on the stage at the end are Job
and the Deity, the best man and his God.

The concluding chapter of Job's speech (ch.31) has a particular function in the economy of the book. Job is not satisfied with accusing, beg-
ging, and hoping; he takes more efficacious action, compelling God to
leave His uncommitted, whimsical transcendence and to take a stand, to
relate Himself to his problems. Ancient man, as he conceptualized his
world, had a means of challenging God: the oath. Man swears to a fact or
a promise; if he perjures himself, God, Who is evoked in the oath, is
bound to punish him; if it is a terrible oath, punishment will be terrible.
(It is hardly necessary to remark that ordinarily an oath was not sworn in
order to challenge God but to affirm a statement or a promise.) It is
otherwise with Job. Ch. 31, 40 verses long, is his oath.[4] It is the most terrible oath in the Bible, for this reason: A full oath has the following form.
"If I did or shall do this, or if I did not or shall not do this, then may God
punish me." Ordinarily, however, the apodosis ("then may God punish
me") is omitted.[4a] The very likely reason for this ellipsis is that one shied
away from conjuring up punishment in the unlikely event of an unintentional factual inaccuracy of the material content of the oath. Although
uttered in good faith, such an inaccuracy may set in motion the mecha-
nism of punishment for perjury that the oath envisages. Caution trun-
cated the oath in biblical and postbiblical Israel and among her neigh-

---

[4] Vss. 35—37, probably to be placed after vs. 40, are not part of the oath but draw the
sum total of Job's pleadings from ch. 3 through ch. 31. For the form of this oath, cf. S. H.
Blank, *JJS* 2 (1951), pp. 105—107.

[4a] On occasion, a symbolic act, a rite or a gesture may have taken the place of the apodosis. In a text from Alalakh in northern Syria, 18th cent. B.C., we read: "Abba-AN
placed himself under oath to Yarimlim cutting the neck of a sheep (and saying): 'If I take
away what I have given to you'" (D.J. Wiseman, *JCS* 12 [1958], pp. 126—129, lines
39—42).

THE MEANING OF THE BOOK OF JOB

bors.[5] Job throws caution to the winds. Over and over he explicitly calls upon himself every conceivable punishment if what he says is not true.

He talks long but says in effect only one thing: that he has led an essentially good life, that he has not sinned. For all that he is not verbose. It is worth the reader's notice that the sins which he abjures are not, for the most part, monstrous crimes but minute deviations from the loftiest standards of ethics and piety. Here are a few examples: "If I have disdained the cause of my manservant or maidservant when they brought a complaint against me ... " (vs. 13). "If I have withheld anything that the poor desired or have caused the eyes of the widow to fail ... " (vs. 16). "If I have 'rejoiced'[6] at the ruin of my foe or exulted when evil overtook him ... " (vs. 29). "If I have concealed my transgression as people (are wont to do) by hiding my iniquity in my bosom because I stood in great fear of the multitude ... and kept silence ... " (vss. 33 f.). "If my land has cried out against me ... if I have eaten its yield without payment and brought low the spirit of its owners"[7] (vss. 38 f.).

The challenge to God is overt and clear. God is bound to act. If Job has perjured himself, God is to punish him even more than he is already punished, if that is yet possible. If not, he is pure; the oath proves it. Then he should be restored *in integrum,* for so judicial procedure requires. If neither of these immediate and plain alternatives result, God is challenged personally to respond to the oath. (Indeed, what Job desires

---

[5] The custom in Jewish Palestine of the first few centuries A.D. is described by S. Lieberman, *Greek in Jewish Palestine* (1942), ch. 5, especially pp. 121–24. It is as interesting as it is not surprising that the simple people were even more cautious than the rabbis in the formulation of the oath.

[6] Read 'וְהִתְרְעַעְתִּי' with the Targum (ויבבית), commentaries; MT וְהִתְעֹרַרְתִּי.

[7] The meaning of "my land" in conjunction with "its owners" is that Job had distrained real estate of defaulting debtors and, himself consuming its yield, had brought the impoverished original owners to the verge of despair. Had Job behaved in such a manner, he would have been fully within his legal rights, yet by virtue of his own highly developed conscience guilty of a cruel and antisocial act. M. Dahood, taking his cue from Ugaritic, has repeatedly insisted (for example in *Biblica* 46 [1965], pp. 320 f.) that בְּעָלֶיהָ is dialectical for פעליה(='פֹּעֲלֶיהָ'). This is possible but gratuitous. In general, we would observe that resort to dialectical features, nonstandard sound shifts or the like should not be had except with caution and primarily for the purpose of avoiding forced exegesis or unsupported emendations.

above all else is the personal encounter with God, divine revelation.)
Would that He produced counteraccusation; Job will make a crown and
an ornament out of it—so certain is he of his case. He will stand up before God like a prince, he will not blink an eye (vss. 35—37). Job has
grown to Promethean stature. The miracle is that it is not growth at the
expense of piety. This is the most striking case in the Bible of a man so
strongly asserting himself against God while yet remaining so loyal to
Him.

From this vantage point, looking back over the disputation of Job and
the friends and forward to the answer of God, we have no difficulty iden-
tifying the problem of the book in a preliminary way. It is the suffering of
the innocent. There is broad agreement about this,[8] although the issue is
sometimes blurred by the omission of the qualifier "of the innocent." The
omission reduces the problem to suffering alone, but this is surely unintentional because the suffering of the noninnocent is deserved suffering,
i.e., punishment. The friends indeed attempt repeatedly to construe Job's
suffering as punishment. But no one has yet seen in this argument more
than a straw man.

The problem of the suffering of the innocent is everywhere in the
book. Where is the answer? It is a priori probable that it is found at the
end. An answer comes after a question and not in the middle while the
questioning is going on. This is a truism, to be sure, but its evocation is
forced upon us by proposals that the answer lies in the middle of the
book, e.g., in chs. 19[9] or 28[10] or even in the speeches of Elihu.[11] As to
the end, the prose epilogue presents no serious candidature. It contains
little more than the story of Job's restoration to his former state of happi-

---

[8] For a different opinion, cf. *infra*, p. 25.

[9] For some of the champions of this proposal, notably those who hold that 19:25—27
refer to Job's resurrection or redemption, cf. Fohrer, com., pp. 318 f. Further recent
attempts to detect the solution in ch. 19 are mentioned by Kuhl 1953, p. 304. Add K. Ful-
lerton, ZAW 42 (1924), pp. 116—36.

[10] The opinions are cited and discussed by Kuhl 1953, p. 282; Rowley, pp. 166 f. Add
Tur Sinai, com., pp. 238, 388. It should be remarked however, that a number of scholars
who accept this view place the chapter at the end of the divine address.

[11] K. Budde, com. (1913), pp. XLV—XLVIII; others are listed by Kuhl 1953, pp. 261
f.; Kuhl 1954, pp. 312 f.

ness and the pronouncement of his vindication. Thus by elimination we are directed to the final chapters of the poetry (hereinafter "final chapters"), 38:1—42:6, God's long speech and Job's short response. We assume that the answer is found in either or both of their components, and it will be our task to demonstrate that this assumption is correct, that here indeed lies the answer of the book. As the business of the demonstration begins immediately and extends to the end of the article, this assumption is henceforth our working hypothesis, one we hope will be vindicated in the course of this discussion.

Some critics, however, say that the final chapters are not part of the original book. Their argument runs as follows: The logic of literary structure as well as other considerations require that these chapters contain the answer of the book; this is their *raison d'être*. But they do not contain it (by which the critics mean: we have not detected in them an acceptable answer). Ergo, the chapters have no justification for existence; they were added later. Ergo, the book has no answer to its problem.[12] This is lazy man's logic. The sentence "I have not detected the meaning" should signify to the philologist "I have not yet detected it," and this should spur him to further search in place of recourse to the easy alternative of denying the authenticity of the passage.

Yet since most of those who deny that the answer of the book is contained in its final chapters say that the book has no answer at all,[13] we have first to address ourselves to the question: does the book have an answer? This question we answer in the affirmative for the following reasons.[14]

First, were the book to contain no answer, we should be faced with a literary work posing a problem of the greatest moment without offering or even attempting a solution. The reader would be cut loose from his moorings of tradition and faith and left adrift. The Book of Job without an answer to its problem would constitute a literary torso, an anthology of verbalized doubts; it would betray an utter lack of appreciation of the

[12] The latter conclusion is, of course, not shared by the comparatively small group of interpreters who are referred to in nn. 9—11.

[13] Cf. n. 12.

[14] Cf. also R. A. F. MacKenzie, *Biblica* 40 (1959), pp. 437—41.

controlling conceptions which are everywhere in evidence in the work to allow this judgment to stand.

A second reason for postulating an answer to the problem of the suffering of the innocent in Job is the plain and obvious design of the book. It converges forcefully on the final chapters. Job's long concluding speech (chs. 29–31) containing his oath sums up his position but is not an absolute end. This speech is a transition, an expression of expectation; it culminates in his challenge to God as he subjects himself to the penalties enumerated in the oath; it is the strongest expression of his longing for confrontation. The final chapters bring the fulfillment of the desire to meet God; for a revelation, an answer is granted there. To declare these chapters unauthentic is to reject the expected when it occurs.

A further support for the thesis that the problem of the book is answered is to be found in the beginning of the epilogue. It reads: "After having spoken these words to Job, the Lord said to Eliphaz, the Temanite: 'My wrath is kindled against you and your two friends; for you have not spoken of Me what is right, as has My servant Job'" (42:7). As several scholars have observed, this verse refers to a revelation which God has just granted to Job. Job's wish has been fulfilled, his incessant questions have received a reply. Which means that explicit reference to an actual revelation is made in a different part of the book. God's answer to suffering Job is or contains His answer to the suffering of Job, i.e., it constitutes the solution to the problem of the book.[15] The answer of the book is anchored in its ground plan.

Some scholars, however, for whom we may take C. Kuhl as a spokesman, share the extreme skepticism of the critics mentioned before. Overwhelmed by the difficulty of understanding God's reply, by the seeming unrelatedness of its content to Job's words, they say that God's answer is His theophany, the mere fact that He appeared to the man who deemed himself cast out from the presence of God. The theophany itself is genuine, but its verbal content, the long divine address, is a later addition.[16]

---

[15] Neither this nor the preceding arguments prove the genuineness of the present answer, 38:1–40:14 (for its extent, cf. n. 26); they admit of the highly improbable hypothesis that the original answer of the poem was replaced by the present one. (Whether an originally independent prose story had a different disputation, followed by a different speech of God, [Fohrer, com., pp. 37, 538] need not detain us.)

[16] Kuhl 1953, pp. 270 f.

At first glance, this opinion has much to recommend itself. The theophany rehabilitates Job. Job has suffered, but this suffering is no sign of his rejection. True, he as well as the friends have so interpreted it, but their interpretation is now corrected. Moreover, theophany, personal contact with God has been his greatest desire; now it is realized. Furthermore, revelation is the supreme good in biblical religion. Of Moses, Deuteronomy says (34:10): "There has not risen a prophet in Israel like Moses, whom the Lord knew face to face." Yet Job has come close to this. In general it may be said that all doubts, anguishes, and antagonisms to which a man may be prey disappear in the presence of a vision. Job himself says as much in his last response: "I had heard of You from hearsay, but now my eye sees You. Therefore . . . " (42:5 f.). The vision has transferred him into a new state. It is the fullest answer.

The importance of the revelation in the Book of Job is immense. It can be overemphasized in only one way: if it is made exclusive, if it is interpreted to be the whole answer. This, however, is a misinterpretation and must be rejected for the following reasons:

(1) The event of a revelation, distinct from its specific, articulate content, is personal, untransmissible, and unrepeatable. A report of a revelatory event as such is pure autobiography. Had the author of the book restricted himself to autobiography at this critical juncture, he would have proclaimed that his own problems were solved, but to his readers he would say implicitly: "If you are grievously afflicted, wait for a personal revelation; there is no salvation outside of revelation." Such an answer would be altogether incongruous.

(2) The design and the construction of the book do not lend themselves to Kuhl's interpretation. The book in its first thirty-one chapters[17] is the result of a supreme conceptual, literary, and poetical effort. Is it conceivable that the author invested this stupendous intellectual energy in the question only to seek, receive, and transmit the whole solution on a nonintellectual level?

The reasoning and the conclusions of the preceding paragraphs are essentially formal, as this summary shows: the Book of Job presents a problem (it is the problem of the suffering of the innocent); the problem

---

[17]I accept the prevailing critical opinion that the Elihu pericope (chaps. 32–37) is secondary and therefore do not consider these chapters.

has an answer; the answer is contained in the final chapters; and the final chapters are authentic. The conclusions being formal, they must now be put to the test of substantiation through the interpretation of the final chapters that, according to our postulation, contain the answer.

"The Lord answered Job out of the storm" (38:1). Job is granted his request; God answers him. The answer comes from the storm, and since, in the Bible, a storm often precedes or accompanies a theophany, we are prepared for a theophany to occur with the answer. The occurrence is affirmed in Job's response: "Now my eyes see You" (42:5).

The divine speech has two introductory verses.

> Just who darkens the plan by words without knowledge? ³Gird up your loins like a man; I will question you, and you shall declare to Me (38:2 f.).

We shall learn soon which plan (עֵצָה) Job darkens. But irrespective of which and whose, his approach, possibly his very position, is rejected at the outset; he speaks "without knowledge." In vs. 3b, God formally accepts the challenge. Earlier Job offered God two alternatives: "Call, and I will answer; or let me speak, and You reply to me" (13:22). Now God chooses the first alternative. In contrast with the continuation of the verse, its beginning, "Gird up your loins," is figurative, possibly referring to an ancient custom, which C. H. Gordon calls "belt-wrestling."[18]

Now comes the substance of the speech. We know from vs. 3 that it will be presented in the form of a question, a question which breaks down into a series of detailed questions. The first group, vss. 4—11, concerns creation; within it, the first subgroup, vss. 4—7, contains questions about the creation of the earth, which means in the cosmology and language of the time, the dry land.

> Where were you when I laid the foundation of the earth? Tell me if you have understanding. ⁵Who determined its measurements—if you know that, or who stretched the line on it? ⁶In what were its bases sunk, or who laid its cornerstone, ⁷when the morning stars sang in unison and all the divine beings shouted for joy? (38:4—7).

"You, Job, were not present at the creation of the earth and, conse-

---

[18] Cf. *HUCA* 23:1 (1950 f.), pp. 131—36.

quently, you know nothing about its nature." Take the problem of measurement. How can the infinitely large earth be measured? With which measuring line? After the measuring, the laying of foundations. This is even less comprehensible. On what basis is this immense earth set? On the watery sea, as the Psalmist says (24:2)? Or maybe even on no basis at all, as the Book of Job itself has it ("He hangs the earth upon nothing," 26:7)? All this is complete mystery. What makes it even more mysterious to man is that other beings, divine or celestial, are presumably able to answer these questions for they were present and involved when these things happened, they celebrated the great event—only human beings were not there and hence do not share the knowledge.

'Who'[19] shut in the sea with doors when it burst forth from the womb,
[9]when I made clouds its garment and dense fog its swaddling band,
[10]making breakers[20] 'its'[21] limit,[22] fixing bars and doors, [11]and said:
"Thus far shall you come and no farther; here shall your 'proud'[23] waves
'be stayed'[23]"? (38:8—11).

The author of Job was a well-educated man, familiar with the Jewish and non-Jewish literature of his time. His book abounds in allusions to the myths of the ancient Orient. One of the most prominent of them is the story of the fight of the supreme god, the leader of the present pantheon, with the sea which appears in the image of a gigantic dragon; the god is victorious and, according to one version, fashions the sky (and the earth) out of the body of the dead monster.[24] This myth is alluded to in other parts of the book (3:8; 7:12; 9:13; 26:12 f.).[25] Yet nothing of it is present in this passage. The sea is not God's adversary; it is a giant baby, just born, that had to be confined at the moment of birth (vs. 8), when a baby must be wrapped in swaddling clothes. The stripes of fog on the surface

[19] Read 'מִי סָךְ', commentaries; so also the Vulgate (quis conclusit); MT וַיָּסֶךְ.
[20] וָאֶשְׁבֹּר, denominative from מִשְׁבָּרִים "breakers, surf at the reefs of the shore."
[21] Read 'חֻקּוֹ', commentaries; MT חֻקִּי.
[22] Cf. 14:5.
[23] Read 'יִשְׁבֹּת גְּאוֹן' commentaries; MT יָשִׁית בִּגְאוֹן.
[24] Cf. the Assyro-Babylonian epic Enuma Elish IV:93 ff.
[25] Cf. e.g., Fohrer, com., pp. 502 f., who offers an inclusive treatment of this and other mythological imagery.

of the sea are its swaddle (vs. 9). All this is subsumed under the question of vs. 4: "Where were you then?"

The text now turns from the creation of the world to its survey and management (38:12—39:30).[26] The form of the questions is maintained throughout. We are first shown the inanimate world (38:12—38). At the beginning there is the daily rise of the morning.

> Have you ever in your life commanded the morning, have you directed[27] the dawn to its place [13]to take hold of the skirts of the earth so that the wicked are shaken out of it—[14]it changes like clay under the seal and 'it is dyed'[28] like a garment—[15]so that light is withheld from the wicked, and their uplifted arm is broken? (38:12—15).

Has Job ever performed such a routine thing as bringing on a new day? Following up the broad question by special attention to one corner of the tableau, which is nothing but a manifestation of His interest in the world as it is, God describes the dawn by what it does to the earth. The latter looks like a broad piece of cloth, of indistinct color first, but the color changes soon and keeps changing with the brightening of the day. As the sun rises, the contours of the earth are beginning to stand our clearly like the impression of a seal on soft clay.

Next comes a paragraph which may be called "The dimensions of the universe."

> Have you reached the springs of the sea[29] or walked in the recesses of the deep? [17]Have the gates of death been laid bare to your sight, or have you

---

[26] I incline to the critical opinion that 40:15—41:26 are not authentic; cf. the references in Rowley, p. 166, n. 1; also Fohrer, com., p. 39. But the point this article is trying to make is not affected by one's critical position regarding this section; cf. also Rowley's view, p. 166. Other insertions and disorders in the final chapters will be critically recognized in their proper places.

[27] Cf. the same meaning of a probably related form of this verb in 1 Sam. 21:3.

[28] Read 'וְתִצְטַבַּע' or 'וְתִצָּבַע', commentaries; MT וְיִתְיַצְּבוּ.

[29] The nouns in vss. 16—18 may refer to names of gods or demons in various ancient Oriental mythologies and accordingly be rendered as "Sea," "Deep" (or "Primeval Flood"), "Death," "Murk," and "Netherworld"; or "Yamm," *"Tiham," "Mot," "Ṣalmut," and *"Arṣ." (*Tiham, and *Arṣ may be hypothesized by their appearance [in feminine forms] in the cognate literature. Tiamtu, etc., is well known from the Assyro-Babylonian civilization. Remarkably, ארצית [=Erṣitu] appears in Jewish folklore [M. Gas-

seen the gates to murk? [18]Have you examined well (the universe) as far as the farthest (ends) of the netherworld? Speak, if you know any of this! [19]Where is the way to the abode of the light, or where is the place of darkness, [20]that you may lead either one[30] back to its realm or discern the paths to its home? [21]You surely know all this[31] for you were already born then, and the number of your days is great indeed (38:16–21).

"The first questions, all left unanswered, showed clearly enough," God continues, "that you were not present at the creation of the world. Have you at least seen its full expanse?" The question, like all the others, is rhetorical and has an ironical ring; the expected answer is no. Job knows only a small section of the world. The sarcasm of vs. 21, however, momentarily disregards the conclusion of vss. 4 ff.: "You know all this because at the time of their creation you must have been alive—or so you behave."

The theme of the dimensions of the universe is continued in the next paragraph, dealing with precipitations and winds.

Have you reached the storehouses or the snow or have you seen the storehouses of the hail [23]which I have reserved for times of trouble, for the day of battle and war? [24]By what route does the west wind[32] escape[33]

---

ter, ספר מעשיות, here after S. Krauss, *HUCA* 4 (1927), p. 352; Krauss, however, misinterprets the word].) I cannot decide whether the author, oscillating between the semantic foreground ("sea") and background ("Sea," "Yamm"), intends either of these pairs of meanings ("sea" or "Sea" [or "Yamm," respectively] and in like manner all the others) or both of them. The language of classical Hebrew poetry admits of both, and it is often beyond our means to settle on a single meaning ("sea" or "Sea/Yamm") or the double meaning ("sea-Sea/Yamm"). (A comparable problem is presented in Sumero-Akkadian cuneiform, where, for example, ᵈŠamaš, for all the presence of the divine determinative, in many contexts conveys to the modern reader nothing more than "sun.") The problem of the significance of Near Eastern mythology in Job will be discussed further on, pp. 16, 33.

[30] "Either one" is an attempt to render the distributive function of the Hebrew personal suffixes; this function is present in חַרְבּוֹ and קַשְׁתּוֹ (Isa. 41:2).

[31] The force of כֻּלָּה after יָדַעְתָּ of vs. 18 extends to יָדַעְתָּ of this verse. The word is not repeated, perhaps in order to avoid crowding the stich.

[32] Vocalize 'אוּר' (?) <Aram. אוריה <Akkad. *amurrū* (Tur Sinai, com.).

[33] Akkad. *ḫalāqu* means both "to flee, escape, slip away" and "to perish." M. Dahood considers the second meaning for some biblical passages (*Biblica* 45 [1964], p. 408). The first, however, provides the basis for interpreting Jer. 37:12 (already Redaq, Rosenmüller,

or the east wind fan out over the earth? ²⁵Who has cleft a channel for the
rain flood or a way for the thunder cloud ²⁶to cause rain on land where
no man is, on a desert where no people live ²⁷to satiate waste and desolate
terrain and to sprout fresh grass?³⁴ ²⁸Has the rain a father, or (is there
one) who sired the drops³⁵ of the dew? ²⁹From whose womb does the ice
come forth, or who gives birth to the rime of heaven, ³⁰when the water
'becomes solid'³⁶ like stone, and the surface of the waters is 'hidden'?³⁶
(38:22–30).

Vss. 28–30 raise a new point. God asks Job: "How do rain, ice, and frost
come into being? Give a realistic answer. Do not give Me myths for
facts." Mythological fragments or just allusions to myths are one of the
secondary features of Job, probably more prominent in it than in any
other biblical book.³⁷ But what was only an inkling in the passage about
the sea (vss. 8–11), here becomes explicit. Myths in Job, as in general in
the other (poetic) books of the Bible, are literary devices, a stylistic feature betraying the broad education of the author, but hardly constitutive
elements of his belief. "Has the rain a father?" The myth says yes; explicitly of implicitly, rain is the semen of the weather god. The Book of Job
says no. This no, which is clad in the by now familiar form of a rhetorical
question, destroys a world of fancy and coherence which everybody
understands and in which he can orient himself,³⁸ without explicitly substituting another one of comparable serviceability.³⁹

---

and Gesenius [*Thesaurus*] from the context, as well as Geller and Tur Sinai based on the
Akkadian); Lam. 4:16 (following verbs of motion and naming the ultimate agent of it:
"the face of the Lord chased them away" [cf. Num. 10:35]); 1 Sam. 23:28 (an etiological
connection of the story with the "Rock of Escape"). There is no basis for judging the
masoretic vocalization of the verb here and in the Jeremiah passage.

³⁴ מֹצָא, literally "plants" or "growth"; *mw'yt'* "plant." Cf. Gen. 1:12.

³⁵ The meaning of אֶגְלֵי is conjectural. (A. Guillaume's etymology, *Abr-Nahrain* 1 [1959
f.], p. 6, had justly been questioned by [Driver and] Gray, com. four decades before it was
proposed.)

³⁶ Very uncertain. The translation of this verse follows a number of commentaries in
(1) emending the text by exchanging the order of the verbs and (2) assuming for יִתְלַכָּדוּ the
meaning "hold together" (41:9 || יִדְבָּקוּ), hence "pack, solidify," metaphorical for "freeze."
Moreover, "waters" as the rendition of תְּהוֹם has no better support than Ezek. 31:4 and Ps.
42:6. (It cannot mean here "primeval flood," or "sea," "rivers," since neither the one nor
the others—in and around Palestine—ever freeze.)

³⁷ Cf. *supra*, p. 13.

³⁸ Cf. *infra*, p. 33.

³⁹ But note that vss. 34 and 37 suggest (different) explanations of the origin of rain.

Vss. 31–38, not reproduced here, contain final questions about the inanimate world, in particular about various celestial phenomena. Beginning with vs. 39 to the end of the descriptive interrogation (39:30)[40] we find ourselves on the road through the kingdom of animals. Several of its members, from the lion down, pass before our eyes. Each member or group of members represents one side of animal life, and God questions Job about it. First providing food for wild animals; this is demonstrated at the lion.

Can you hunt the prey for the lion or satisfy the appetite of the lions[41] [40]when they crouch in their dens or lie in wait in the thicket? [41]Who provides his prey 'in the evening'[42] when his whelps roving without food cry to God? (38:39–41).

Man is not wont to give much thought to the food supply of wild animals, but it is a problem all the same. Would Job assume the responsibility of providing food for one of their kind who normally has no difficulty in getting what he needs?

Next comes procreation; the text speaks about mountain goats and deer.

Do you know when the mountain goats give birth, or do you observe the calving of the hinds? [2]Can you number the months that they fulfil or know the time when they give birth, [3]when they crouch to bring forth their offspring and cast their young? [4]Their kids become strong, grow up in the open, and go forth never to return (39:1–4).

Here it is not the question of responsibility and care but something less. It is only knowledge, obtained through observation of some phases of animal life. But alas, the animals are too swift for observation, or the phases are too long.

The next paragraph, speaking about the zebra(?),[43] the onager, and the wild ox, concerns the freedom and taming of wild beasts.

---

[40] Cf. n. 26 about 40:15—41:26.

[41] (כְּפִיר(ים, another of the several Hebrew words for lion.

[42] The vocalization 'לָעֶרֶב' (cf. 4:10 f.; Ps. 104:20 f.) is preferable to masoretic לָעֹרֵב, commentaries; the raven is quite out of place before 39:26 or rather 39:30. Also, יִתְעוּ is more appropriate as applied to young lions than young ravens, so much so, that many who retain לָעֹרֵב find it necessary to emend the end of the verse.

[43] The identification is not certain.

Who has let the zebra go free or who has loosened the onager's bonds [6]to whom I have given the steppe for his home and the salt land for his habitat? [7]He scorns the tumult of the city, he does not hear the driver's shouts. [8]He 'ranges'[44] the mountains as his pasture and searches after every bit of green. [9]Is the wild ox willing to serve you? Will he spend the night at your manger? [10]Does a rope[45] bind the wild ox to the furrow? Will he at your heels plow up the valleys?[46] [11]Can you depend on him for the greatness of his strength and shunt your work upon him? [12]Can you rely on him to come back,[47] 'to'[48] your threshing floor[48] bring home your grain? (39:5—12).

"Zebra and onager owe you nothing," says God, "not even their freedom. They are far beyond your ken and completely beyond your reach." Speaking of the wild ox, God continues the line of this argument but gives it a practical turn: "The wild ox could be quite a useful beast with his strength, but you are unable to domesticate him. You know little about the world and can do less about it. You are unable to effect so small a change in the order of the created world as would be the transferral of a wild beast to the category of the tame. It is your will against the will of the beast, yet it is his which prevails."

The rest of the road through the animal kingdom (39:13—30), passing in succession the ostrich (vss. 13—18), the horse (vss. 19—25), and the hawk and the vulture[49] (vss. 26—30), need not be traversed here. The

---

[44] Vocalize 'יָתוּר', commentaries: MT יְתוּר

[45] Literally "his rope," i.e., the rope which would bind him. But the text of the stich is suspect. רֵים, not in the LXX, is perhaps a vertical dittography from vs. 9. If so, the translation is: "Can you bind 'I' his rope (as he plows, or: in order that he plow) in the furrow?" Cf. Tur Sinai, com.

[46] The passage would be consistent with the use of a two-handle plow which requires two plowmen, one handling the plow, the other leading the ox; or, since it is highly unlikely that such plows were used in biblical Palestine (cf. J. Feliks, החקלאות בארץ ישראל בתקופת המשנה והתלמוד [1963], p. 29), it might have reference to the custom of drawing border furrows which require two plowmen irrespective of the type of plow (cf. Fohrer, com., after Guthe); or to a special plowing, before or after the main plowing, similarly requiring two men, which may be the intention of יְשַׁדֵּד (cf. Isa. 28:24; and see the comment of Feliks, supported by rabbinic passages, *ibid.*, pp. 37 f.; "to harrow" is wrong).

[47] The *ketiv* ישוב is adopted; the *qere* is יָשִׁיב

[48] Read 'וְהָרֵעַ גָּרְנְךָ', commentaries ('and' is not expressed in the translation); MT וְזַרְעֲךָ וְגָרְנְךָ. The word זֶרַע assumes the extended meaning "(seed grain >) grain =harvest."

[49] The identification of נֶשֶׁר, "vulture" or/and "eagle," is not settled; cf. G. R. Driver, *PEQ* 86 f. (1955), pp. 9 f.; 90 (1958), pp. 56 f.; M. Dor, לשוננו 27 f. (1963 f.), pp. 290—92; Z. Ben-Ḥayyim, *ibid.*, pp. 293 f.; זיכרונות האקדמיה ללשון העברית (תשכ״ג-תשכ״ד) 1965, pp. 222—30.

form of a string of (rhetorical) questions is preserved throughout. At the end of the journey God looks back as He draws the sum of His questioning. The beginning of the concluding section of His speech (40:2, 8—14)[50] is transitional in form in that it continues, in vss. 2, 8 f., the rhetorical questions of chs. 38 f.; but they are no longer questions about the world.

> Will the reprover enter suit against Shaddai? Let him who admonishes God give answer. [8]Will you really nullify My judgment, put Me in the wrong so that you may be vindicated? [9]Or is it that you have an arm like God and like Him can thunderously roar? [10]Deck yourself with majesty and dignity, clothe yourself in state and glory. [11]Give free scope to your raging anger. Seeing anyone haughty, bring him low; [12]seeing anyone haughty, abase him and tread down the wicked in their tracks. [13]Conceal them alike in the earth, wrap their faces in concealment. [14]Then I, too, will acknowledge that your right hand is all-prevailing (40:2, 8—14).

"Will the reprover enter suit?" The reprover, of course, is Job, and reproof is exactly what he administered to the Deity throughout the disputation. These words of reproof were the overflow of an embittered soul; but is he really prepared to enter into litigation with Him? "Let him who admonishes God give answer. Yes or no? Do you now, having failed to answer even one of My questions about the world, yet desire to contend with Me? (40:2). Would you nullify My judgment so that you may be vindicated? Is this an issue which concerns your person alone? Are you so wrapped up in yourself as to be closed to all else? Or would you now perhaps admit the possible existence and validity of standards of which you had not dreamed or the possible nonexistence or invalidity of standards in which you have believed or which you have taken for granted? (40:8). Have you any of the divine attributes required to govern the world? (40:9. At this juncture it is might, not knowledge, which Job would have to possess for the task but does not.) If you have, don the robes of office, take up the scepter (40:10). Then, having dressed for the part, begin your rule: put the wicked in their place! (40:13). Do that, and

---

[50] The critical omission of a number of verses and the rearrangement of the remaining ones, which also affects Job's answer, represent the opinion of the scholars named by Kuhl 1953, p. 269; it is convincingly argued by Fohrer, com., pp. 37—39. But again (cf. n. 26), the meaning of this part of Job and thereby of the whole book does not depend on the critical surgery performed on the text here. The transmitted text as well as a number of different critical rearrangements are all compatible with the interpretation offered here.

I will recognize your potency" (40:14). The issue is now clearly drawn. Does Job have the power? Will he pick up the gauntlet?

It is precisely at this point, no earlier, no later, that Job must respond. This structural requirement is one of the reasons for the critical rearrangement of the text. Job's answer, however, is more than an indispensable element of the literary structure. It is the outgrowth of the peculiar form that the problem of the suffering of the innocent takes on in the book: the narration of the experience of a particular person.[51] The reader of this narration who has seen Job as more than a spokesman for a philosophical viewpoint, who has involved himself in the person of Job throughout the long, heart-rending disputation, must ask at its end: "Has the revelation of God in and of itself had any effect on Job? And if so, what? How does Job see himself and his problem now that God Himself has spoken? In other biblical revelations nothing is the same after the event; God calls and man responds. Is Job a biblical book in this dialogical sense of God's call and man's response? Is Job after the revelation a wiser, better man?" The answer to these questions lies in Job's last words, in the fact that he spoke at all, and in what it was he said.

> Then Job answered the Lord:[52] [4]'I am indeed of small account; what shall I answer You? I lay my hand on my mouth. [5]I have spoken once but will not 'do so again,'[53] twice indeed, but will say no more. [42:2]I know that You can do everything, that nothing You purpose is impossible for You. [3b]Verily,[54] I made pronouncements but understood not, about things too

[51] There is a view recorded in the Talmud (not, however, unopposed) that Job was not a historical personage (Bava Bathra 14b and parallels). My own opinion is that the understanding of the book as fiction should not be accepted except in the narrow sense that events did not happen exactly as told. The book is too close to human experience to be taken as a total invention. In any case, the intensity of direct involvement shines through the haze rising out of the questions of historical literalness.

[52] On the arrangement of the text, cf. n. 50. The arrangement has received some oblique support with the publication, in 1971, of the Job targum (11QtgHi). The order of the text at the apparent end of the dialogue in that version is as follows: 42:1–2; 40:5; 42:4–6. While troublesome 42:4 is there, the replacement of 42:3(a) by 40:5 is certainly an improvement; not identical with the present proposal, it is of a piece with it.

[53] Read 'אֶשְׁנֶה', commentaries; literal translation "'do it twice'"; MT אֲעֶנֶה.

[54] לָכֵן as in Gen. 4:15; 30:15; 1 Sam. 28:2. F. J. Goldbaum, *JNES* 23 (1964), pp. 132–34, sweepingly generalizes a special application of the word, viz., the introduction of a vow.

wondrous for me, beyond my ken. [5]From hearsay I had heard of You, but now my eye sees You. [6]Therefore I retract[55] and repent in dust and ashes (40:3—5; 42:2, 3b, 5, 6).

The talk is coming to its end. Toward the conclusion of His address (40:2) God has called upon Job to answer. But this Job declines to do: "I cannot. I can no longer carry on. I am too light" (קַלֹּתִי; RSV: "I am of small account," which is a paraphrase). The root קלל is antonymous to כבד which yields the noun כָּבוֹד "weight, value, substance, essence of personality."[56] Biblical man's כָּבוֹד was most precious to him; take away his כָּבוֹד, and you deprive him of his better part. Job concerned himself with כָּבוֹד on two separate occasions in the earlier parts of the book (19:9; 29:20). But when God now asks him about the world and invites him to perform certain acts, Job who has no answer and is unable to meet the challenge disclaims all כָּבוֹד and says קַלֹּתִי. His position has crumbled, he cannot stand up and gird his loins like a man, he brings the disputation to a halt, he "will say no more" (40:4 f.). But if he does not know the answers to God's specific questions about the world, he has gained knowledge about God and thus indirectly about the world in general. God began His speech with the rhetorical question intending Job: "Just who darkens the plan by words without knowledge?" (38:2). God made and is upholding the world according to His plan, but Job misinterpreted it in his words, i.e., according to the light of his own conceptions. Now Job has become wiser. He sees that nothing God purposes is impossible—either of conception or of execution (42:2) Repudiation of his former position is now for Job both a necessary logical and existential consequence (42:3b).

Job's misinterpretation of God and the world was due to his conceptions which were by and large those of Israelite tradition. His argument with the friends rested on this ground common to all of them, and their disagreement was about secondary features and particularly had regard to the application of the philosophy of tradition to his fate. Tradition, the

---

[55] Cf. L. J. Kuyper, *VT* 9 (1959), pp. 91—94.

[56] כָּבוֹד as a social concept is "honor." "Die Ehre ist, objektiv, die Meinung Anderer von unserm Wert, und subjektiv, unsere Furcht vor dieser Meinung" (A. Schopenhauer, *Parerga und Paralipomena*, "Aphorismen zur Lebensweisheit," ch. 4. [*Sämtliche Werke*, vol. 4, Leipzig, Inselverlag, Grossherzog Wilhelm Ernst Ausgabe, no date, p. 426]).

text calls it שֵׁמַע אֹזֶן,[57] was immensely important in ancient Israel. When it
was tradition of religious doctrines, and when these doctrines were combined into a comparatively consistent whole, we speak of traditional theology. There is no part in the Old Testament which represents the most
common variety of traditional theology better than the talk of Job and the
friends. But let us remember that insofar as Israelite tradition was biblical it was given to eruptions, notably at the appearance of God. Job's
experience of divine revelation has raised him above the hearsay of tradition; he has "seen" God. This "seeing" is not, to be sure, mere sensory
perception by the eye but a personal meeting. And this meeting means for
man that he has achieved the closest contact with the Deity and is now
among His most faithful and intimate ones. Job had desired confrontation with God; he has received much more: communion. Be it clear, however, that this communion is not mystical oneness of man and God;
"Gott bleibt Gott, Mensch bleibt Mensch."[58] It is the closest possible
meeting of two personalities which remain distinct.

The communion of Job with God resembles the communion of the
prophets with the Divine. As such it has important consequences for the
understanding of the book, consequences in regard to which I find myself
in disagreement with Fohrer despite the fact that he, too, recognizes the
similarity of the experience of Job and that of the prophets.[59] The
prophets are taken into God's counsel. "God does nothing without
revealing His counsel to His servants the prophets," says Amos (3:7).
God deliberates with Amos (7:1—9; 8:3), with Isaiah (6:8—13), and
others as He deliberated aforetime with Abraham (Gen. 18:17—21,
23—33) and Moses (Exod. 32—34). Not only is the intellectual element
characteristically present in their communion with God, the communion
involves: usually the understanding of, often the approval of, sometimes
an active sharing in His plan. Job's communion with God is not bought
with an intellectual sacrifice, at the cost of renouncing his wish to understand the constitution of the world. True, of its creation, its expanse, its

---

[57] Words for hearing, asking, telling, remembering, and the like express the concept of
tradition in biblical Hebrew; e.g., 2 Sam. 7:22; Ps. 44:2; 78:3 f.; Deut. 4:32; 32:7; Job
8:8, 10; Exod. 13:8, 14; Judg. 6:13; Ps. 77:6 f.

[58] Fohrer, com., p. 535, n.6.

[59] Fohrer, com., p. 53

details—of animal life and of all the other things—he has no more knowledge now than he had before. But he now has gained an insight into its constitution, even as the prophets were granted new understanding in the communion with God (42:5).

"Therefore I retract and repent in dust and ashes." These are Job's final words. Outwardly nothing has changed for him. He is still sitting in the dirt: "He took a potsherd with which to scrape himself and sat in the ashes" (2:8). The ashes are the same, but it is a changed man who is sitting in them.

What has changed him? The revelation—by which we mean two things: the fact of the revelation itself and its content; and it is this content that is the answer to the problem of the work, the meaning of the Book of Job. The question is, however, just what is the content, what is God's reply?

A review of a few interpretations is in order before I offer my own interpretation. The criteria governing the selection are durability, newness, or the importance of the interpretations.

The interpretation that probably enjoys the greatest popularity is the one that might be labelled "education through overwhelming." Job is shown the immensity, complexity, and mystery of the universe; these greatly exceed his comprehension. For all this he can and does relate himself to this stupendous world by recognizing in it its creator, ruler and sustainer. God is not only infinitely mightier but also wiser than he. God's is that inscrutable business, the government of the world. While man thinks only of his own needs and problems, God sustains a whole world, providing for all His creatures. As Job is made aware of the world's material and spiritual dimensions—dimensions forever beyond his grasp—he is reduced to submission. The long catalog of the complexities and wonders of the universe, culminating in the evidence of the providential care for the animals, seems to bear out this interpretation; but its faults are so fatal—and glaring at that—that the fact of its wide acceptance must in itself be regarded as a problem in the history of the interpretation of the book. Job has never doubted God's power or wisdom. He has, in fact, repeatedly spoken of them, albeit mostly with bitterness because of God's capricious misuse of His superior might and wisdom to thwart justice (see, for instance, chs. 9 and 12). Although the complexities of the governance of the world have not been Job's concern, we are given no reason to doubt his readiness to recognize them. They are not, however, the issue, nor is God's ability to keep things going. The issue is: Why do I suffer? Why do the righteous suffer?[60]

Distantly related to this interpretation is the one given by M. Buber,[61] with which can loosely be associated that of G. von Rad.[62] Buber does not fail to see that the problem is not the dimensions and mysteries of the universe and that parading its complexities will not provide the answer. He sees that the problem is justice. But when it comes to the answer, Buber would have us believe that the answer is as follows: God teaches Job that divine justice, to be exact the justice of God which is manifest in creation, is greater than human justice; that it is not retributory and ega-litarian but allotting, spending, freely flowing; that God gives each crea-ture that which is appropriate, *suum cuique*. But this is no answer at all. For Job's question remains: Is it "appropriate" for the innocent to suffer and for the wicked to prosper? God's allotment of fates is not the issue; this Job has never doubted. What the issue does concern is the fate of the individual, its why and wherefore. What is the reason for God's not shap-ing this fate in accordance with the standards that He himself has set? In other words, not the *cuique* is the question but the *suum*. But what is particularly disturbing in Buber's interpretation is the very application of the term justice to God's generosity (a generosity which would here con-sist of a liberal allotment of suffering to the righteous). Nothing is gained by such assignment of private meanings to terms which in ordinary and universal usage—the Book of Job not excepted—denote the opposite.

Robert Gordis has another interpretation, whose essence may be stated in his own words. "Nature is . . . a cosmos, a thing of beauty . . . Just as there is order and harmony in the natural world . . . so there is order and meaning in the moral sphere . . . When man steeps himself in the beauty of the world his troubles . . . dissolve within the larger plan . . .

---

[60] It would be altogether consistent with the interpretation under scrutiny to make God answer this question with the counterquestion: "Are things not complicated enough the way they are now? Why do you want to make them more difficult with your ques-tion?"

[61] *The Prophetic Faith* (1949), pp. 194 f.; in the German original, *Werke*, vol. 2 (1964), pp. 441 f.

[62] *Theologie des A.T.*, vol. 1 (1957), pp. 414 f.

The beauty of the world becomes an anodyne to man's suffering—and the key to truth . . . and it is before this truth that he [Job] yields."[63] The operative words in the above argument are " . . . beauty becomes an anodyne to man's suffering—and the key to truth." If the question is justice, would anyone propose that the demands of justice are met by the administering of an anesthesia to the victim of an unjust sentence? And if the question is pain and torture, the beauty surrounding the tortured may in its contrast intensify the pain. It was just Bialik's sensitivity to a beauty in nature that indeed led him to write in בעיר ההרגה, a poem about the pogrom of Kishinev in 1903:

כִּי קָרָא אֲדֹנָי לָאָבִיב וְלַטֶּבַח גַּם־יָחַד:

הַשֶּׁמֶשׁ זָרְחָה, הַשִּׁטָּה פָּרְחָה, וְהַשּׁוֹחֵט שָׁחַט.[64]

The last interpretation to be examined, that of G. Fohrer, actually attacks the question of the problem itself.[65] The problem of the book, says Fohrer, is not: Why does the righteous man suffer? but: What is the proper conduct of man in suffering? It does not concern theodicy but man's life and his conduct. The question of theodicy is not even raised, for it is one which cannot be answered. From this it follows that the answer of the Book of Job cannot be found in the address of God but only in the final reply of Job. "In der vorbehaltlosen Hingabe an Gott und in der persönlichen Gemeinschaft mit ihm trägt und erträgt Hiob sein Geschick . . . Hiob wird in das grosse Leben und Leiden der Welt eingegliedert, zugleich aber durch die Gemeinschaft mit dem göttlichen Urgrund der Welt herausgehoben. Das ist das rechte Verstehen des Leides und das rechte Verhalten des Menschen in ihm: demütiges und hingebungsvolles Schweigen aus dem Ruhen in Gott. . . ."[66]

---

[63] In *Great Moral Dilemmas in Literature* . . . , R. M. MacIver ed. (1956), pp. 177 f.; *Judaism* 13 (1964), pp.48–63; *The Book of God and Man* (1965), pp. 155 f. The quotation is from *Judaism*, pp. 62 f.

[64] "The Lord called forth spring and killing at once: The sun shone, the locust bloomed, and the butcher butchered" (lines 21 f.)

[65] *ThZ* 18 (1962), pp. 1–24; com., pp. 532, 536, 557–59; cf. the opinions referred to on pp. 557 f., n. 21.

[66] 'In his unconditional surrender to God and personal communion with Him Job endures his fate . . . Job is integrated into the great life and suffering of the world, yet at the same time raised above it by his communion with the divine ground of the world. This is the proper understanding of suffering and man's proper conduct in it: submissive silence flowing from the repose in God' (Fohrer, com., p. 558). S. Terrien denies with

My earlier remarks indicate how far I am able to go along with Fohrer.[67] Job's reply and the way he replies are essential to the book. The book is more than the exposition of a concept; it is the life story of a man,[68] written with his life blood. The end of the story, his reply to the divine questioning, is indispensable, for without it the beginning and the middle are without justification. It completes the confrontation and complements the revelation. The fault of Fohrer's interpretation, as I see it, lies in its exclusiveness, i.e., in refusing to see in the Book of Job a theoretical treatise. It is my view that while it is not only a theoretical treatise, it is certainly that, and basically that. My criticism of those scholars who, disregarding the content of God's speech, restrict the answer of the book to the fact of the revelation,[69] also applies, in some measure, to Fohrer. Indeed, man's conduct in suffering may not exist even as a secondary theme.[70] But be that as it may, the primary theme is the suffering of the innocent. For the overwhelming majority of readers and commentators this is, and always has been, the problem of the book.[71]

Fohrer that the main theme of the book is the suffering of the innocent, the problem of theodicy; cf. his contribution to *The Interpreter's Bible*, vol. 3 (1954), pp. 877–1198, particularly pp. 897, 902; and his *Job* (*Commentaire de l'A. T.* 13; 1963), particularly pp. 35 f., 45–49. Terrien differs from Fohrer in that he refuses to deconceptualize the essence of the book as radically and systematically as does Fohrer. But this difference seems, at times, to be only one of degree. In a context which only slightly mitigates the boldness of his statement he says: Man "transgresse les limites de son humanité chaque fois qu'il prononce un jugement sur le caractère de la divinité" '(Man) transgresses the limits of his humanity whenever he pronounces a judgment about the essence of the divine' (*Job*, p. 45). Cf. also Rowley, pp. 176, 183.

[67] Cf. *supra*, p. 22.

[68] Cf. *supra*, p. 20.

[69] Cf. *supra*, pp. 10 f.

[70] It would be wrong to posit that in presenting Job's communion with God and his retraction the book sees a normative model for man's conduct in suffering.

[71] At this juncture it may be remarked that the epilogue, which could be expected to be relevant to the answer of the book, fails notably to offer confirmation of any of the foregoing interpretations or any other interpretation known to me. The epilogue vindicates Job in general but also explicitly in relation to the friends: "After having spoken these words to Job, the Lord said to Eliphaz, the Temanite: 'My wrath is kindled against you and your two friends, for you have not spoken of Me what is right as has My servant Job'" (vs. 7). It is in this verse and in some of the following that the author takes the occasion, the only time in the entire work, to state explicitly his opinion of the friends and

In a text of such demonstrated difficulty as is the speech of God (witness the numerous contradictory interpretations) the meaning often eludes a verse-to-verse approach. We shall, therefore, have recourse to another approach: first, we shall derive the answer to the problem of the book from its total conceptual content; second, seek the verification of the answer in the text of the divine address; third, apply two controls to the answer, one external to the address, the other to the book.

Job and his friends, worlds apart in many respects, share one belief; the acrimoniousness of their disputation and its minute details are due to this shared premise: the world is founded on justice, i.e., *quid pro quo*, reward and punishment, which will hereinafter be referred to as the principle of retribution. This principle pervades the world. Job and the

---

their philosophy and to sum up his evaluation of Job and his philosophy and conduct. But he does not even begin to explain why that which Job has spoken of God—as compared with that which the friends have—is right. (דִּבֶּר אֶל with the rare meaning "to speak of, concerning" [cf. 1 Sam 3:12] is a case of the otherwise frequent interchange of אֶל and עַל; the standard phase with this meaning is דִּבֶּר עַל.) Of even greater moment is the fact that he does not in any way relate the epilogue's vindication of Job to what must be regarded as absolutely true, namely, the divine answer. This may be accounted for in terms of the literary prehistory of the book (if the hypothesis is accepted that the author used an existing prose frame and adapted it imperfectly) or of the genre and purpose of the prose epilogue (i.e., the narrative hurries to the eventful end and seeks to avoid retarding complications). Whatever the reason, the reader may regret that the author is not more helpful in his last verses.

A characteristically modern approach deplores the very existence of the epilogue coming, as it does, after the heights of the poetry achieved in the final chapters. Admitting the literary requirement of a complete narrative frame, beginning and end, and even the desirability of the idyllic tones of the finale, a number of readers yet regard this finale as anticlimatic (cf. Kuhl 1953, pp. 204 f.; Rowley, pp. 159 f.). This approach elicits two comments. One, it cannot be assumed as a matter of course that the ancient Israelite would have been disturbed by this anticlimax in the same manner as the contemporary Westerner reared on the canons of Greek literary style and theory. The Israelite may indeed have welcomed it with relief. Secondly, the epilogue provides the needed resolution of the plot. Job was afflicted with physical ailments and social ostracism and suffered spiritual torments. He was freed of the last of these afflictions in the final chapters of the poetry; the physical and social penalties remain. The problem of the book, which is spiritual, is solved, and Job is vindicated—as will be shown—before the epilogue. But he remains in his physical pain and in social disgrace. His pain was a necessary device in the drama of ideas. This drama now over and pain having played out its role, that pain should be removed. The epilogue does just this.

friends hold fast to this belief because they have been raised in it; because everybody has it; because man has an intense need to abide by it. The need is so great that he goes to the remotest extremes to uphold it. When reality does not agree with the principle of retribution, whose function is to structure and interpret reality, so much the worse for reality. Man distorts his experience of reality, disregards facts, imagines figments, fashions *ad hoc* theories and erects superstructures, all so as not to give up or substantially change the principle. A parade example of this phenomenon is the discussion of Job and the friends. What accounts for this phenomenon? The fact that this principle of retribution is the touchstone of man's life and his conduct within his society. Whether in the rearing of children or the administration of justice, it is this principle which guides him. From it flow some of his noblest deeds. And so it is natural that God is conceived as guaranteeing it in the governance of the world.

But give up the principle, reject causality in the physical-ethical world, and the problem of Job, the man and the book, disappears. Where justice is possible, injustice is, too. Where it is not, where the principle of retribution has no validity, there can be no injustice. In the absence of this principle, for Job to expect a lot corresponding morally with his deed is absurd. Where there is no ground for expecting anything, it is pointless for him to complain of his disappointment: that though he has been pious and upright, his lot is bitter. Nor is there any point to the inference drawn by the friends from Job's lot to his conduct. To repeat: only the awareness that the complex world of matter and ideas, unlike the simple world of pure matter, is not governed by the category of cause-and-effect, i.e., only the elimination of the principle of retribution, can solve the problem of the book.[72]

This is the inescapable conclusion from the conceptual content of the

---

[72] N.N. Glatzer, *supra* (n.1) pp. 194—97 and 247 f., quotes two excerpts from modern authors who sketch answers to the problem of Job in a way reminiscent of the answer proposed here. One is the classicist Gilbert Murray; the quotation is from his *Aeschylus; The Creator of Tragedy* (1940), pp. 91—95. The other is the chemist and educator James B. Conant; the quotation is from his *Modern Science and Modern Man* (1952), pp. 88 f. A recent answer, to be grouped with those of Murray and of Covant, is E. M. Good's "Job and the Literary Task ...," *Soundings* 56 (1973), pp. 470—84.

book and an analysis of its problem. Its verification must be sought in God's address. God says to Job: "You were not present when the universe was created. You do not know its blueprint or the stuff that went into its making." No less than three times God refers to the "foundation," "the basis," and "the cornerstone" of the inhabited world, the earth (38:4, 6). "What, then, makes you assume that it is justice which is its foundation?" "Moreover," God continues, "you do not know the mundane phenomena of the natural world." And He draws progressively tighter circles around Job, proceeding in order of diminishing expanse from the realm of the heaven and the underworld to that of those wild beasts which Job, for all his desire, cannot domesticate. Arriving at what is most familiar to Job, He finally asks: "Perhaps, at least, you know your own homestead?" No answer. "If, then, you know nothing and can do nothing, why ever should you assume that retribution, justice (צֶדֶק) is a constituent element in the plan (עֵצָה [38:2], מְזִמָּה [42:2]) of the world?" (38:2). Thus God leads Job through the macrocosm and microcosm, but nowhere does Job see justice. From the linguistic approach, it is striking that √צדק and other roots which express the idea of justice, viz. √ישר and √חמם, while rather frequent in chs. 1—31,[73] are not found at all in the story of Job's journey through the world.[74] And let us note, the centrality of the idea of justice in the book and the broadness of the canvas on which the universe is painted preclude the deprecation of this observation as an argument from silence.

But we are not left with negative argumentation alone. The divine address contains some passages that have not, it seems to me, received due attention in the commentaries. It is striking that the description of the inanimate world, comprising almost all of chapter 38, is interrupted by an evaluative and teleological proposition centering on man: "Have you ever in your life commanded the morning, have you directed the dawn to its place [13]to take hold of the skirts of the earth so that the wicked are shaken out of it, [15]so that light is withheld from the wicked,

---

[73] The Elihu chapters (32—37) are disregarded; cf. n. 17.

[74] √צדק occurs 19 times, √ישר 7 times, √חמם 16 times. √צדק, with the legal meaning "to be vindicated," occurs in 40:8 after the journey through the world; the occurrence is therefore not counted. √חמם in 31:40 means "to finish," and this passage is also not counted.

and their uplifted arm is broken?" (38:12 f., 15). This can mean one thing only: there is no provision for retribution, nor any manifestation of it in the order of the world. The dawn of every day provides an occasion to punish the wicked, but this possibility is not in practice realized and is therefore not in the plan of the world. "Consider this fundamental fact," Job is told: "The sun rises over the righteous and the sinners alike. Can you change that?"

The end of God's speech is similar in meaning. Here is an excerpt: "Will the reprover enter suit against Shaddai? [8]Will you put Me in the wrong so that you may be vindicated? [9]Or is it that you have an arm like God? [12]Seeing anyone haughty, abase him and tread down the wicked in their tracks. [14]Then I, too, will acknowledge that your right hand is all-prevailing" (40:2, 8—14). Everything is rhetorical or hypothetical. God and Job know that he cannot possibly do these things: it is not in the plan, not in the plan for the wicked to be punished. If Job were able to perform these things, his criticism of God would be justified, not only by the demonstration of his own prowess but, more important, by the demonstration that retribution is at least potentially operative in the world and need only be actualized. Failing a demonstration of this ability, the assumption of punishment of the wicked and reward of the righteous is without ground, and Job has no right to blame God.

The third passage I shall cite is the least conspicuous but the most interesting: "Who has cleft a channel for the rain flood or a way for the thunder cloud [26]to cause rain on land where no man is, on a desert where no people live [27]to satiate waste and desolate terrain and to sprout fresh grass?" (38:25—27). As God describes the meterological phenomena, he is implying: "Consider this, Job: precious rain, that would be so beneficial to human beings, is wasted on land uninhabited and uninhabitable. In the natural world, where the category of cause-and-effect is operative, man is not as central as you fancy." This is, in effect, God's polemic with Job. It is, by the same token, the author's polemic with the point of view found in the rest of the Bible, for Job represents the general biblical point of view. Rain, in the Bible, figures prominently as a vehicle of reward and punishment. It is given for good deeds and withheld for evil ones. Here, however, the phenomenon is shown not to be a vehicle of morality at all—the moral purpose ascribed to it just does not exist. (Be it noted that the text does not state that the rain falls partly on the desert and partly on the sown. The point is that it falls on the desert where it has no relevance for man.)

God says: "No retribution is provided for in the blueprint of the world, nor does it exist anywhere in it. None is planned for the nonhuman world and none for the human world. Divine justice is not an element of reality. It is a figment existing only in the misguided philosophy with which you have been inculcated. The world in which you and the friends are spun is a dream. Wake up, Job!" And wake up is what Job does at the end.

Let us now adduce controls for our thesis. One control, whose substance is acknowledged by all, yet whose significance in the total picture is commonly ignored, is the knowledge that we, the readers of the prologue, possess—we know that Job did not suffer in retribution for what he had done. We know that his presuppositions were wrong in part and those of the friends in toto; that their discussion, earnest though it was, was largely out of touch with reality. The Book of Job is, from the first chapter, the classical statement that a man's lot is not the consequence of his deeds. The prologue, for one thing, shows that in the one exemplary case with which it is concerned divine justice, retributuion, does not enter into the heavenly considerations. Against this reading of the whole book in the light of its prologue it may be argued that, our earlier remark notwithstanding,[75] allowance should be made for a narrative feature which exists purely for the sake of the plot and is probably not intended to have a bearing on the ideas of the book. The argument, however, while legitimate in principle, "makes allowance," i.e., it reckons with a literary flaw in a work so artistic as to make such allowance gratuitous. Be that as it may, the innocence of Job is a feature not confined to the narrative of the prologue but one providing the basis of the entire work; without it there is no problem of Job, indeed there is no Book of Job.

The other control is historical and circumstantial. It is stronger than the previous control for being external to the book and weaker because, resting on its date, it is prey to the uncertainties of literary history. Yet for all the difficulty of dating, the overwhelming majority of scholars, for a variety of reasons, dates the Book of Job between the sixth and the

---

[75] Cf. *supra*, pp. 1–3.

fourth centuries B.C. Now that is the very period in which the earlier doctrine of collective retribution (represented, for instance, in the Pentateuch) had lost its sway without yet being replaced by the doctrine of individual retribution in the world-to-come. (From time to time there was attempted an application of the earlier doctrine of retributory justice to the individual rather than to the group. These attempts, notably in wisdom texts *sensu proprio,* remained ephemeral, the doctrine foundering on the rock of reality: the wicked flourish, and the righteous perish.) Now the earlier and the later doctrines have an effective answer to the problem of the suffering of the innocent. The former, the collective answer, operates with a social unit large in the number of its components, the individual Israelites, and extended in time, the people of Israel through the generations. When dealing with a group as large and long-lived as a nation it is possible to work out solutions in accordance with the principle of collective retribution. The latter, the belief of retribution in the other world, admits by definition no difficulties: retribution, deferred to a future life, cannot be contradicted by experience.

(In the later history of Judaism and in Christianity these religions continued to experiment with various combinations of the forms of retribution—individual, collective, and otherworldly. Enjoying the shelter of flexible retributory creeds, they have not been troubled by the problem central to the book in a measure at all commensurable with the concern of modern readers who find themselves unable to accept the theological shelter which ideological versatility makes possible for these religions. Hence it is that in modern times, when nontraditional religiosity has come to the fore, the Book of Job figures so much more prominently than was the case hitherto either in the thinking or the liturgy of Judaism and Christianity.)

Thus it would seem clear that the sixth through the third centuries represented that one period in the history of biblical religion which is not covered, or, at best, very scantily covered, by one or the other form of the idea of divine justice. It is in this period that the problem of the suffering of the innocent is most likely to have been answered in a way other than, hence opposed to, that of divine justice = retribution. And this is the very period to which the Book of Job is commonly dated. It is through the combination of our view, viz., that the solution which the book offers to the problem is the radical denial of the principle of retribution, and the accepted determination of the date of the book that the gap in the history of thought on this problem is neatly filled. At some time during the sixth through the third centuries a book was written which said to man: Neither hope for reward for good deeds nor fear punishment for evil deeds; moralists cannot shake the wicked from the surface of the earth and God will not. The laws of the natural order and those of the moral order are not of a piece. If you decide to do what is good, do it because it is good.

Let us now, laying aside our concern for checking conclusions, extend our consideration of the adventure of ideas. The Book of Job continues the intellectual and religious enterprise, begun in the earlier books of the Bible, of emptying the world of much that had been put into it during the preceding millennia by human fantasy operating to satisfy human concerns. These books demythologized the world.[77] The Book of Job, in this respect, does not lag behind any of them. It features, as has been observed before, an abundance of images from the then current myths but does not fail to provide its own understanding of them:[78] the world is not as the myths would have it. If, therefore, the myths do not describe reality, their appearance or allusions to them in the book is a matter of literary style and artistic convention somewhat in the manner of the tropes and mythological figures in the libretti of Metastasio.

But the Book of Job does more than demythologize the world; it also de-moralizes it, which is to say, makes it amoral. It completes the process whose first phase is known to the reader of the Bible from the opening pages of Genesis: the removal from the conceptual world of an order of superhuman beings independent of the Deity. And it extends it by the denial of the realization of moral values—values deriving from the Deity, to be sure—other than realization effected by man. This new world is as harsh as it is simple, for in it man is deprived of the protection he enjoys in a world saturated with myth and morality and populated with powers to which he might turn with a view to rendering them favorable to his well-being, foremost by his leading a meritorious life.

[77] "Myth" and its derivatives are used here in the narrow sense, referring to identifiable myths of the ancient Near East, their cognates, and their possible reflexes in Israel.

[78] Cf. the remarks to 38:8–11, 28 f., *supra*, pp. 13, 16.

The number of alternative explanations offered for the meaning of the Book of Job confronts each interpreter with the question: If what you say is right, why does the book not say so in so many words? An easy answer is that the dramatic and poetic nature of such a work, containing layer upon layer of depth and hinting at yet others, precludes a plain and direct proposition. The interpretation offered here suggests an additional answer, which might be adduced in support of the interpretation: the very radicalism of the book's answer, shattering a central biblical doctrine and a belief cherished in ancient Israel, would itself demand the protection of a veil. The book is, to be sure, uniquely daring in many other respects and according to any interpretation: the pronouncements of Job against God, agonized and agonizing, must have evoked a shudder in the biblical audience. Yet these outbursts do not constitute a new and radical doctrine; they can be passed off as cries of a man in pain. But the answer of God, presenting a doctrine as radical as it is new, a doctrine in dia-metrical opposition to the teaching of tradition, may never have been tolerated or preserved for us but for the protection of its form, its eschewal of the direct, categorical pronouncement.

If we look once more at the structure of the work, the unity of frame and colloquy, whether primary or secondary,[79] now appears in a bright light. Two questions were posed in the prologue; one, What is piety? the other, Is there piety?[80] We had some reason to answer the second question in the affirmative. The final chapters strengthen the affirmation: it is to Job, the man who, above all other men, exemplifies piety (1:8), that God reveals Himself. In this context, revelation connotes more than rela-tivity and rank ("there is none as pious as he") denote; it constitutes, in effect, the affirmation by God that Job is pious. Our main interest, how-ever, is in the first question, the essential feature of whose answer was put forward in the prologue without equivocation: piety, whatever its other attributes, must be disinterested. Egoistically motivated connection between the religio-moral and the natural worlds, common since the beginning of the history of the human kind and evident in many parts of the Bible, is forever precluded by this unequivocal answer of the pro-

---

[79] Cf. n. 2.
[80] Cf. *supra*, pp. 2 f.

logue; for to make this connection is to deprive attitude, behavior, or action of the dignity of piety. God's answer, however, goes a step further. It severs any causal connection, hitherto assumed in the world at large and prominent everywhere in the Bible, between these two worlds; a person's fate is dissociated from, and unrelated to, his religio-moral attitude or actions. The prologue says that one ought not to, the divine address says that one cannot, expect anything for one's behavior.[81] Job behaved piously throughout, but his behavior had, in the narrated time[82] of 1:13—31:40, no consequences compatible with the accepted idea of reward and punishment; yet he most ardently hoped for these consequences and was utterly shaken when his hopes were not realized. God tells him in chs. 38—40 that these consequences nowhere and never follow, and that it is, therefore, futile to hope for them. In his final reply (40:3—5; 42:2 f.,5 f.) Job acknowledges this fact and thus, free of misconception, is now prepared for a pious and moral life uncluttered by false hopes and unfounded claims. To resort to a simile: the unity of the book may be likened to a switchback traversing rugged territory yet ever maintaining the general direction toward the goal; on a lower bend, the answer of the prologue—on an upper bend, the divine answer.

The Book of Job, a supreme expression of religious faith, presents the purest moral theory in the Bible. Now it would be a grave error to interpret its denial of divine retribution as constituting a legitimate excuse for man from his obligations to establish justice on earth. Justice is not woven into the stuff of the universe nor is God occupied with its administration but it is an ideal to be realized by society and in it. As to God himself, while the book does not say so explicitly, it does not exclude the possibility of God's obligating Himself to abide by human standards in

---

[81] This generalization has two aspects. (1) The prologue, to be sure, deals only with reward, the expected result of pious behavior, and not with punishment; only the discourse extends the doctrine to include punishment (4:7—11; and elsewhere). (2) Strictly speaking, the prologue does not say that man ought to expect nothing for his behavior; it says only that his behavior ought to be independent of the fulfillment or nonfulfillment of his expectations. The generalization is nonetheless, in my opinion, unobjectionable. The prologue is a narrative which singles out parts which characterize the whole and does not constitute a discursive, comprehensive treatment of the whole.

[82] Cf. M. Weiss, *Biblica* 46 (1965), p. 182.

regard to specific occasions and contexts. Thus God, while often the author of the standards for human conduct, is Himself bound by them only in exceptional cases.

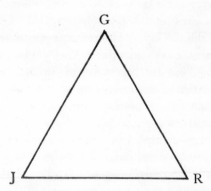

Let us imagine an equilateral triangle, at the three vertexes of which we have G standing for God Who turns His face to man and is accessible to him, J for Job, the upright man, and R for the philosophy of retribution or justice in the world. The Book of Job, then, tells of an attempt to maintain these ideas simultaneously—an attempt which ends in failure. It is the purpose of the book to demonstrate the impossibility of the coexistence of these three ideas and the consequent logical necessity to give up one of them. The friends cancel J, maintaining G and R. God eliminates R, maintaining G and J. Job all but gives up G, as he maintains J and R. Now it is the limiting phrase "all but" that makes a religious book of what would otherwise have been merely a theological treatise. It epitomizes Job's struggle with himself and with God. He knew in his bones that he was just. At the same time he shared the concept of his age that it is the business of God to maintain the category of cause-and-effect in the moral as well as in the natural world. Unable to compromise the fact of his innocence or to divest himself of the concept of his age, he distorted perforce the image of God. But this distortion accomplished nothing; he yet felt that he was wrong, he hoped and, for moments, even held the conviction that God had His face turned toward him, if not with favor then at least with interest, that God would one day "long for" him (14:15). He wanted therefore to "come" to God (23:3), to "see" Him, i.e., His true image (19:26 f.). In his unflagging but futile attempt to interpret the vicious triangle he became ever more enmeshed in contradictions. He maintained J and R and despaired of, yet did not surrender, G. At times observation of reality led him nonetheless to the conclusion that R was wrong, i.e., that the world is not governed by justice. At these moments he came close to one aspect of God's position. Yet only close; he could only conceive of the dichotomy justice/injustice, until God showed him that this dichotomy is not adequate for the structuring of reality, for it lacks the third required element: nonjustice. These three elements should indeed be grouped in a dichotomy, but in the form: justice-injustice/nonjustice. The left side of the dichotomy, justice-injustice, is societal, the right one, nonjustice, is extrasocietal. The error of Job and the friends lay in this that they permitted the societal aspect of the dichotomy to encroach on the extrasocietal one. This is the error of R. But once the error is recognized, R is eliminated, and G and J remain—this is God's answer. Job accepts the answer. Unencumbered now by the old doctrine of justice and retribution, he receives confirmation of his former hope that God does turn His face to man, that He is accessible to him—confirmation provided by the theophany. To put it differently: He Who speaks to man in the Book of Job is neither a just nor an unjust god but God.

Of Job, enmeshed in his contradictions, who at the end recanted everything he had said, God says to the friends: "You have not spoken of Me what is right as has My servant Job" (42:7). The error that Job upheld and was compelled to renounce was yet closer to the truth than the arguments of the friends for all the support of many authorities that these arguments enjoyed. This is the judgment of the book. From the contradictions of Job there is a way to truth, from the consistencies of the friends, none.

Deeper and more beautiful yet are the words of the Midrash (*Pesiqta Rabbati, Aḥare Mot* [3], ed. M. Friedmann, 190b): אלו לא קרא תגר כשם שאומרים עכשו בתפילה אלהי אברהם אלהי יצחק ואלהי יעקב כך היו אומרים ואלהי איוב "Had he [Job] not clamored so—as it is now the practice to say in prayer 'God of Abraham, God of Isaac, and God of Jacob,' so one would say 'and God of Job'."

The Basic Meaning of the Biblical Sabbath

A n attempt will be made here to determine the basic meaning of the sabbath as it is conceived in the Old Testament. The undertaking might appear unnecessary. The Bible, in presenting sabbath commandments and prohibitions, associates with them several statements, more or less explicit, that offer a rationale for the keeping of the sabbath. But scholarly opinion differs in regard to questions of the originality or derivative nature of the formulations of these rationales. It is, therefore, advisable not to base our inquiry into the essential meaning of the sabbath on these foundations. As our study progresses, we will have occasion to examine them.

We take our departure from the sabbath section of the Decalogue, a text whose centrality for our study is determined by the ease with which other important texts can be related to it.[1] We begin with the citation of the two versions of the Decalogue statement of the sabbath law.

Ex 20: 8—11	Deut 5:12—15
8 Remember	
	12 Take heed of
the sabbath day and keep it holy.	the sabbath day and keep it holy, as the Lord your God has commanded you.
9 You have six days to labor and do all your work,[2]	13 You have six days to labor and do all your work,[2]

---

[1] Note every sabbath text of the Old Testament is relevant to our study. We shall consider only those passages that are of material consequence for our search.

[2] Thus *The New English Bible* (1970), whose interpretation implicit in this translation, I fully indorse as against the poorly argued proposition of J. D. W. Watts, *ZAW* 74 (1962), pp. 141—145.

10 but the seventh day is a
   sabbath of the Lord your God;
   that day you shall do no work
   at all—neither you, your son,
   your daughter, nor your slave,
   your slave girl, nor

   your cattle, or the alien
   within your gates.

11 For in six days the Lord
   made heaven and earth, the sea
   and all that is in them, and on
   the seventh day He rested;

   therefore the Lord
   has blessed the sabbath day
   and declared it holy.

14 but the seventh day is a
   sabbath of the Lord your God;
   that day you shall do no work
   at all—neither you, your son,
   your daughter, nor your slave,
   your slave girl, nor
   your ox, your ass, nor any of
   your cattle, or the alien
   within your gates,
   so that your slave and slave
   girl may rest as you do.[3]

15 Remember that you were a slave
   in Egypt, and the Lord your God
   brought you out with a strong
   hand and an outstretched arm;
   therefore the Lord

   your God has commanded you
   to keep the sabbath day.

Both versions are etiothetic in large measure. This is abundantly clear from כי "for" and למען "so that", respectively, and if it were necessary, the effect of these words is strengthened by על כן "therefore". The formal parallelism, however, only serves to highlight the problem raised by the content. Thus, in Exodus it is God's resting after the work of creation which is given as the reason for Israel's keeping the sabbath, whereas in Deuteronomy the rationale lies in the slave's need for rest and the memory of Israel's slavery in Egypt and subsequent salvation.

The Decalogue, to be sure, is not the only text where these themes are put forth as rationales of the sabbath. The theme of God's rest is mentioned in Gen 2:(1—)2f. and Ex 31:17, and that of social ethics in Ex 23:12. The third rationale is indicated in Ez 20, where admonitions to

---

[3] See n. 7.

keep the sabbath and rebukes for not keeping it (vss. 12 f., 16, 20 f., 24) are imbedded in a text which emphasizes God's salvific act of bringing Israel forth from Egypt.[4] But it is the presence of several motivations in the two versions of the Decalogue which raises the problem, which of them is original in the Decalogue and whether indeed anyone represents the basic meaning of the sabbath. Three rationales are given,[5] but only one can have been original in the Decalogue format. Having no criterion to determine which is the original, we must, for the present, put them all aside.

It is a well argued and commonly held view that the Decalogue in its present form is the result of a long process of growth, and that the sabbath section in it is one of those which have absorbed several accretions in the middle and at the end. This view not only supports our decision to disregard all rationales since, ex hypothesi, none is original, but it also makes it inadvisable to assume that any of them contains the basic meaning of the sabbath for it would follow from it that the basic meaning is contained in an addition to the Decalogue but not in the original text.[6]

---

[4] While, in Ez 20, this rationale is only implicit, two others are fully spelled out there. Common to the latter is the concept of symbolism: the sabbath is a sign (אות). The first says that the sabbaths (Ezekiel prefers the plural) are a sign that Yhwh sanctifies Israel (vs. 12), the second that they are a sign that He is their God (vs. 20). Sabbath and holiness are associated expressly or contextually in a number of biblical passages beginning with the Decalogue; the "sign" adds its peculiar symbolism to the association. The rationale that the observance of the sabbath is a sign of Israel's acceptance of Yhwh as its God is not distant from the idea that the sabbath is (a sign of) the covenant (ברית; Ex 31:16 f.).

One need not dispute these rationales to recognize that the basic meaning of the sabbath is not found in them. Holiness is all-embracing; pertaining to religion in general, it is not the specific meaning of a specific religious phenomenon. Thus, sacrifices are holy, but holiness is not their meaning; nor is it even their rationale: man does not offer sacrifices because they are holy. Neither is the other rationale, the sabbath as a sign of Yhwh's divinity, the answer to our quest. Cessation of work at frequent intervals can no more be traced back to the idea of the divinity of Yhwh or the covenant, of which it is called a sign, than circumcision, which is similarly characterized (Gen 17:7, 9—11 f., 13 f.). These symbols of the covenant are arbitrary. That which signifies and that which is signified have no natural, extrasymbolical relationship with one another.

[5] It may be that two of them, namely those of the Deuteronomy text, ought to be reduced to one by regarding one of them as basic and the other as subsidiary to it.

[6] While a remote possibility initially exists that both the original and one of the additions may contain the basic meaning, we shall see that such is, in the event, not the case.

Of the texts mentioned on the preceding pages, Ex 23:12 is of special interest. It corresponds rather closely to Deut. 5:14 end in regard to the rationale of social ethics. It reads: "You have six days to do your labor but on the seventh day you shall abstain (תשבת), *so that* (למען) *your ox and your ass may rest* (ינוח), and the son of *your slave girl* and *the alien* may have a respite." Deut. 5:14 end shall be repeated here to facilitate comparison; identical or similar expressions are *in italics:* "(*your ox and your ass . . .* and *the alien* within your gates) *so that* (למען) your slave and *your slave girl may rest* (ינוח) as you do"[7].

One may be predisposed to look to the Exodus verse for the primary meaning of the sabbath. The verse is from an early text, the so-called Book of the Covenant, and one's first search for basic or primary meanings is naturally in early literature. Also, the apodosis of the sentence begins with "so that", and where a reason is given or an intention pronounced, the underlying idea cannot be far away; if the text is early, it is not improbable that the idea is identical with the basic meaning. Finally, and other than in Deut. 5:14, there is no indication that this etiothetic clause is not genuine.

For all this, however, the basic meaning is not found here.[8] In fact, no meaning of the sabbath is contained in the verse.[9] As to the expressed rationale, it is clearly secondary; that is, it applies only to beasts and persons in various states of dependence. As concerns them, the sabbath law

---

[7] The close relationship between Ex 23:12 and Deut 5:14 invites a comment on כמוך "(so that your slave . . . may rest) as you (do)" of Deuteronomy. For one thing, it has no correspondent in Exodus and, more important, it is stylistically infelicitous. Since the text does not say, "You shall rest", it is awkward to say that the slave shall rest "as you do". And if one would suggest for the sake of the argument that in the sabbath legislation resting is the same as not working, he would have the law say, "You, your son, or your slave must not work, so that your slave, like you, shall not work". This would place the emphasis where it manifestly cannot belong—on the slave.

One can only surmise as to the intention of כמוך "as you (do)". Perhaps it means to convey a certain balance: "Your slave . . . may rest as you do—and remember that you were a slave in Egypt."

[8] M. Noth, *Das zweite Buch Mose* (1959), p. 154 (English translation [1962], p. 190), is aware of this, while G. Beer, *Exodus* (1939), p. 119, gropes toward it.

[9] There is, perhaps, a faint indirect hint at a meaning in the contextual association with the šemiṭṭa law of the immediately preceding verses, for which see n. 17. I characterize the hint, if any, as indirect and faint because from these verses no meaning of the šemiṭṭa itself can be extracted.

is a social law of charity and benevolence. The need for legislation of this kind is obvious. The independent Israelite, however pressing his need for work, is free to interrupt his labors, at least for a little while, whenever he is exhausted or thinks he can afford it. It is his laborers and his beasts who need the protection provided by the law of a minimum and regular physical rest. The free Israelites, the partners in the covenant, the recipients of the Torah, to whom primarily the sabbath is given—these are not named as beneficiaries of the sabbath rest. The lawgiver states the salutary effect of the injunction. His eagerness to make this point is underscored by his having made a similar statement in the preceding verse, which deals with the *šemiṭṭa* year. Still, his formulation of the sabbath law contains no more than a secondary reason, for he does not preach to the beasts or the aliens. A primary reason, a motivation affecting directly those who are commanded to observe the law, is not offered.

The failure to mention the Israelite citizen in the etiothetic clauses here and in Deut 5:14 is noteworthy. Both passages combine to convey the sense, which is unmistakable for all its being implied and negative: "Rest"[10] does not describe what Israel does or should do on the sabbath. As far as Israel is concerned, sabbath rest and restfulness is not a biblical commandment. Any notion to the contrary must be traced to post-Old Testament literature.[11]

We now return to the Decalogue. Having seen that the basic meaning of the sabbath is not found in the etiothetic passages, we must also note that the list of persons and beasts (Ex 20:10b/Deut 5:14bα) is merely an expatiation on the "you" to whom the prohibition is addressed and therefore of no relevance to our search. We are left, then, with the first two and a half verses treating the sabbath, Ex 20:8—10a/Deut 5:12—14a: "Remember/Take heed of[11a] the sabbath day and keep it holy (/as the Lord

---

[10] Verb or noun; נוח or another, infrequent root.

[11] The nearest the Old Testament comes to this notion is in the Decalogue of Exodus: "For in six days the Lord made heaven and earth . . . and on the seventh day He rested."

[11a] The verbs שמר and זכר constitute a pair of near synonymous variants. Treaty and covenant texts show repeatedly that there is an almost indifferent choice between these verbs for expressing the idea of keeping (the treaty or covenant). The same is true of the Akkadian equivalents *ḥasāsu* "to remember" and *naṣāru* "to keep" in similar contexts. See M. Weinfeld in *Theologisches Wörterbuch zum A.T.* I, coll. 788 f., and, in greater detail, לשוננו 36 (1971/72), p. 92, n. 71, and pp. 96f.

your God has commanded you). You have six days to labor and do all your work, but the seventh day is a sabbath of the Lord your God; that day you shall do no work at all."

This quotation has four clauses. The first characterizes the sabbath as holy, a characterization which offers no clue to the reason.[12] Therefore, if that reason is expressed in the Decalogue, we must search for it in the adjoining three clauses. These may now be compared with two other texts. The first, Lev 23:3, reads: "On six days work may be done, but on the seventh day there is a sabbath of complete abstention (שבת שבתון), a sacred celebration. You shall do no work at all; it is a sabbath of the Lord in all your habitations." The verse is from the introduction to the festival calendar of Leviticus (23:1—44), a part of the law collection of Holiness. The similarity is striking.[13] Indeed, because of the very closeness in the formulations a comparison of these two laws contributes little to the understanding of the Decalogue section; there just is not very much in Lev 23:3 that is not in the Decalogue. And here our search would have to rest but for another law from the Holiness collection, Lev 25:3f. With the addition of this text the points of similarity and dissimilarity, the features of repetition and novelty make for a productive comparison: "You have six years to sow your fields, six years to prune your vineyards and gather the yield, 4but in the seventh year the land shall have a sabbath of complete abstention; it is a sabbath of the Lord. That year you shall not sow your fields nor prune your vineyards."

A synoptic arrangement of the three Hebrew texts brings out into relief both the similarities and the differences. Texts A, B, and C are, respectively, the Decalogue section, Lev 23:3, and 25:3f.

Text A	Text B	Text C
ששת ימים	ששת ימים	שש שנים
תעבד		תזרע שדך

---

[12] See n. 4.

[13] The question as to how to account for the similarities between the sabbath section of the Decalogue and Lev 23 as well as for other similarities pointed out in this article cannot easily be answered within the framework of the various documentary hypotheses. The Decalogue-Lev 23 question is given a detailed consideration by H. Graf Reventlow, *Gebot und Predigt im Dekalog* (1962), pp. 50—56. The present discussion is not predicated on any one of the proposed answers.

		ושש שנים
		תזמר כרמך
ועשית כל מלאכתך		ואספת את תבואתה
	תֵעשה מלאכה	
ויום השביעי	וביום השביעי	ובשנה השביעת
	שבת שבתון	שבת שבתון
		יהיה לארץ
	מקרא קדש	
שבת ליהוה אלהיך		שבת ליהוה
לא תעשה		
כל מלאכה	כל מלאכה	שדך
	לא תעשו	לא תזרע
		וכרמך
		לא תזמר
	שבת הוא ליהוה	
	בכל מושבתיכם	

Let us focus on Text C for its differences, differences within similarity being our desideratum. This text deals not with the sabbath day but with the sabbath year; i.e., it is a *šemiṭṭa* text.[14] The idea of *šemiṭṭa* as it applies to landed property, the content of Lev 25:1—7, is readily accessible: reclaiming the land for its true lord and owner, God. Its clearest formulation appears in v. 23: "For the land is Mine."[15] To be sure, the quotation is from the jubilee law, the continuation of the *šemiṭṭa* law, with which it forms a unit.[16] But this fact should not stand in the way of

[14] The laws use the verb שמט equally with fields (Ex 23:11) and debts (Dtn 15:2f.) as direct objects, corresponding to Middle Hebrew שמיטת קרקעות and שמטת כספים. No English word covers both uses adequately.

[15] I dealth with the idea of *šemiṭṭa* in the Yeivin jubilee volume (ספר שמואל ייבין [1969/70]), pp. 283—288, in an article entitled "עניין שמיטה אצל הר סיני."

[16] That is, a unit of content; the laws are of the same kind. Whether it is also a literary unit is of little importance for our concern. Opinions about the literary question diverge widely; cf. O Eissfeldt, *Einleitung in das A.T.*² (1956), p. 282 (English transl. [1965], p. 235; Eissfeldt largely follows B. Baentsch, *Exodus-Leviticus-Numeri* [1903], pp. 422—430), and is, in turn, followed by K. Elliger, *Leviticus* (1966), pp. 335—349. M. Noth, *Das dritte Buch Mose* (1962), p. 7, believes that it is hardly possible to reconstruct the literary history of the laws of Leviticus.

our realizing that the same idea must underlie the verse that precedes our *šemiṭṭa* text in column C. Vs.2 says, "The land shall observe a sabbath of the Lord." The integral nature of the text as a whole is reinforced by the repetition in wording two verses later: "The land shall have a sabbath of complete abstention; it is a sabbath of the Lord." Man, in refraining at regular intervals from exploiting the land for his own needs, thereby places it under the lordship of God. And with the land he places himself, its possessor and cultivator, under divine dominion. This is not fancy. The passage from the jubilee section (vs. 23), affirming God's lordship over the land, is complemented in the same section by a parallel affirmation of His lordship over Israel: "For the Israelites are My slaves" (or: "servants", vs. 55). This last verse is not the conclusion merely of the last item in the chapter but expresses the rationale for the entirety of its provisions, including the content of our column C.

It is only a short and logical step, then, to proceed from the striking similarity of form and content in the *šemiṭṭa* text of column C and the sabbath texts of columns A and B to a conclusion concerning the correspondence of meaning.[17] The key phrase is "a sabbath of the Lord". As

---

[17] The Holiness collection is not the only legal text to link sabbath and *šemiṭṭa* laws. The Exodus text discussed earlier (see also n. 9) is another. In the ensuing synopsis, text D is Ex 23:12, and text E is vs. 10f.

Text D	Text E
ששת ימים תעשה מעשיך	ושש שנים תזרע את ארצך
	ואספת את תבואתה
וביום השביעי תשבת	והשביעת תשמטנה ונטשתה
למען ינוח שורך וחמרך	
וינפש בן אמתך והגר	ואכלו אביני עמך
	ויתרם תאכל חית השדה
	כן תעשה לכרמך ולזיתך

(Translation of text E: "[10]You have six years to sow your land and gather the yield, [11]but in the seventh year you shall let it lie fallow and leave it alone. Let the poor among your people eat of it, and what they leave the wild animals may eat. You shall do likewise with your vineyards and your olive groves.")

The following comments are in place: 1. The great similarity between the *šemiṭṭa* texts of Exodus and Leviticus recommends the employment of the former for the interpretation of the latter. 2. The close formal and hence, presumably, conceptual relationship between sabbath and *šemiṭṭa* texts is not limited to the Holiness collection. 3. In contrast

containing the essential name of the sabbath day, this phrase is so integral as almost to miss notice for the idea which is its centrality. It is because that which is central to text C is not a matter of a holy day but of the land and man's cessation of its cultivation that the prominence and repetition of the phrase "a sabbath of the Lord" clearly conveys the idea of God's lordship over that land. This accordingly alerts us to the full significance of "a sabbath of the Lord" as referring to the meaning of the sabbath day. Just as in the *šemiṭṭa* year man desists from utilizing the land for his own business and benefit, so on the sabbath day he desists from using that day for his own affairs. And just as the intervals in regard to the *šemiṭṭa* and the jubilee years are determined by the number seven, so too is the number seven determinative in regard to that recurring day when man refrains from his own pursuits and sets it aside for God. In regular succession he breaks the natural flow of time, proclaiming ($\sqrt{}$קרא, Lev 23:3, as in the case of *šemiṭṭa*, Deut 15:2) that the break is made for the sake of[18] the Lord.[19]

Early biblical law rarely gives reasons[20] and theorizes even more rarely. It would not be in the normal range and character of the Bible to verbalize the idea of the sabbath as recovered and interpreted here. But the importance of the sabbath and its frequent mention in the Bible have presented a challenge to rationalization since ancient times. The absence of an explicit etiothesis drew later biblical authors and redactors to fill this literary void, to offer rationales associated with prominent concepts or events—respite from work, the creation of the world, or the exodus from Egypt. The inclusion of these rationales, whatever their extrinsic merit, has had the effect of obscuring the intrinsic and basic meaning of the sabbath institution.

---

to Leviticus, the sabbath and *šemiṭṭa* texts of Exodus form one context, which makes the similarity immediately evident, supplying an additional indication of the close relationship between the two institutions. The cumulative effect of these details further encourages the interpreter to use one phenomenon for the understanding of the other.

[18] Hebrew ל is both "of" and "for (the sake, benefit of)."

[19] It redounds to the credit of G. von Rad to have ascertained the significance of *šemiṭṭa* for the meaning of the sabbath; see his *Theologie des A.T.* I (1957), p. 25, n. 2 (English trans. [1962], p. 16, n. 3); *Das fünfte Buch Mose* (1964), p. 42.

[20] A few etiological stories or references to them, e.g. Gen 32:33, are among the exceptions.

This meaning which we have ascertained from the laws finds support in a postexilic prophecy: "If you restrain your foot on the sabbath so as not to pursue your own affairs on My holy day,[21] if . . . you honor it by not going your own ways, not looking after your own affairs, and not making various decisions,[22] then . . . " (Isa 58:13). Man normally is master of his time. He is free to dispose of it as he sees fit or as necessity bids him. The Israelite is duty-bound, however, once every seven days to assert by word and deed that God is the master of time. God's dominion over time parallels and complements that over the land—witness the synoptic texts—and Israel's cognition of both is a condition of her usufruct of the land. In the words of the prophet: (If you do not pursue your own affairs on the sabbath) "then I shall set you atop the heights of the land and give you your father Jacob's patrimony" (vs. 14). Unlike the apodictic statement of the Decalogue, the expression here is in conditional form and the language poetic and persuasive. Nevertheless, there can be no doubt that it is the sense of the later text no less than that of the earlier that on one day out of seven the Israelite is to renounce dominion over his own time and recognize God's dominion over it.

One may phrase it more simply: Every seventh day the Israelite renounces his autonomy and affirms God's dominion over him. The former expression, however, is fully justified. The Bible elsewhere presents us with the proposition that time is indeed God's domain. Two psalm passages of identical structure speak of Him, respectively, as the lord of space and the lord of time: "Yours is the heavens, the earth is Yours also", and "Yours is the day, the night is Yours also" (Ps 89:12 and 74:16). Furthermore, be it noted, biblical expressions concerning God's dominion over space or territory, which are accepted at face value because dominion over space is a clear and simple notion, are often metaphors for His dominion over the inhabitants of that territory (e.g., Lev 25:23; Ex 19:5); on occasion, His lack of interest in uninhabited space is

---

[21] Thus, מעשות, 1Q Isa[a], which is the regular but not necessarily original, form. The receptus (עשות) translates literally: "If you draw your foot back from the sabbath to do your own pleasure . . ." The translations "to do your pleasure" and "to pursue your own affairs" are equally valid, but I cannot indorse the suggestion that חפץ can be narrowed down to mean "gainful work, business", as have C. Westermann, *Das Buch Jesaja Kap. 40—66* (1966), pp. 270 f.; *The New English Bible*, pp. 891 f., and others.

[22] Cf. M. Weinfeld, לשוננו 36 (1971/72), p. 9.

recorded (Isa 45:18). In other words, God's dominion over space and His dominion over time are largely two aspects of the same thing: His dominion over man and especially over Israel. There is, therefore, nothing incongruous nor bold in the conclusion that every seventh day the Israelite is to renounce dominion over time, thereby renounce autonomy, and recognize God's dominion over time and thus over himself. Keeping the sabbath is acceptance of the sovereignty[23] of God.[24]

Out of all proportions to the intrinsic importance of the idea of the sabbath and the strict and frequent prohibitions to work is the sparseness of its ritual;[25] a sacrifice of two lambs and two tenths of an epha (slightly over four quarts or four and a half liters) of flour with oil is all that the people offers at its central, or a major, sanctuary on a sabbath.[26] Adding

[23] Sovereignty and divinity (cf. n. 4) are different and unrelated. Every god has, or is, divinity; some gods also have sovereignty, which , however, they have not acquired by extending or intensifying their divinity.

[24] The preeminence which the sabbath assumes with this interpretation is indirectly reinforced in N. Lohfink's study: "Zur Dekalogfassung von Dtn 5," *BZ* N.F. 9 (1965), pp. 17—32. Lohfink proposes that the deuteronomic version of the Decalogue, as contrasted with that of Exodus, is not an accumulation of accidental and unrelated small variants but the result of a rewriting, mainly but not exclusively, of the sabbath commandment with the intention of making that commandment, rather than the first (Deut. 5:7[-8—10], the chief commandment of the Decalogue. Arriving at his proposal by a linguistic and structural analysis of Deut. 5:6—18, he displays exemplary method, and the result is quite plausible. It is in the second part of the article, where he leaves the study of literature and turns to writing history, that he is much less impressive. But whatever the historical circumstances of the proposed reediting of the Decalogue in Deuteronomy, the recast was greatly facilitated, if not actually rendered possible, by the cognate concepts behind the first (vs. 7) and fourth (vss. 12—15) commandments. One commandment could take the place of the other because the core of both is the recognition of God's dominion over man and man's owing exclusive loyalty to God.

[25] The view of H. J. Kraus, *Gottesdienst in Israel*, (1962), p. 99, that there is no indication of a sabbath ritual in preexilic times, overstates the issue. Even if we neglect the order of sacrifices in Num 28:9f. and the law of the bread display in Lev 24:5—9 in disregard of arguments of Y. Kaufmann that these laws (P and H) are preexilic, there is the eighth-century reference in Isa 1:13 to sabbatical activities in the temple. Nevertheless, Kraus well epitomizes the situation. Yet the remarkable thing is that the Leviticus and Numbers passages, whatever their time of origin, contain all recorded rituals of the historical sabbath, and they are not only few but also scanty.

[26] Instead of this sacrifice, the author of Ez 46:4 envisages a more substantial one for the temple of the future.

the sabbatical rite of the twelve loaves of the bread of display[27] does not change the picture materially; the loaves are only to be laid out each sabbath and are not to be offered in a sacrificial way. Scantiness is what characterizes the cult of the sabbath, especially when compared with the more substantial and variegated rituals, sacrificial and nonsacrificial, of the festivals, and this scantiness is remarkable both in view of the importance of the day and the importance of the cult in the religion of Israel. We would expect so important an occasion to have eventuated in a more prominent act. But it did not. One is inclined to suggest that the sabbath stands somewhat apart from the other phenomena of Israelite religion.

This reflection is strengthened by another consideration. All regularly recurring events in ancient Israel were bound up with the cyclical changes of nature—the seasons or the revolutions of the moon or the sun. The impact of the climactological and astronomical divisions of time on the economic, social, and religious life of Israel, as anywhere in the ancient Near East, was overwhelming and elicited significant responses. Man who structured social time in accordance with the natural divisions of time was likely to be in harmony with nature. The structure all but guaranteed that the rhythm of society and culture should beat in unison with the rhythm of heaven, earth, and underworld.

For the sabbath, however, there is no room in this physico-human periodicity. Having no bond with nature other than the change of day and night,[28] the sabbatical cycle is indifferent to the harmony of the universe.[29] It represents a neutral structuring of empty time.[30] Since the

---

[27] For the age and the nature of this ceremony, see B. A. Levine, "Prolegomenon," p. xxxv, to G. B. Gray, *Sacrifice in the Old Testament* (1971).

[28] See n. 30.

[29] The weekly cycle of the sabbath has nothing to do with the lunar month, and no attempt is known, such as by intercalation, to bring the two into accord. It is of interest to note that the Babylonian and Assyrian calendars have a comparatively large number of significant days (the name of one of them, *šapattu*, formerly excited speculation as to its relation to Hebrew *šabbat*, but this speculation has led nowhere). If these days are selectively integrated into one system, the resultant frequency (the time from day A to day B to day C, etc.) approximates the frequency of the Israelite Sabbath. But these days are anchored in the lunar month, and their frequency alternates with its alternating length. Clearly, the moon reigns supreme. (The following facts pertain to the rotation of the moon: "The siderical month [the time of the return of the moon to the same star] is 27 days, 7 hours, 43 minutes, and 12 seconds; the synodic month [from new moon to new

rhythm of the sabbath is the only exception to the prevailing natural rhythm, and since the exception in no way derives from time as such nor is traceable to any aspect of time experienced in the ancient Near East, it is likely that the opposition between the sabbath on the one hand and nature on the other hand was not unintentional. The intention was, I suggest, to fill time with a content that is uncontamined by, and distinct from, anything related to natural time, i.e., time as agricultural season or astronomical phase. (The sabbath is celebrated every seventh day, but the concomitant structuring of time affects the six other days as well, hence all time.) That content, displacing the various ideas and phenomena asso-

---

moon], which alone matters for the calculation of time, is 29 days, 12 hours, 44 minutes, and 3 seconds" [E. Jenni, *Die theologische Begründung des Sabbatgebotes* ... (1956), p. 11, n. 20.])

[30] The Old Testament concept of time is warmly disputed. Pedersen and Boman would reject the very thought of empty time in connection with ancient Israel; see J. Pedersen, *Israel* ..., I/II (1926) pp. 487—491; T. Boman, *Das hebräische Denken* ...³, (1959), pp. 109—121 (English transl. [1960], pp. 129—141). With these scholars others may be grouped, among them J. Marsh, *The Fulness of Time* (1952), and J. Muilenburg, *HTR* 54 (1961), pp. 225—255. The positions of Boman and Marsh have been severly criticized by Barr, in my opinion with full justification and success; seé J. Barr, *The Semantics of Biblical Language* (1961), Index, s.v. Boman (especially pp. 72—79); *Biblical Words for Time* (1962), Index, s.v. Boman, Marsh (especially pp. 20 ff.), and von Rad (pp. 30f). See also E. Jenni in *The Interpreter's Dictionary of the Bible* 4 (1962), p. 646. But this disputation does not bear on the issue at hand. We are not asking, to begin with, how the Israelites conceived of time, nor do we go on to fashion our explanation in accordance with a hypothetical answer; rather, we note the unbroken succession of time units of equal length that are independent of natural and cultural phenomena other than the change of day and night and the freely chosen number seven; these two are of neutral value and refer to no specific content. As to the day-and-night change, this is an unavoidable element given this plan (general cessation of work) and this material (time); no division of time into units of medium length designed to regulate the life of society can disregard this change. As to number seven, it is so ubiquitous (see, for instance, J. Hehn, *Siebenzahl und Sabbat* ... [1907]; B. Jacob *JOR* N.S. 14 [1923 f.], pp. 158—161; N.H. Snaith, *The Jewish New Year Festival* [1947], pp. 115—117; R. Gordis, *Poets,Prophets, and Sages* [1971], pp. 95—103 = *JBL* 62 [1943], pp. 17—26; O. Loretz, *Schöpfung und Mythos* [1968], pp. 63 f., n. 34; and in general, F. Heiler, *Erscheinungsformen und Wesen der Religion* [1961], pp. 167—169), almost indiscriminately so, that it cannot carry the weight of any distinct idea. It is a preferred number for ordering and quantifying, comparable to our twenty-five or dozen (25 has nothing to do with married bliss nor 12 with eggs). In fine, our observation about the succession of time units is correct, and the definition of the sabbatical cycle as neutral structuring of empty time is secure.

ciated with natural time, is the idea of the absolute sovereignty of God, a sovereignty unqualified even by an indirect cognizance of the rule of other powers. As man takes heed of the sabbath day and keeps it holy, he not only relinquishes the opportunity of using part of his time as he pleases but also foregoes the option of tying it to the secure and beneficial order of nature. The celebration of the sabbath is an act completely different from anything comparable in the life of ancient Israel. The sabbath is an isolated and strange phenomenon, not only in the world but also in Israel itself.

A late author expressed in his peculiar way the aspect of the sabbath as a neutral structuring of empty time. In the quotation from Sirach that follows (early second century B.C.), the answer to the question extends God's differentiation of time to the seasonal festivals. But such wordiness should not be permitted to obscure the intent of the question itself, focusing as it does on the sabbath:[31] "Why does one day outrank the others, when all daylight in the year comes from the sun? [8]By God's wisdom they were distinguished; He differentiated seasons and festivals. [9]Some he blessed and declared holy and others He made ordinary days" (33/36:7—9).[32]

---

[31] The text is the first part of a parable comparing people with times. At first glance, the author seems to speak of holy days in general, but on closer reading it turns out that he means the sabbath exclusively or chiefly: (1) The part of the parable to be elucidated (vss. 10—13 [ff.?]) is not concerned with some unknown chosen people or peoples but with Israel (and the priests within Israel), i.e., a special *comparatum* and not an indefinite number of indistinct *comparata;* we should assume the same individuation for the *comparandum.* (2) The words "He blessed and declared holy" are an obvious allusion to the sabbath text Gen 2:3. A further, secondary argument is mentioned in the next note.

[32] See G. H Box in : R. H Charles, *The Apocrypha and Pseudepigrapha of the O.T.* I (1913), p. 429, for text, translation, and interpretation. The rabbinical parallels, quoted or referred to in a note, support the comment that it is (chiefly) the sabbath which is meant. In addition consult M. S. (H.) Segal, ספר בן סירא השלם (1952/53), p. רו and רי-ריא, for reconstruction of and comment on the text. Segal uses a Hebrew manuscript discovered after Box.

Hagar and the
Birth of Ishmael

A threefold promise attends the Abraham stories. It is stated at the beginning: offspring, land, and blessing (Gen 12:1–3,7). The blessing is an elusive thing, and the time of its realization is mainly the future. Possession of the land is real, but it, too, will not come to pass in Abraham's lifetime. Offspring, however, is a thing of the present; it is to happen in the span of the Abraham narrative. Of the three promises it is the most immediate and basic; the other two depend on it for their realization. But it, too, is steadily delayed as the tale goes on until Abraham has become old. In Gen 15 things seem to be coming to a head. Abram, this is then still his name, doubts the fulfillment of the promise, while God reiterates it in the most forceful and self-obligating manner. The reader[1] who advances to chapter 16 expects that God's word will be consummated now.

Not only the reader expects this, the *narrationis personae* expect it also and they decide to do something about it. Ten years they have stood by (16:3),[2] allowing things to take their course. But when nothing has

---

[1] The original audience of the Old Testament narratives was typically a listening audience. But since language, including scientific terminology, does not and need not reflect change, including change in the matter of cognition, in the extralinguistic world, modern "reader" instead of "listener" (as well as "author" and "book") is used throughout.

[2] The "ten years" together with the rest of vs. 3 and vss.1a and 15f. are regarded by almost all critics as part of P, and P is regarded as the latest, and indeed a very late, constituent of the Pentateuch (Hexateuch, etc.). By this hypothesis, these verses should be eliminated if one is interested in the original (?) story. Yet their elimination has been disputed by Volz, in my opinion quite successfully; see P. Volz (and W. Rudolph), *Der Elohist als Erzähler* (1933), pp. 136f. The most Volz would grant is the possibility of "ten years" being a gloss. It is noted, however, that Old Assyrian texts of more recent publication tend to support the genuineness of a phrase: "x years" of barrenness antecedent to concubinage. See Excursus 1, text B (p. 70) and note 38.

happened the natural way, they have recourse to a social institution of wide acceptance.

(VS. 1)   Three of the four protagonists are named in the first verse. Abram and Sarai are known from before; the third, Hagar, is here first introduced and identified. Her identification as slave girl/handmaid of Sarai in combination with the statement of Sarai's barrenness sets the stage for the ensuing conflict.

The conflict grows out of the mores of the age, whose potentialities Sarai and, secondarily, Abram undertake to actualize for their benefit. These mores and their legal trussings are documented for Mesopotamia and have repeatedly been adduced by students.[3] The pertinent sources, all legal, are collected and analyzed in Excursus 1.

From elements of these sources, most dating from the four centuries 1800—1400 B.C. variously assigned as "the time of Abraham,"[4] some even earlier, the following plot emerges:[5] A marriage has remained childless for a number of years. Hoping to compensate for this, the wife gives her husband a slave girl on whom he may sire offspring. While in status a wife to the master of the house, she remains a handmaid to the mistress, and a child borne by her is to be considered the offspring of the mistress. When the girl (upon bearing children) becomes insolent to her mistress, the latter punishes her.

The plot, entirely composed from elements of Mesopotamian texts, has put us ahead of our biblical narrative,[6] demonstrating that the first six verses of Gen 16 are imbedded in the life and law of the ancient Orient, and that the actors behave in accordance with its norms.

We recognize at this point that a tale with a similar beginning is told

[3] Recent comments are by R. Yaron in P. Peli, ed., *Proceedings of the Fifth World Congress of Jewish Studies ... 1969* (1972), pp. 7—9 (Hebrew section), and R. Frankena, *Oudttestamentische Studiën* 17 (1972), p. 63.

[4] A poorly preserved Neo-Assyrian marriage document (*Iraq* 16 [1954], p. 38:41—50; Nimrud, 7th century) shows some remote pertinence.

[5] The drawing of a composite picture for comparison is unobjectionable if it is realized that the cuneiform documents, including the so-called codes, reflect various cases from real life representing different combinations of a few constants with a rather large number of free variables.

[6] In our fabricated story the handmaid has already given birth to the children; in Genesis she is, for obvious narrative reasons, still pregnant.

in 30:1—5, where childless Rachel gives her handmaid Bilhah to her husband Jacob. There, however, no comparable conflict develops, and no need arises to fortify the positions of any of the parties to the conflict. The difference in Gen. 16 accounts for certain stylistic peculiarities. Its beginning sounds circumstantial, if not repetitive; yet this is what the situation calls for: emphasis on the legal basis of developments to come. *"Abram heeded Sarai's request.* So *Sarai, Abram's wife,* brought her *slave girl* Hagar the Egyptian . . . and gave her to her *husband Abram as a wife"* (vss. 2f.). Hagar, seeing that she is with child, forgets her station "and regards her mistress with scorn." While in itself understandable and a natural development to the modern reader, Hagar's behavior must have been extraordinary in her time. Had it not been, it is likely that the institution of substitute childbearing would not have existed; Bilhah and Zilpah, furthermore, did not react this way; and, in any case, the honor of bearing a child to the master would probably have satisfied most slave women and compensated them for any contingent deprivations. Hagar, apparently not feeling compensated, behaves as she does, whereas the other characters view the development solely in terms of legalities. This is the root of the narrative's conflict. Too much is missed when the conflict is interpreted as merely a clash of two wills. It is very much a conflict of two rights. The opposing parties seem persuaded that they have rights, and if I correctly sense the text, it too is premised on the existence of these rights. (vss. 2b—3) (vs. 4)

In vs. 5. the legal form has a litigious ring. A law suit is indicated with Sarai's crying to Abram, "I have been wronged, and through no one's fault but yours!" He, the master of the house, is permitting her handmaid to infringe on her position as mistress. As he has failed her, Sarai, in providing the protection due to her, this has become a case between her and him, and let God be the judge. Hagar, who has caused the trouble, is, at this point, not herself a litigant, more a circumstance than a protagonist. The case is clear-cut; Abram bows to its logic. He renounces whatever rights he may have had on Hagar as a wife (vs. 3); she is again Sarai's maid, and nothing more. "Deal with her as you please," he says. Whatever protection under custom of agreement Hagar might have had before, she has forfeited by her conduct. The consequences of Abram's answer follow with the directness and characteristic speed of the old biblical narratives: The mistress punishes and the slave (vs. 5) (vs. 6) runs away. The house is emptier. Sarai has lost her handmaid and "her" offspring and Abram the hope for a son in whom God's blessing may have been fulfilled.

(vss. 7f.) Hagar comes again to the fore in her flight through the wilderness; the Egyptian slave (vs. 1) is on the way to her homeland.[7] As she stops by an oasis, a man addresses her, identified by the text as "messenger of the Lord," but in all likelihood unrecognized as such by Hagar initially.[8] But as he calls her "Hagar, slave girl of Sarai," she cannot fail to realize that he is an extraordinary phenomenon. The reader, of course, knows more. The speaker having been identified for him, he knows that, as she is hailed as Sarai's slave, the flight has ended. Divine will has thwarted Hagar's attempt to escape slavery.

Rare must be the modern reader whose sympathies are not with Hagar, who is not disappointed by the divine decree that aborts her flight. Such sympathy, however, may be out of keeping with the intent behind the narrative. The interpreter is in a difficult situation. It is of great importance to understand the likely response of the audience for whom the tale was—first—intended. The author's anticipation of this response must have been a factor in his composition; the what and the how of his work are in part determined by it. But I find no indication in the text as to the anticipated response of that audience to the reinstitution of Hagar's slavery by the messenger of the Lord nor as to the evaluation of the reinstitution. This lack of guidance is one of our handicaps in the understanding of this as of other biblical texts, especially narratives. To fill the lacuna with our own reaction is to be unaware of the problem or gratuitously mislead ourselves.

The speech continues simple and pithy. The question posed by the man to Hagar could easily come from the mouth of any lone traveller meeting another by happenstance. When it is addressed to a woman

---

[7] "On the Way of/to Shur." Shur is the south-to-central western part of the Sinai peninsula, touching on the border of Egypt. (Hagar has not advanced nearly as far, she is still on the fringes of the Negev; see p. 75.) "The way of/to Shur" thus contributes to the Egyptian theme of this chapter; see p. 69. The phrase is unique in the Bible (1 Sam 15:7 [and Gen 25:18?] perhaps mean the same) but it reappears in the modern Arabic name *darb-eš-šur;* see, e.g., C.L. Woolley and T.E. Lawrence, *The Wilderness of Zin* (1936), pp. 57f.

[8] See p. 64.

travelling by herself in the forbidding desert, it may have an overtone of concern and solicitude: "Where have you come from and where are you going?" This apparently innocent sounding question is of a definite narrative moment. The response elicited answers only the first part of the question (she knows whence and from whom she flees, but her precarious situation precludes any confidence that she will reach her destination), thus affording the interrogator the opportunity himself to provide the missing part of the answer. Insofar as it goes, Hagar's reply to the address and question is accurate and fitting. Almost in challenge to the questioner she replies: "She whom you declare my mistress—she is the one I am escaping; no longer am I her slave."

Her pluck is to no avail; the man sends her back straight off. Point- (VS. 9) edly he catches up from her reply the word "mistress" and, reconfirming the status quo ante, reaffirms the relationship of slave girl and mistress (vss. 8,9). More drastic yet, he demands acceptance of harsh punishment, the very cause of Hagar's flight: "Go back to your mistress and submit to abuse at her hand." The demand for complete submission bears the seal of authority, an authority and finality conveyed by the repeated formula "The messenger of the Lord said to her." We have already observed, however, that only the reader is so soon aware of the authoritative finality. Since the beginning of the encounter the narrative has moved on two levels of awareness, that of the audience and that of the *narrationis personae,* with unequal speeds. Thus the audience waits in suspense for the moment when Hagar will learn what the audience already knows, the awesome identity of her interlocutor.

This interpretation is in conflict with an opinion proposed over one hundred years ago by Wellhausen and adopted by many scholars since. It retains and appreciates vss. 8 and 9, deleted by Wellhausen and his followers.[9] The reasons cited for the deletion are: (1) The repetition of "The messenger of the Lord said to her" is seen as a stylistic flaw serious enough to make the integrity of the text suspect; (2) the commandment

---

[9] J. Wellhausen, *Die Composition des Hexateuch* (1889), pp. 21f. (first published in *Jahrbücher für deutsche Theologie* 21 [1876], p. 410). From O. Eissfeldt, *Hexateuch-synopse* (1922), p. 257*, it seems that A. Kuenen preceded him. Opinions on vs.8 are divided. H. Holzinger, *Genesis* (1898), p. 152, makes a convincing case for the genuineness of this verse. In the following I shall therefore deal only with vs.9 (and vs.10).

that Hagar return to Sarai (of vs. 9) is merely a device of the redactor to
prepare the story of 21:9—21; (3) the commandment to submit to Sarai's
abuse (of the same verse) is not in keeping with the assurance (of vs. 11)
that God has taken note of her (complaint about the) abuse.

A fourth consideration, with which the writer is in agreement,
leads to the deletion of vs. 10, which has no place anywhere in this
chapter and is particularly incongruous in its place before vs. 11. In
contradistinction to the similar passage 22:17a, which is well integrated in its context, the broad sweep of 16:10 is glaringly inconsistent
with the precise statements that surround it.

The reasons, however, which are evoked for eliminating (vs. 8
and) vs. 9 do not hold up under examination. No. (1), the repeated introduction of the speaker and the speech, is no criterion of criticism at
all. A witness to the naturalness of such repetition is the autobiography of Darius I, inscribed on the rock of Bisutun, a text in which
every paragraph begins with "King Darius says (thus)." In the Old
Testament compare Gen 17:9,15; 19:9; 42:1f; Ex 3:14a,b(-15) and 1
Ki 3:23f.[10]

No. (2). The argument is this: In the original form of the story,
assigned to J, Hagar remained in the desert and bore her son there.
Since, however, the Hagar story of 21:9—21, assigned to E, begins in
Abraham's house, the assumed original end of ch. 16, played out in the
desert, was eliminated in order to allow for her return home. The return, though, is not reported, yet the audience is prepared for it by
the command (in vs. 9) of the messenger that Hagar go back; it follows that the verse is a redactorial expedient (R^{JE}) for the purpose of
that preparation.

Of this observation one thing is correct: Hagar must return home,
and this for two considerations. The first consideration, for which I
may refer to B. Jacob,[11] pertains primarily to the narrative of ch. 16:
Ishmael is to be born and reared in Abram's house—and also named
by him—in order to be reckoned fully as his son. Jacob adds this com-

---

[10] H. Gunkel, *Genesis*^{3} (1910), p. 209, and others would delete Gen 19:9a because it
violates a rule of style. The main effect of such proposals is speciously to strengthen feeble
rules in their struggle for survival. A special reason affirming the genuineness of the
introduction of the speaker is stated in n.15.

[11] See B. Jacob, *Das erste Buch der Tora* (1934). p. 977, after Dillmann. See also infra,
pp. 66 f.

ment: If the boy were not born in Abram's house—and thus unequivocally recognized as his son—Genesis would have had no reason to mention Hagar and Ishmael and there would have been no pair corresponding to Sarah and Isaac, which correspondence, however, belongs to the economy of the narrative. The other consideration lies in the continuation of the Abraham stories. Hagar could not be expelled from Abraham's house in 21:9—21, and no narrative of the expulsion would have had a place in Genesis, without her prior return there told in an earlier chapter. This reason is independent of the postulate that ch. 16 is J and 21:9ff. E. As for a comparison of the two reasons, it would be unprofitable to speculate which one is the main reason. Art does not always submit to such measuring and ranking.

But it must also be said that reason No. (2) is a tangled proposition. It is designed to account for a fact (the narrative detail of vs. 9) as well as to sustain another and unrelated hypothesis (that of the relation of the Ishmaelites to the well of Beer-laḥai-roi[12]), but it succeeds rather in making us look for something in the text and disappointing us because we do not find it. If the original end of the story is to be excised and something is to be told in its stead about Hagar's return (thus the hypothesis behind reason No. (2)), the simple solution of this simple task would be a plain statement about her return inserted at its proper narrative place after vs. 14.[13] But such does not exist. What is present in vs. 9 relating to Hagar's return is a mere foreshadowing of the event, her return, a poor substitute for the event itself. The hypothesis must be rejected for creating more problems than it proposes to solve. The probable cause for mentioning Hagar's return in vs. 9 is to afford the narrator an opportunity to take up the theme of ill-treatment. This brings us to the remaining reason.

This reason, No. (3), is of greater interest than the others because of the issue involved. The argument against the genuineness of vs. 9 is the supposed contradiction between the injunction for Hagar to accept more ill-treatment and the comforting and solicitous assurance of vs. 11 that God has paid attention to her past ill-treatment. Readers who are disinterested in critical questions will nevertheless perhaps welcome the

---

[12] The second hypothesis is too solicitously accommodated. The putative connection of the Ishmaelites with Beer-laḥai-roi does not require Ishmael to be born there. About this hypothesis, see p. 74 f., with n. 53.

[13] Cf. U. Cassuto, *La questione della Genesi* (1934), p. 315.

deletion by critics of vs. 9; they may feel offended that God exacts such hard punishment from the wretched bondwoman. Now there is a common reason to both exegetical difficulties, the critical one and the theological one: the neglect of the legal and social setting of the narrative; though dutifully noted, the setting is insufficiently utilized for the interpretation.[14] The various legal and sociological expressions occurring throughout the chapter as often as is compatible with good style unmistakably delineate the background of the story and impress its reality upon the audience. The background is as much a part of the scenery as the foreground. Nor are we free to change the stage furniture. It is a period piece,and it is not for us to introduce anachronistic notions about social change. Hagar's flight for freedom is not sanctioned, nor should we expect otherwise. The aesthetic and moral value of this story is to be appreciated in terms of its achievement given the elements of its time.

The time of the patriarchs speaks a clear language, its literature no less than its reality. In its narratives, as in those of other early books of the Bible, the social order is considered well nigh immutable. But for all this, Hagar is not to be left in her misfortune. Hers is the story of what God may do for man in adverse circumstances. She is told to return and submit to maltreatment by her mistress, but, this said, the narrative goes on to affirm that God is aware of her maltreatment and will compensate her. In other words: Once we accept, as accept we must, the social and legal order of the time as the setting of the story and allow the author the intention to tell of Hagar's comfort and compensation, the purported contradiction between vss. 9 and 11 disappears; maltreatment, divine awareness, and promised compensation are narrative elements whose interaction creates a narrative tension which is dramatically acceptable and probably so designed. In the exposition of the second part of the story sight must not be lost of the available modes of the narrative nor of the possible intentions of the narrator; we must be alive to a contingency of a relaxation of tension at the end. The degree of this relaxation, or whether it exists at all, is an aesthetic, perhaps a moral question but cannot serve as a criterion of a verse's authenticity.

[14] General readers and nineteenth and early-twentieth century commentators can, of course, not be blamed for the neglect.

With vs. 9 Hagar's hope has reached its nadir; in vs. 11 a steep ascent   (VS. 11)
sets in. The messenger, introduced as before,[15] prophesies the birth of
her son. The announcement is strengthened by the form of the message.
There is in the Bible a literary genre of divine annunciation of future
childbirth, and in the older books its presence betokens happiness.[16] Vss.

[15] Be it noted that the author could not continue "Submit to the abuse at her hand"
(vs.9) with "You are with child" (vs.11) without interposing a transition or introduction.
(The same holds true for a continuation of vs.10, if one would retain that verse.)

[16] The following table, though perhaps not exhaustive, is representative.

Elements of the Genre of Annunciation

	Mother addressed or mentioned	הנה	Pregnancy הרה	Birth ילד	Son בן	Name שם (+קרא)	Future deeds of the child
1. Gen 16:11f.	x	x	x	x	x	x	x
2. Gen 17:19	(x)	—a	—	x	x	x	(x)b
3. Gen 18:10	(x)	x	—	—	x	—c	—
4. Ju 13:3,5,7	x	x	x	x	x	—	—
5. 1 Ki 13:2	—	x	—	x	x	x	x
6. 2 Ki 4:16d	x	—	—	—	x	—	—
7. Isa 7:14f.	x	x	x	x	x	x	x
[8. Isa 9:5e	—	—	—	x	x	x	(x)f]
9. 1 Chr 22:9f.g	—	x	—	x	x	x	x
[10. Luke 1:13—33h	x	x	x	x	x	x	x]

Remarks: (a) אבל instead of הנה. (b) The child will be the receiver of the covenant (ברית).
(c) The fame is played upon in vss. 12f. (d) This item is rudimentary. It is included in this
list because it bears the unmistakable imprint of No. 3. (e) This is not an announcement of
a birth which will happen in the future but of one which took place in the recent past;
cf. וַתֵּהִי. (f) The reference in parenthesis is to the symbol expressed by ותהי המשרה על שכמו
of vs. 5 and not to the actions of vs. 6; these will be performed by God and not by the
child (cf. N. H. Tur-Sinai, פשוטו של מקרא 3:1 [1967], pp. 34 f.). (g) This annunciation is
perhaps influenced by No. 8. (h) The dependence on No. 7 is obvious.

(Announcements and similar texts which do not follow the pattern are, e.g., Gen
25:23; 1 Sam 1:17; Isa 8:1—3; Mi 5:1f. Cf. H. Wildberger, *Jesaja* [1965ff.], p. 289; and a
reference to R.W. Neff in *ZAW* 82 [1970], pp. 459f.)

The following observation about the table may be made: In the older books (Nos.
1—4) God or a divine messenger makes the announcement, in the later books (Nos. 5—8) a
prophet. Also, as mentioned before, the older books transmit the original intent and
mood of the genre, which are reassurance and joy (Nos.1—4,6 [likewise 8—10]); in the
later books the form may serve the opposite purpose, which is announcement of doom
(Nos. 5 and 7).

11f., a particularly fine specimen of the genre, thus guarantee the divine origin of the announcement and therefore its truth. But the narration is well controlled: In distinction to the other instances, the interest here does not shift immediately to the child to be born. Hagar remains the center of attention, and the name bestowed on her son bespeaks the comfort offered to her: "Ishmael (ישמעאל "God hears"),[17] that is, the Lord has paid heed to (כי שמע יהוה אל) your (complaint of) abuse."[18]

(VS. 12)   The next verse enhances her comfort. With והוא "As for him," the text turns to the splendid future of her son. The most likely translation is: "He shall 'fight' (or 'kill', or 'rob')[19] people; his hand against everyone, and everyone's hand against him; he shall camp in defiance of[20] all his kinsmen."[21] A worthy son of his proud and defiant mother (G. von Rad).

[17] This is the interpretation of the name according to the biblical etymology. Whether it is also its workaday meaning, or whether this name and a more or less substantial number of other *yqtl* names are wish names ("May God hear") is a moot question; see J.J. Stamm in *Assyriological Studies* 16 (B. Landsberger jubilee volume, 1965), p. 415.

[18] I do not insist by this translation that the preposition אל "to" is meant to play a minor, assonantal role in the etymology, but it is quite possible that it does. M. Dahood integrates the word more tightly into the etymology by emending אל עניך ‖ כ שמע יהוה "For the Lord has heard ‖ El has answered you" (Biblica 49 [1968], pp.87f). He is a little too eager, it seems. He emends the text for no better reason than adding one line to biblical poetry, however lonely the line, unsupported as it is by a poetic context; he invents a grammatical form (עֲנֶיךָ‎*, Tiberian pointing); and the meaning so obtained is unlikely, as I shall attempt to show later, p. 69.

[19] Vocalize 'פֶּרֶא'; N.H. Tur-Sinai, פשוטו של מקרא 1 (1962), pp. 42f. While admitting that no Semitic root with this meaning is known (a hesitating reference to Hos 13:15 should be disregarded), Tur-Sinai construes the words as predicate and object and compares אכלת אדם את "you devour people" (Ez 36:13, said of Palestine). The explanation was approximated by Resh Lakish (3rd cent.): והוא בחז בחז נפשות "and he shall kidnap people" (Breshit Rabba, a.l.).

[20] Ex 20:3; Isa 65:3; Deut 21:16 (E. König, *Die Genesis* ... [1919], p. 494).

[21] The first four words of vs.12 are commonly translated "He shall be an onager of a man," purportedly conveying the sense that the messenger blesses Ishmael with the life of a nomad who roams the desert like a swift and free onager (cf. Job 39:5–8). One appeals to old Arabic literature for the imagery behind this interpretation (Jacob [n.11], p.413), but the expression so interpreted is at odds with the Hebrew language. "An onager of a man" in the proposed sense, translating the construct פרא אדם, is an Anglicism (Germanism, etc.) and not biblical Hebrew. (In Job 11:12, פרא and אדם belong to different parts of the sentence; see most commentaries.) כסיל אדם (Prov. 15:20; 21:20) and צאן אדם (Ez 36:38), occasionally referrred to, are not pertinent. Since every כסיל is a man, just as is every אביון, the word אדם in the phrases כסיל אדם and אביוני אדם (Isa 29:19) does not substantially

The independence that she has sought so ardently and will not attain he will have as a gift of God; if it is a hard life, it is a free one.

With these wonderful words the man disappears, and Hagar is again (vs. 13) alone in the wilderness. Under the impact of the encounter she says to the deity whom she discerned in the man but sees no more, ""You are a God of (my?) seeing"; that is to say, "Did I really see 'God and have yet remained alive' after seeing (Him)?""[22] If there is testimony to revelation, this is it. The expression conveys a context of excitement, thanksgiving, and overcoming of incredulity.

Name giving and interpretation, begun in vs. 11, are concluded in vs. (vs. 14) 14, with vs. 15 following up as a confirmation. Whatever the origin and early function of vss. 11–14,[23] as part of the narrative their purport is:

---

change the meaning of כסיל or אביונים. Rather, the phrases seem to have an elative function: "(a fool among men>) a perfect fool"; "the neediest of the poor"; cmp. Middle Hebrew גדולי הדור "the greatest men in the generation," טובי העיר "optimates" (דור, אדם and עיר are collectives). צאן אדם (Ez 36:38) is singular and incomparable: The expression is carefully prepared first by (ארבה אתם) כַּצֹאן אדם ("I shall make them numerous) people like a flock," then continued by כְּצֹאן קדשים, כְּצֹאן ירושלם "like the flock of the temple service, like the flock of Jerusalem," until simple צאן אדם "flock of men," i.e., a multitude of people, is reached. E.A. Speiser's comparison, (in his *Genesis* [1964], p.118) of פרא אדם with Akk. *lullû* need not be considered, if only because *lullû* does not have the meaning assumed by him; cf. W.G. Lambert and A.R. Millard, *Atra-Ḥasîs* (1969), p. 152.

[22] This translates the emended text הגם אֱלֹהִים' ראיתי' ראיתי' וָאֶחִי' אחרי ראי. This emendation of J. Wellhausen, *Prolegomena zur Geschichte Israels*[5] (1899), pp.329f., and note, has a threefold distinction. (1) It is graphically simple (הלם < אלהים'; 'ואחי' is partially a haplography before similar אחרי); (2) it accounts for the vision of God in this verse (and the others) and for the idea of life expressed in the name of the well of the next verse; (3) it gives words to the wonderment and gratitude of a person who sees God and yet remains alive; see p. 66. If any meaning at all is to be derived from the actual text, it is essentially the same as that of the emendation: "Did I here (??) really see the rear (?) of the one who saw me?" The word "rear" cannot be taken literally since Hagar talked to the man and had a frontal view of him; it may therefore mean, as it does in 33:23, a less than full view of the deity (see J. Lindblom, *HUCA* 32 [1961], p. 102, n.21, and here, infra, p. 66). But the uncertainty of this and any other interpretation favors an emendation, and no other emendation that I know measures up to Wellhausen's. With the two vocalizations רָאִי and רֹאִי the masoretes probably intended to secure two meanings for "seeing," determined by two different (implied) subjects; the subject of רָאִי "vision" is Hagar, that of רֹאִי "(the) one seeing me" is God. This may perhaps also be the intention of the text but it is doubtful because God's awareness of man here assumes the form of hearing rather than seeing.

[23] The issue is discussed in Excursus 2, pp. 72ff.

events are fleeting but people and places endure. The child to be born and his offspring, even as the well itself, will in their names testify that such and such happened to Hagar.

In vs. 13 we have not only name giving and interpretation but also change of name (or appellation). From vs. 7 through vs. 11 Hagar's interlocutor is the "messenger of the Lord" (מלאך יהוה); in vs. 13 he is called "the Lord" (יהוה) by the narrator and "God" (אל [and אלהים'[24]) by Hagar. But he is "the messenger of the Lord" initially only for the reader. There is no hint that Hagar recognized him as such upon first appearance. On the contrary, there is reason to believe that she did not. Manoah, the father of Samson, though prepared by his wife (Ju 13:6, cf. vss. 8—11), does not recognize the messenger as supernatural (vs. 16). Sometimes even the reader is not informed about the "man's" identity (Gen 32:25), an identity which is gradually established by the action (vss. 27,29); at other times, this information is provided early in the story (18:1), but the reader finds it difficult to apply it at every turn; or the speaker is identified as "messenger of the Lord" for the reader (22:11, 15) but appears as God/the Lord to the *narrationis personae* (vss. 12, 16—18). The variety of expressions is greater than is indicated by these sample texts. But in most of them a trend is recognizable in the narrative movement from the vague and ambiguous to the definite and clear, from the seeming natural to the actual supernatural, from the lower to the higher.

Several, possibly complementary, explanations might be, or have been, proposed for this phenomenon in our passage. They are a genetic explanation (the numen of a small area was absorbed by a higher deity, but the former now and then reappears as the messenger of the latter); a less specific historical explanation (gods in the ancient Near East have messengers or viziers who sometimes accompany their masters and sometimes travel alone but represent them); a theological explanation (in keeping with the tendency to hold the God of Israel at a remove from the world some of His functions are assigned to messengers). However attractive one may find these explanations, they do not adequately render the essence of the narrative. If a narrative is well told, if all its elements

---

[24] See n. 22.

are integrated, the first two explanations merely maintain that the author had at his disposal certain raw materials whose prehistories are still discernible. The third explanation is the weakest. There are, in biblical narratives, many instances of a direct involvement of God in worldly affairs and many others where He delegates His authority to representatives, but the exegesis of the narratives has failed to account theologically for His direct involvement in one place and indirect involvement in another. The explanation is subject to no control and contributes nothing specific; it is as arbitrary as it is useless.

But the essential weakness of all these explanations is that they are extranarrative. The primary questions in regard to narratives are those which yield to intranarrative answers. Messengers, natural or supernatural, in whom God is concealed and from whom He emerges are the narrative's way of expressing man's uncertainty about the divine at a given moment, indeed the elusive nature of the divine in its encounter with him. A man who has had such an experience may give it words and tell a singular tale of revelation. It is not a tale about a whole nation assembled amidst thunder and smoke like that of the revelation on Mount Sinai but about a lone man's experience at a river ford or the entrance of a tent. That experience in the telling reflects his growing awareness, culminating in the assurance that he has indeed met God.

During the encounter the words of the man have become progressively more wonderful and impressive: he knows Hagar's name and station, he commands, he utters a birth annunciation; at the end she knows who he is. In terms of an actor-audience analysis of the narrative, in vss.7–12 the reader knew more than the protagonist since the speaker was identified for him as a "messenger of the Lord" and was not indentified for her; in vs. 13 both have achieved a similar measure of awareness. As for the reader, the narrator drops the "messenger" and says simply "(the name of) the Lord (Who talked to her);" as for her, she calls him "God."[25] At this moment, he vanishes. As man comes to realize the presence of God, as he recognizes Him, God has disappeared.

---

[25] The change from "Lord" to "God" may be due to a variety of reasons: grammar ("יהוה of"?); linguistic traditions (a deity of vision is properly אל ראי); different kinds or different degrees of awareness and identification of the divine (what Hagar experienced is not what the audience knows).

In Homer, too, this feature of a revelation appears distinctly. One example:[26] As the battle for the ships takes a desperate turn for the Greeks, Poseidon, in the guise of Calchas, the diviner, approaches Ajax son of Telamon and Ajax son of Oileus, and, explaining the seriousness of the situation, stirs them to action. He concludes, "Would that a god move your hearts to withstand Hector and encourage the others." Thereupon he touches them with his staff and disappears, almost like a falcon taking off. Says Ajax the son of Oileus, "One of the Olympian gods bids us to fight. This was not Calchas, for I saw the motion of his feet and thighs from the rear as he departed. Unmistakable are the gods" (*Iliad* 13:43–75 [ff.]).

What the Bible adds to the feature it shares with Homer and other religious documents is that if man sees God one moment too long, one shade too clearly, he dies. The danger is stated repeatedly (Ex 33:20–23; Gen 32:31; [33:10[27];] Ju 6:22f.; 13:22f.; see also Nu 4:20) but without a clear demarcation of what constitutes too long and too clearly. The permeating presence of this notion, the uncertainty and fright which man therein experiences present the firm conceptual and narrative ground of vs. 13 as emended: "Did I really see 'God and have yet remained alive' after seeing (Him)?" We would note, however, that the idea may be descried, though blurred, even in the unemended text.[28]

(vss. 15f.)   Hagar does not die. She minds the words of the messenger of the Lord and returns. The detail of her return is not given but only her bearing a son to Abram, that is, in his house. If there is a reason for this narrative speed, it would appear that only the essential is to be narrated, that the son is Abram's as well as hers. This is further solace to Hagar, her story reaching a new and last peak. The elements of the outcome could have been discerned in the previous verses but here they are concentrated and attain a clarity which provides added movement to the narration. In these two short verses the matter of Abram's parenthood is mentioned

---

[26] Cf. the outstanding interpretation of this passage as well as of others by W.F. Otto, *Die Götter Griechenlands*[6] (1970), pp. 206–211.

[27] The verse probably says: "I (Jacob) have seen your (Esau's) face as one sees the face of God (and thereby forfeits his life), but you received me favorably (and spared me)." The reference to 32:8f.,11,31 is rather obvious.

[28] See n.22.

three times; no accident is the remark about his giving the boy a name—by naming him he recognizes him as his son.

No less conspicuous is the fact that Sarai plays no further role. Abram is mentioned four times and Hagar three, but Sarai not at all. This is emphasis by omission, all the more so since the reader might readily expect her to appear and act in light of the forecast of vs. 9 "Go back to your mistress." The conclusion is inescapable: Sarai is deliberately removed from the stage. Her plan has failed, and her grief over childlessness remains unalleviated. Might the sympathy of the audience not well rest now with Sarai?

Given the mores of the time, Gen 16 is an unusual story. The mistress gives her handmaid to her husband for companionship with the express purpose of securing offspring for herself. In accordance with the expectation the status of the girl remains unaffected by this arrangement; the messenger of the Lord has made this clear: "Go back to your mistress and submit to abuse at her hand" (vs. 9). Yet against all expectation, the offspring is apparently not legally and socially the mistress's but the maid's. This quite exceptional development then would confront us with a case, rare in an early biblical book, of a change in the social order, minor though the change may be. The existing order is accepted but it is not narrowly interpreted; room is left for human adjustment and divine grace. The tale begins with Hagar's deprivation and ends with her glory.

The foregoing interpretation of the Hagar story has been concerned almost exclusively with what is told in ch. 16. Except for the opening two paragraphs no consideration has been given to the fact that the story is a chapter of the Abraham narrative nor to the meaning it derives from its integration into the Pentateuch. This consideration is now due. Let us then undertake now to view the story as a part of a whole.[29]

As we have noted in those opening paragraphs, the paramount element which ties the Hagar chapter to the Abraham narrative as a whole

---

[29] While our concern in the following paragraphs will be the meaning of ch. 16 as part of a larger unit, not a few scholars have shown interest in the meanings of parts of this chapter, meanings which these parts had or may have had during their putative preliterary, independent, and probably extra-Israelite existence. This issue will be examined in Excursus 2.

is God's promise to Abraham, in particular the promise of offspring on whom the blessing, first mentioned in 12:2f., may rest. Ch. 16 as an independent and self-contained account can be read with no reference to this promise; the opening statement about Sarai's childlessness seems to function as the introduction to a homely incident in the family history of a revered ancestor.[30] But the reader of the Book of Genesis cannot but be aware that the members of this family, while existing as private individuals, bear in their persons and in their history a significance transcending their individual biographies. While Abram and Sarai act in their own private spheres and seem to have as much freedom as they could wish, given normal human limitations, they are fated here to fail of achievement because they do not, in fact, have such freedom. All are vehicles of destiny, Abram first and foremost. Through him an overarching purpose is to be realized. But Hagar is not the proper consort. It is for this very reason that she is the protagonist who achieves the most. That is, she is the freest of all protagonists for the very reason that she has no function in the realization of that great purpose. She does not, to be sure, secure freedom from slavery, but this is not the central issue of the story, the narrative of her flight notwithstanding. What matters is that she gains more than she could have ever hoped to achieve.

On the outcome for Sarai I have already remarked. As for Abram, it was an attempt that ended in failure, a failure he could not but recognize.[31] Was it his intention, in acceding to his wife's wish, to give God a helping hand in bringing about an early fulfillment of the promise? If so, his intention was frustrated, his help was rejected, the fulfillment was further delayed. In the economy of the book the sixteenth chapter is more than the story of an exercise in futility, which it certainly is on the family level. It is, and primarily so, a set-back in the historical dimension. It could have seemed no other to its original audience, the descendants of Isaac. For them it was, and so it must be for us, the story of the delay of

---

[30] A careful reading of the statement would, however, challenge this impression. The text begins with the letter waw, for which the *RSV* accounts by "Now Sarai, Abram's wife, bore him no children". R. Knox, *The Holy Bible* (1944), has it more clearly: "And still Abram's wife Sarai bore him no children." This waw does its bit to integrate ch.16 into the rest of the narrative.

[31] This is reflected in 17:18.

Isaac's birth, a delay ironically enough occasioned by the impatience of his parents and their precipitous enterprise.

It is also the story of their cousin and his mother. When this story had taken (preliminary) shape, Israel's interest in the Ishmaelites was probably not terribly strong, even if allowance is made for the transfer of the name from the tribe(s) which had disappeared to nomads in general.[32] But the interest in his mother's kin persisted unabated throughout biblical times, and the mention of Hagar's relation to Egypt in this chapter and in the book at large receives more than its ordinary narrative due: 16:1,3,7[33]; 21:21 (it is Hagar who brings an Egyptian daughter-in-law into the family and thus achieves a preponderance of the Egyptian element); 25:12.[34] The significance of this fact gains prominence in the larger frame of Genesis and the Pentateuch. The slavery of Israel in Egypt is predicted in the chapter preceding Hagar's story, and the characteristic expression employed in the prediction is the root ענה "abuse" (15:13). It is repeated in ch. 16 to describe Sarai's behavior to her slave and the motive for the slave's flight (16:6), to express the command of the Lord's messenger to Hagar (vs. 9) and the plight which aroused the compassion of the Lord (vs. 11). But the affinity between the Egyptian slavery and the slavery of the Egyptian does not stop here. In the context of the preceding chapter, slavery predicted is slavery ordained; this is the form and the meaning of the divine speech (15:13f.; cf. 46:3f.; also Ps 105:17f.). The substance, slavery and abuse, is the same in both chapters, but the subjects and objects of the verb ענה are interchanged: Sarai as subject and Hagar as object here; Hagar's descendants as subject and Sarai's as object there. And while this feature may escape a casual reader, this would hardly be the case for the educated Israelite. For him there could be no overlooking the verse pregnant with meaning for every Ishmaelite: "the Lord has paid heed to your (complaint of) abuse"[35] (vs.11). He knew well the homologous formulation applying to Israel and occur-

---

[32] Cf. F. Zimmermann, *JBL* 71 (1952), pp.113f.

[33] See n.7.

[34] Cassuto (n.13), pp.315f., has called attention to the element of Egyptian slavery in the Hagar story.

[35] The sing. fem. עָנְיֵךְ, referring to Hagar, offers no difficulty to this identification. Hebrew often uses this form for peoples.

ring in the proclamation that accompanies the annual offering of the first fruit: "... The Egyptians ill-treated us and abused us (ויענונו) ... but the Lord paid heed to our call and took notice of our abuse" (וישמע יהוה את קלנו וירא את ענינו, Deut 26:6f.; cf. Ex 3:7). What the Egyptians would later do to Sarai's children, Sarai did to a child of Egypt. But God listened to both; His compassion is with all His creatures (Ps 145:9).

Excursus I[36]

Mesopotamian Sources to Gen 16:1—6

No single extrabiblical text corresponds fully to the situation of this biblical narrative, but a combination of the following five documents provides a backdrop of great similarity.

A.   If a man's slave girl, pretending equality to her mistress, speaks insolently to her, her mouth shall be scoured with a sila of salt.[37]

B.   Laqipum has married Ḥatala the daughter of Enišru ... If (Ḥatala) does not procure offspring for him within two years (!), it is incumbent upon her to buy a slave girl (and give her to her husband as a concubine). Subsequently, after having some-how (?) procured an infant for him (through the slave girl), she (Ḥatala) may sell her wherever she pleases.[38]

---

[36] To p. 54.

[37] Sumerian. Laws of Ur-Nammu (2112—2095 B.C. [middle chronology; the dates are from J.S. Brinkman in A.L. Oppenheim, *Ancient Mesopotamia* (1964), pp.335—352]), B§29/22'/B2'. O.R. Gurney and S.N. Kramer in *Assyriological Studies* 16 (n.17) p.16; translated also by J.J. Finkelstein in *The Ancient Near East*, ed. J.B. Pritchard (1969), p.525; translated and commented by E. Szlechter, *RA* 61 (1967),pp.109,118. Instead of "speaks insolently to," one may translate "curses."

[38] Old Assyrian, 18th century. *ICK* I 3; translitereated, etc., B. Hrozný in *Symbolae ... Koschaker* (1939), pp.108f.; translated and commented by J. Lewy, *HUCA* 27 (1956), pp.9f. For *šarrum* (line 13) "son of a slave girl," see Lewy, p.7, n.32. It is of interest to note, as Lewy does, p.10, n.44, that in a subsequent letter (*ICK* I 69:7—12) Laqipum advises Ḥatala, "If you do not like the slave girl, sell her and keep the money." Laqipum is

C.   If a man has married a *nadītu* (priestess) and she has given a
      slave girl to her husband, the slave girl then bears children,
      whereupon she goes about making herself equal to her mistress,
      her mistress may not sell her since she has borne children; she
      may put a slave mark on her and count her among the slaves. If
      she has not borne children, her mistress may sell her.[39]

D.   Bunini and (his wife) Belissunu have bought (a girl named)
      Šamašnuri ... To Bunini she is a wife, to Belissunu a slave. If
      Šamašnuri says to her mistress Belissunu, "You are not my mis-
      tress," one shall cut her hair and sell her.[40]

E.   ... If Gilimninu (the wife) fails to bear children, she shall get a
      woman from the Nullu Land (i.e., a slave girl) as a wife for Šen-
      nina (the husband). In that case Gilimninu alone (?) shall have
      authority over the offspring.[41]

The following elements can be gathered from these texts (the
features bearing similarities to Gen 16 are italicized): (1) *An*—apparently—*monogamous marriage*[42] *is expanded by the introduction of
a second—and secondary—wife* (henceforth "girl") *when it turns out to
have remained childless for a number of years* (B,[E]). (2) *The childlessness of the marriage* is a consequence of the social state of the wife (C)[43]/

---

as good as his word; he may even go further, as we do not know whether the maid bore a
child in the meantime. He reassures his wife of her rights adding that the proceeds of the
sale are hers; this is natural since, according to the marriage deed, she laid out the money
for the purchase of the maid. Another Old Assyrian marriage contract stipulates a duration of three years of childless marriage before the husband (!) may buy a girl for concubinage (Lewy, pp.6f., lines 18–22).

[39] Old Babylonian. Laws of Ammurapi (1792–1750) §§146f.

[40] Old Babylonian, time of Ammurapi. *CT* VIII 22b; translated, etc., by M. Schorr,
Urkunden des altbabylonischen Zivil-und Prozessrechts (1913), p. 121.

[41] Nuzi, about 15th cent. *HSS* V 67. For the background and bibliography, see
Speiser, *Genesis* [n.21], pp.120f., and also R. Borger, *Handbuch der Keilschriftliteratur*
... 1 (1967), p. 43. The translation of the last sentence is based on the reading *gi-lim-ni-
nu-[m]a*(?) *ú-ma-ar* after Speiser, but the rendering and interpretation are less certain
than one might gather from his commentary.

[42] The special arrangment whereby an Old Assyrian trader has one wife in Cappadocia
and one in Assyria (Lewy [n.38], p.9, n.40) can be disregarded.

[43] *Nadītu* (LUKUR) priestesses were forbidden to have, or prevented (?) from having, children.

has a natural cause (B,E). (3) *The girl is provided   by, and—
presumably—belongs to,* both spouses (D)/ the husband (the text referred
to at the end of note 38)/ *the wife* (B,C,E). (4) *The girl is a wife to the
master of the house and a handmaid to the mistress* (D). (5) *Authority
over the offspring of the girl rests with the wife* (E, uncertain but likely
reading). (6) *The girl* makes herself equal to her mistress (C)/*is insolent
to*[44] *her mistress* (A). (7) *Punishment of the girl consists in* her reduction
to full slavery (within the present household or by selling her away) (C,
D)/*infliction of corporal pain* (A).

E X C U R S U S   2[45]

The Names in Gen 16:11—14

Explanations have been given for the names and namings in these
verses which go beyond, and are sometimes out of consonance with, the
immediate understanding of the Hagar story. They shall be surveyed and
evaluated here.

Ishmael (vs. 11[f.]). The etymology and its narrative matrix are sometimes said, though not without reserve, to be of Ishmaelite origin.[46] The
following considerations militate against this opinion: (1) There is no
positive reason for a hypothesis of an Ishmaelite origin of the etymology
and its setting. The Bible is full of etymologies of personal names, yet nobody would suggest ordinarily that they originate with the distinct
groups of descendants of the bearers of the names. (2) The etymology is
part of the annunciation of the future birth of the child, which represents a

---

[44] "Curses" instead of "is insolent to" (cf. n.37) is less similar to ותקל ... בעיניה (Gen.
16:4), but note that the meaning of קלל (verb, piel; noun) on occasion extends to the field
of imprecation; cf. H.C. Brichto, *The Problem of "Curse" in the Hebrew Bible* (1963),
pp.174–176, 195–196 (ff.), 220f.

[45] See n.29.

[46] E. g., Gunkel (n.10), p. 912, considers it a possibility; O. Procksch, *Die Genesis*
(1913), p.110, refers to Gunkel; M. Noth, *Überlieferungsgeschichte des Pentateuch* (1948),
p. 119, n.312, thinks it is plausible.

genre known only in biblical literature.[47] Which is to say: The minor
hypothesis of an Ishmaelite origin of the name etymology presupposes
the further and major, but utterly unsupported hypothesis that the genre
of annunciation was also at home with the Ishmaelites. The whole construct is a case of the tail wagging the dog.

El-roi (vs. 13). Proposals about the origin of this etymology often presuppose a definite image of the nature of El-roi. The prevailing opinion
has it that El-roi is a stable and identifiable deity who has his own place
and/or community of worship. It is usually assumed that he is a local
numen of the well, even of a sanctuary situated there; Kilian calls vss. 13f.
a cult etiology.[48] This opinion is taken for granted without further support. But there is little to justify such confidence. Almost all students of
ancient Oriental religion have neglected Usener's theory of momentary
gods (*Augenblicksgötter*) to the detriment of research. A momentary god
is experienced once and for a limited duration in an extraordinary, often
surprising object or event.[49] Good illustrations of the concept are τὸν
παρόντα δαίμονα "the god who, at present, has power over me"[50];
aius locutius "the speaking voice," that spoke just once; and *fortuna
huiusque diei* "Fortuna of this particular day."[51] Usener developed his

---

[47] See n.16. The Ugaritic passage *hl ǵlmt tld b[———]n* (*UT* 77:7; *Corpus* 24:7) should
be left out of consideration; it is too damaged to provide a useful base for judgement, and
what surrounds it is even more obscure. We do not even know whether it contains a prediction of a future event (thus G.R. Driver, *Canaanite Myths and Legends* [1954], p. 125),
a report about a past event (thus J. Aistleitner, *Die mythologischen . . . Texte aus Ras
Schamra* [1959], p.63), or a description of a general and recurring situation.

[48] R. Kilian, *Die vorpriesterlichen Abrahams-Überlieferungen* (1966), p.86. W.W. Graf
Baudissin, *Kyrios als Gottesname . . .* 3 (1929), pp.131f.,136, hesitatingly disagrees with
the general view; cf. also F.M. Cross, *HTR* 55 (1962), p.233, n.28. The issue is hardly affected by the moot problem of local El numina in Canaan and their role in the life of the
"patriarchs," for which one may compare H. Weidmann, *Die Patriarchen und ihre
Religion . . .* (1968), pp.113—125.

[49] H. Usener, *Götternamen* (1896), pp.279—301, see also p.276. The theory has been
accepted, among others, by E. Cassirer, *Philosophie der symbolischen Formen* 2 (1923),
p.208, and G. van der Leeuw, *Phänomenologie der Religion* (1933). pp.134—136, 140. J.
van Dijk briefly discusses momentary gods in Sumerian religion (in J.P. Asmussen . . . ed.,
Handbuch der Religionsgeschichte I [1971], p.461).

[50] Usener (n.49), p.293.

[51] The Latin examples are from L. Deubner in Chantepie de la Saussaye, *Lehrbuch der
Religionsgeschichte* 2⁴ (1925), pp.443 and 465.

theory with Indo-European material, but there is no reason to assume that the phenomenon is limited to the Indo-Europeans. A "god of appearance" who figures exclusively in a story about an encounter or a vision that is neither induced nor expected fits the concept in a most natural way; he is an *Augenblicksgott* almost by definition. Usener's theory illuminates the text in a welcome manner, but the text does not depend on it for understanding; it would get the same interpretation in the absence of this or any comparable available theory. On the other hand, the El-roi of the widely cherished view maintains his extraliterary existence in the desert only by the grace of the theory of local Els of Canaan, and how good is this theory for the detection and establishment of putative facts?

Beer-Laḥai-roi (vs. 14). This etymology is predicated on the name El-roi and not vice versa (El-roi got his etymology in the preceding verse), and this observation agrees with the text: "Therefore (i.e., by virtue of what is told in vs. 13) one calls the well . . ."[52] On the hypothesis that El-roi is a deity of permanence, worshipped in the second millennium and perhaps associated with this well, the etymology of the name of the well may have preexisted the main part of the narrative. If one decides for the alternative hypothesis that El-roi is a momentary god whom the author introduced into (though not necessarily invented for) the narrative, the etymology of the name of the well is likewise original with the narrative.

Support has been sought for the assumption of an independent tribal origin of the etymology of the well by linking the well to the Ishmaelites. This link cannot be established. (1) The only person of reported relation

---

[52] H. Cazelles, *Ugaritica* 6 (1969), p.34, with n.43, sees in Laḥai the name of an obscure local deity and refers to similar *laḥwi* of Mari and Chagar Bazar (see H.B. Huffmon, *Amorite Personal Names* [1965], pp.50, 79, 192. To Huffmon's names two more may be added from Mari texts, published by G. Dossin in *RA* 65 [1971]: *la-aḥ-we-e-sa-ar* (!) [p.40, line 21] and *la-aḥ-wi-be-lí* [p.59, line 72]). This proposal is encumbered by (grapho-phonetic and) semantic difficulties; for the latter see Huffmon, p.78, and W. von Soden, *WdO* 3 (1966), p.181. Cazelles may, however, draw minor support from *šlmlḥy*, recorded on an ostracon from Elath, Persian period, and studied by J. Naveh, *BASOR* 183 (1966), p.27. *šlmbʻl*, שלומיאל, and שלמיהו suggest that *lḥy* is the divine element in this personal name. It needs no emphasis that no way leads from these essays to the biblical etymologies.

to the well is Isaac (Gen. 24:62; 25:11); the relation of Ishmael is a supposition of doubtful validity, resting solely on an altogether gratuitous exegesis of this narrative.[53] (2) Geography offers no foothold. The well is situated in the Negev (Gen. 24:62), probably somewhere between Hebron and Kadesh Barnea (16:14; Bered is unknown).[54] A wandering tribe cannot be identified by a well that cannot be located. (3) Hagar, the mother of Ishmael, names the god (vs.13) but not the well; the sentence about the naming of the latter has the impersonal "one" as subject.

The examination of the hypothesis that some or all name etymologies of vss.11—14 are of nonliterary and probably extra-Israelite origin has produced rather negative results. The hypothesis is very improbable for the first name, Ishmael. The etymology is one of a fairly large number in the Old Testament, and there is nothing to suggest that it be accorded special treatment and its provenance be sought outside this tale. The hypothesis would also presuppose the otherwise unsupported fact that the Ishmaelites possessed a literary genre identical with, or similar to, the biblical genre of divine annuniciation of childbirth. The hypothesis is but a mite better for the second name, El-roi. The first caveat about the etymology of Ishmael applies to it with equal force, and, furthermore, this etymology is based on the uncomfortably questionable presupposi-

---

[53] Kilian (n.48), pp.84,87, notes the original mutual independence of vss.11f. (the Ishmael passage) and vss.13f. (the Beer-laḥai-roi passage). It would follow from his analysis that the association of the Ishmaelites with the well results from a quirk of literary history, but he avoids the conclusion by assuming, without textual or archaelogical support, that the Ishmaelites worshipped El-roi or sojourned, at least occasionally, by the well. (The preparation of this assumption on p.86 is itself a chain of non sequiturs.) M. Noth (n.46), pp.118—120, is somewhat more cautious as he says that the Isaac and Ishmael clans shared in the water and cult of the well. With G. Fohrer, *Geschichte der israelitischen Religion* (1969), p.50, reference to Ishmael has at long last disappeared from critical exegesis, and only the clan of Isaac remains.

[54] To look for it south or west of Kadesh Barnea (Ain el Qudeirat) would place it outside of the Negev. In Gen 20:1 the Negev seems to extend SW of Kadesh Barnea, but this is impossible for geographical and contextual reasons, in spite of all the exegetical effort invested in the demonstration. Should Shur here (and also in some other passages?) be different from the Shur by the Egyptian frontier (see n.7)? Targums sometime identify Shur with Ḥaluṣa (so far attested only in postbiblical times; see A. Jaussen, *RB* 15 [1906], p.597, and G.I. Davies, *VT* 22 [1972], pp.155f.,158), ca. 20 km SW of Beer Sheba (cf. A. Negev, in בא"י אנציקלופדיה לחפירות ארכיאולוגיות אנלוגיות [1970], pp.152—154). Within a broad area, such a location would well fit Gen 20:1.

tion that the god had permanence and a basis in the cult and/or society. As regards the third name, Beer-laḥai-roi, here again the hypothesis lacks a positive raison d'être. In the first place, it is not plausible that one should look for it outside of Israel; furthermore, it, too, is based on the presupposition of the permanence and substantiality of El-roi. The attempt to trace Gen 16:11—14 back to nonliterary and extra-Israelite origins has produced results of various degrees of improbability, none of them small. Under these circumstances it is unprofitable to speculate about the preliterary and non-Israelite meanings of these verses.

The Biblical Account
of the Foundation of
the Monarchy in Israel

The story of the foundation of the monarchy in Israel is related in 1 Sam 8:4—12:25. Its narrative content is the event of Saul's enthronement, but the conceptual problem behind it is the change from the kingship of God to the kingship of man. It is, therefore, in order to consider the idea of the kingship of God and its realization in early Israel, that is to say, during the two centuries antecedent to the events of the story. The chapters under consideration affirm this idea repeatedly, if chiefly by indirection, in that they are critical of and sometimes even inimical to the introduction of human kingship on the ground that it replaces the divine kingship under which Israel lived heretofore.

Many scholars hold that the biblical view is not historical. In the first two centuries of Israel's settled life and for a considerable time thereafter, they argue, the idea that God is the king of Israel did not exist and, consequently, Samuel and his contemporaries could not have objected in its name to the introduction of the monarchy. The opposition to the monarchy on these grounds, about which we read in the Book of Samuel, must be seen, therefore, as a retrojection from much later times; passages that express it are incongruous with the era of their tale, and the image that they paint is distorted.

What, then, according to the scholars who hold this opinion, is the real reason for this antagonism to kingship in the Book of Samuel? Two answers are offered: one, the influence of Hosea; the other, that of the deuteronomists. In Hosea especially two passages, 8:4 and 13:10f., are held to express the prophet's opposition to kingship.[1] Rather than com-

---

[1] K. Budde, *Die Bücher Samuel* (1902), p. 55; P. Dhorme, *Les Livres de Samuel* (1910), p. 71; R. Kittel, in E. Kautzsch-A. Bertholet, *Die Heilige Schrift des A.T.* I⁴ (1922), p. 419; A. Lods, *Israel des origines au ... VIIIe siècle* (1930), p. 412.

ment on them myself, I cite from the first third of this century, when this opinion was in vogue, the chief commentators on the Book of Hosea: Marti, Gressmann, Nowack, Guthe, and Sellin.[2] Remarkably enough, of these five scholars, four do not construe these key verses as Hosea in opposition to monarchy; indeeed, they are of the opinion that he was not against monarchy at all or that he even held it in esteem, seeing in it a gift of God. Only Sellin maintains Hosea's objection to monarchy and points to the tradition of 1 Sam 8 and 10 as the inspiration of Hosea. In other words, Sellin sees as cause what is commonly held to be the effect.

The other answer, that the objection to the monarchy manifest in our chapters is to be traced to the deuteronomistic school, rests on alleged facts; alleged only, for they do not exist at all. Thus Weiser is unquestionably correct when he points out that neither the Book of Deuteronomy nor the deuteronomistic components of the Book of Kings reject the monarchy in principle.[3] There exists, then, in the literature of the periods of the declining kingdoms of Israel and Judah or of the Babylonian exile no statement of opposition to the establishment of the monarchy. Hence, that opposition, explicitly expressed in chs. 8 and 10 of First Samuel, cannot be argued to be of late origin, nor the story of 1 Sam 8—12 to be composite and imperfectly integrated,[4] on the basis of either of these two putative influences.

Much more worthy of consideration is the view of Victor Maag,[5] who, while not insisting that the concept of the kingship of God was unknown in early Israel, nevertheless attributes no importance to it. The concept eventuated from an encounter between Yhwh and the Canaanite god El only after the formative and determinative period of the history of

[2] K. Marti, *Das Dodekapropheton* (1904), pp. 66,102; H. Gressmann, in *Die Schriften des A.T. in Auswahl* ... II:1 [1910] [2](1921), p. 386, "Textkrit. Anmerk.," p. 16; W. Nowack, *Die kleinen Propheten* [1897] [3](1922), pp. 50,77; H. Guthe, in Kautzsch (n.1) II[4] (1923), pp. 13,21; E. Sellin, *Das Zwölfprophetenbuch* [1922] [2](1929), pp. 87,132.

[3] A Weiser, *Samuel; seine geschichtliche Aufgabe* ... (1962), pp. 27 n.1, 34. The contrary opinion of M. Noth, *Überlieferungsgeschichtliche Studien* I (1943), pp. 54 f. (57,60,62,73), rests on an analysis which, itself being in need of substantiation and demonstration, is unsuitable for a basis to anything.

[4] A list of additions to the original relation is found on p. 83. For the special case of ch. 12, see pp. 98 f.

[5] V. Maag, "Malkut Jhwh," *Congress Volume Oxford 1959* (Supplements to *Vetus Testamentum* 7 [1960]), pp. 129—153.

the religion of Israel. Kingship, human or divine, he argues, played no role in the prehistory or earliest history of Israel. This is critical for the understanding of Israel's subsequent history because, unlike other peoples, Israel was not bent on obliterating or obliviating its nomadic past. Israel's religion is rooted in this past, and this fact is decisive for the problem of the kingship of God, for a god of nomads is not portrayed in terms of royalty. "This God is not a king. He is a leader, protector, a Deity omnipresent, close to man and absolutely authoritative; all this, but not a king. The functions that are the responsibility of a god of a migratory people do not leave Him time or scope to hold sway as a king."[6] The Pentateuch does not characterize as king the God of the patriarchs or the God of the tribes that wandered in the desert and then moved into Palestine, nor does it employ any royal imagery in the description of Him.[7] In the ancient Near East, the place of the king is in a settled society and a

---

[6] "Dieser Gott ist nicht König! Er is Führer, Beschützer, allgegenwärtig den Menschen verbundener, absolut autoritativer Gott: all das; aber nicht König. Die Funktionen, welche der Transmigrationsgott übt, bieten ihm weder Zeit noch *ambiente*, um als König zu thronen" (id., p. 141).

[7] There is a danger of resting too much of the argument on this point. Translating מלך by "(being, becoming, etc.) king," we note that the Pentateuch attributes royalty to God two or three times. Maag mentions two (id., p. 141, n.2): "The Lord is king (ימלך) for ever and ever" (Ex 15:18), and "The Lord their God is with them, a king's (מלך) acclaim bestowed on Him" (Nu 23:21). But he says that these passages in their poetic contexts were borrowed from Canaanite and incorporated unchanged into the pentateuchal prose narrative; the second verse in particular betrays Canaanite imprint in תועפת ראם of the immediate continuation, ראם "wild ox" being identified with the Ugaritic *ṯr il* "Il the Bull." Maag does not mention the third passage, "He became king (ויהי . . . מלך) in Jeshurun when the chiefs of the people were assembled, the convocation (?) of the tribes of Israel" (Deut 33:5). It appears that he does not consider מלך as referring to God; and admittedly, one cannot claim more than probability for the interpretation that maintains this reference. But his exposition of the other two passages should not stand unchallenged. The allegation of Canaanite influence in Nu 23:21f. is unfounded. The bull is a ubiquitous symbol of the divine in the ancient Near East extending as far as South Arabia; nor is it monopolized by an El-type or Baal-type god. The first passage, Ex 15:18, it is true, is part of a text in which one may discern some imprint of "Canaan," if one is willing to use this spongy term. But concerning this comparatively long piece of 18 verses, it is difficult to tell where (in the text) and when (in its prehistory) the influence does, or did, set in. Besides this literary attestation there is probably one personal name giving evidence of the concept of divine kingship in Israel's nomadic past recorded in the Pentateuch. For names, see below, p. 81.

stable world that functions cyclically; he maintains them socially, politically, religiously and, in a way, also cosmically. When Israel established itself in Palestine, its God gradually absorbed new features, among them kingship, but for a very long time the royal aspect of His divinity remained of small account.

I consider Maag's article as a whole a momentous study of the religion of Israel, owning few equals.[8] For our purpose, however, its restrictive semantics lays it open to criticism. To say that מלך, the operative word in the text under discussion, indeed its subject, means "king," and that king is defined as a potentate of a well organized state, large or small, such as Egypt, Babylonia, or Ugarit, is to overlook the hierarchic mobility and shifting semantics of words denoting social phenomena. An examination of Semitic words that are candidates for the English rendering "king" will make my point clear. Let us consider the contrasting uses in Hebrew and Akkadian of the terms *malk and *š/šarr. In Hebrew, the מלך holds the highest rank of rulership and the שר an intermediate one; in Akkadian, šarru is commonly "king," and malku signifies a role of lesser station.[9] But even šarru, prior to, or outside of, the highly organized monarchies of Mesopotamia, has a range of qualifications. The first seventeen entries of the Assyrian king list are "tent dwellers," i.e., nomads, yet they are called šarr(LUGAL.MEŠ)-a-ni "kings" all the same.[10] The "sheiks" of the Haneans (ab-bu-ú ḪA.NA), a tribal grouping in the area of Mari in the eighteenth century B.C., are called šarrānu "kings."[11] As for *malk, Safaitic mlk is "tribal chief, lord," and has no

---

[8] The preceding paragraph summarizes only what relates directly to the present discussion.

[9] This statement, while somewhat general, is not impaired in its validity. For *malku*, see W. von Soden, *Akkadisches Handwörterbuch* (1959 ff.), pp. 595ff.: for *šarru* (and *rubā'u*) in the special situation of the Old Assyrian expansion into Asia Minor, see P. Garelli, *Les Assyriens en Cappadoce* (1963), pp. 207–212.

[10] See I. J. Gelb, *JNES* 13 (1954), pp. 210f., and F.R. Kraus, *Könige, die in Zelten wohnten* (1965), pp. 3f.,13f. It is questionable, however, whether it is appropriate to speak of an "allgemeine Entwertung des Königtitels in altbabylonischer Zeit" (Kraus,p. 13). It is quite possible that nomads and others speaking of nomads used the word with no pejorative connotation. At any rate, the versatility of the word *šarru* at that time is not of great importance for the present issue.

[11] F. Thureau-Dangin, *RA* 33 (1936), pp. 50f. I:15f.; correct reading J.R. Kupper, *Les nomads en Mésopotamie au temps . . . de Mari* (1957), p. 1,n.1, p. 32,n.2.

royal connotation.[12] In fine, words that are commonly, and usually adequately, translated "king," in reality denote the holder of the highest office or position in a more or less independent social unit and do not commit us to a specific definition of the nature of that unit; they do not tell whether the holder of the office heads a tribe or an empire. This sentence, slightly rephrased, can also be stated conversely: The form of an ancient Oriental society frequently does not support inferences as to the title of its head. It would be futile, therefore, to speculate whether Yhwh could or could not have been designated the מלך of the tribes of Israel at a given point in their history.

Onomastic evidence, however, is present which points to the conclusion that early Israel did indeed consider Yhwh as their מלך. Three or four persons born in premonarchical times have names that contain the component מלך: Abimelech (Ju 8:31, and elsewhere), Ahimelech (1 Sam 21:2, and elsewhere), Malkishua (14:49), and probably Malkiel (Nu 26:45 [Gen 46:17]). The premonarchical era of the birth of the first three being beyond question, the element מלך cannot refer to an Israelite monarch. While the names are variously interpreted, the view most commonly held and entitled to preference sees מלך as an epithet of God.[13] The conclusion imposes itself that before the foundation of the monarchy there were Israelites who considered Yhwh as their מלך.[14]

---

[12] A. Jamme, *Orientalia* N.S. 39 (1970), pp. 504–511.

[13] The names mean: "The/My-Father-Is-מלך," "The/My-Brother-Is-מלך," "The/My-מלך-Is-Help"(?), and "The/My-מלך-Is-El/God." The identification of the subject and the predicate of the last name as expressed in this translation is not certain; cf. the name Elimelech.

[14] I cite, to give a fuller picture, alternative interpretations of these names and different inferences drawn from them for the religion of premonarchic Israel. While I do not, except perhaps (1a), own them myself, I would point out that they, too, support in various degrees the thesis that Yhwh was or might well have been regarded as Israel's king in the earliest times.

(1) מלך is not king but leader or holder of a more primitive office. Instances of this meaning of *mlk* outside of Hebrew were cited above. For Hebrew, one can refer to ואשכן כמלך בגדוד (Job 29:25): the head of a גדוד is not a king but an officer, a שר or a lower rank (2 Sam 4:2; 1 Ki 11:24; 1 Ch 12:19). An attempt to show a more frequent occurence of this meaning in Hebrew has been made by S. Talmon in his article "In Those Days There Was No King in Israel," *Proceedings of the Fifth World Cong. of Jew. Studies 1969*, ed. P. Peli (vol.1, 1972), pp. (135–)141–144 (Hebrew; English abstract, p. 242f). The names "The/My-Father-Is-a/the-Leader," etc., could refer either (a) to Yhwh or (b) to man. If (a), the

As was mentioned before, Maag thinks that the idea of the kingship of
God in Israel is the result of Canaanite influence.[15] Now there is not a
shred of evidence for this opinion and, to my mind, it does not possess a
grain of likelihood. Furthermore, were it to be true, it would shed no light
on our subject. The fact of such borrowing, could it be proved, might well
have taken place very long before the establishment of the monarchy in
Israel. Finally, given the paucity and nature of our sources, this kind of
opinion is unsusceptible to refutation. This is not to say that, because it
cannot possibly be refuted, it is sound. On the contrary, it says that the
opinion is devoid of sense. I refer to the methodological principle that
when one cannot state the ready conditions under which a statement can
be falsified, the statement is nonsense in that it lacks content.[16] When, in

---

affirmations are functionally equivalent to what is understood in the commonly prevailing
interpretation. If (b), they show that מלך was a word of social rank in early Israel, and
nothing in this militates against conceiving Yhwh as מלך.

(2) The parents who gave these names to their children in the period of our concern did
not thereby intend a specific expression of the affirmation. That is, the names just took
the fancy of the parents because they had run in the family, sounded good, or whatever.
Thus, at a later time, several men were called Judah, as recorded in Ezra and Nehemiah,
although no etymologically supportable meaning could have been known in the fifth century. Even if this argument is accepted, its force in our case is limited. אב, אח, and אל are
frequent components of early names (שוע is infrequent), entering into combinations with
other words to form other names; within combinations with these words they change
position forming yet other names; and most of them and their components are words of
everyday life, which express ideas of relevance and significance. (The following small
sampling of names should illustrate this; they are drawn from Judges, Samuel, and one
from Chronicles: אביאל and אליאב, אביגיל, אביה and אביה, אביחיל, אביטל אבינדב, אבינעם, אבינר,
אביעזר, אבישוע [1 Ch 8:4], אלישוע, יהושע.). These observations combine to support the proposition that the names were fully alive, and that their plain linguistic contents were most
probably intended by those who gave the names.

(3) The names are a foreign import in Israel and do not reflect its own religion. This
argument is similar to the preceding one and can be answered similarly. Whatever the
likelihood of their being imports, the names were, within Israel, perfectly understandable
and naturally understood in the Israelite way, i.e., they referred to Yhwh (cf. O Eissfeldt,
Kleine Schriften 1 [1962], pp. 179,192 [=*ZAW* 46 (1928), pp. 90,104]). If מלך did not
refer to a deity, the above comment on (1b) applies.

[15] Maag (n.5), p. 142.

[16] For a full statement of this principle, see K.R. Popper, *The Logic of Scientific Dis-
covery* (Harper Torchbook ed., 1965), pp. 40–42, and Index, s.v. "Falsifiability" and
"Falsification"; id., *Conjectures and Refutations* (1963), ch. 1 (pp. 33ff.), and elsewhere.
Cf. also P.B. Medawar, *The Art of the Soluble* (1967), pp. 147–151.

the humanities, this last observation combines with the two preceding ones it condemns the proposition under examination.[17]

The story of the foundation of the monarchy falls into five sections, which we shall call A, B, C, D, and E. Section A is a report of the assembly of the people at Ramah for the purpose of requesting a king (8:4—22 [without vss. 5aβ, 8, 11b—18]); B relates the search for the asses and the anointing of Saul (9:1—10:16 [without 10:8]); C deals with the assembly at Mizpah to present the king to the people (10:17—27); D is the story of the battle at Jabesh—gilead (11:1—11 [vss. 12f. link this section to the next]); E recounts the assembly at Gilgal, which is opened by a long oration of Samuel's (11:14—12:25 [composite and glossed]).

There is a widely held opinion that the attitude of sections B and D towards Saul is sympathetic, and that these sections are, therefore, close in spirit as well as in time to the events they recount, whereas the attitude of the remaining sections is negative and, therefore, remote from the subjects of their stories. This opinion will be criticized on two counts. One, it sets up alternatives and forces them on the composition: the several sections are either wholly for Saul or kingship or else wholly against him or kingship. Such exclusive classification of texts is the result of an unvindicated prepossession; I shall attempt to show later that the texts do not fit into this binary system. Two, this classification of the sections is combined with an assumption about their chronological origins: a section which is understood to be sympathetic to the monarchy and the events that led to it is close to the events, hence an early source; an unsympathetic section is remote, hence a late source. While this simplistic view is not shared by all who hold this position, the extent to which it does pervade the scholarship on the subject leads one to marvel at what passes for method in the study of history, literary or other.

Viewing the five sections in their order we observe that the narrative they make up is built in the form of a simple rondo: a—b—a—b—a, assembly—action—assembly—action—assembly.[18] Assemblies are held

[17] Natural sciences, being much more exact and exercising much greater control over the conditions of their propositions, do not have to set up the above triad of characteristics in order to establish the criticism; the last member suffices.

[18] A similar structure in the Akkadian epic of Atraḫasis I:192—248 was pointed out by W.L. Moran, *BASOR* 200 (1970), p. 48.

to voice opinions and counteropinions; this is their basic function in society, and there is no reason why it should be otherwise in our story. Therefore, the fact of different views that crop up in various sections reporting on the assemblies can hardly be taken in itself as a prima facie case for literary conflation or compositeness. The establishment of the monarchy, as universally recognized, was a radical change in the life of Israel, reflecting an existing crisis and pregnant with the potential to shake the foundations of society and religion. It is only natural that the resulting agitation found expression in the discussions of the assemblies. Now in the three assembly sections, A, C, and E, we have just that: yes and no, doubt and warning, thesis, antithesis and, yes, synthesis. Had the author suppressed the warning and the opposition and cloaked the monarchy with untarnished glory, he would have done less than justice to history and the canons of literary composition. He did nothing of the sort. He grasped the uniqueness of the historic moment, described the tensions, lent them words, and integrated them into his report. Against the historical perspicacity and literary incisiveness which distinguish sections A and C, the account of section B pales into an idyll for all its vaunted flavor of antiquity and rusticity; donkeys always get lost.

We shall now examine the sections individually, beginning with section A (8:4ff.).[19] The elders of Israel come to Samuel at Ramah, evidently because of the growing pressure of the Philistines, to request "a king (מלך) to rule over us (לשפטנו) like all the nations" (8:5). The idea of rule and government is expressed in this story by four roots: עצר, נגד, מלך and שפט. Commentators have for the most part failed to give due consideration to the last two, probably because of their relative rarity in this

---

[19] The section was studied by M. Buber in his exemplary essay "Das Volksbegehren." Throughout the comments that follow I am much indebted to Buber's exposition although I do not accept his views in toto; since I do not cite my agreement at every turn, neither shall I state my criticism. The essay was first published in W. Schmauch, ed., *In memoriam E. Lohmeyer* (1951), pp. 53—66; it was republished in his *Werke* 2 (1964), pp. 727—742. It forms the first chapter of a three-chapter book, called *Der Gesalbte*. The second chapter is entitled "Die Erzählung von Sauls Königswahl," first published in *VT* 6 (1956), pp. 113—173; republished in *Werke* 2 (but called "Wie Saul König wurde"), pp. 743—811. (The bibliographical listing on p. 1233 claims completeness but lacks it; only a Hebrew publication of this chapter is listed.) Hereafter all references to the two chapters—the third is not referred to—are to the republication in *Werke*.

semantic field. This rarity may be an indication of the antiquity of the subject matter and its linguistic expression, and it may, furthermore, point to the peculiar nature of the government about which we read here and which began to disappear rapidly after Saul's kingship.

Verse 5 employs מלך and שפט. Having previously dealt with the former,[20] we now shall turn to the latter. The sense of judging perceived in שפט is not present in any of the sections but the last one, where Samuel's invocation of a judgement, his demand that the fairness of his stewardship be vindicated, is followed by a full-fledged court scene. The nonjuridical meaning of שפט in Hebrew and the cognate languages is now beyond the pale of question;[21] were it not so, the use of the term שפט in these chapters alone would be sufficient to establish it. When the meaning of שפט as "ruling" is added to its sense of "judging," it imposes upon the scholar the task of determining in each case whether one sense is present to the exclusion of the other or whether both are present in equal force or perhaps with one force ancillary to the other.[22] In the case of 8:20 there can be no doubt as to what is meant: "Our king shall govern us (ושפטנו), lead us forth and fight our wars for us." The *hen-dia-trion* of this sentence determines the overriding meaning of שפט in this story: leadership in war. This is the nature of the government that the hour requires; the juridical element is totally absent.

Samuel's reaction to the demand of the people is negative: the demand is ill-conceived; and, furthermore, he is not authorized to grant it. Therefore he turns to God. God's answer consists of three points. To quote Buber: "First, it is not for you to be concerned with yourself but to carry out my directions. Second, they do not request that a successor be appointed to you, who are not their מלך, but to Me, their מלך. And finally ... it is my will that the successor be appointed." Buber continues: "It is clear that, according to the narrative, Yhwh says that until now He has

---

[20] See pp. 80 f.

[21] For שפט in the Bible, see W. Richter, *ZAW* 77 (1965), pp. 58—71. The material is well presented and the conclusions are sound, but one would wish to see them stated more resolutely. For Mari see the fine study of A. Marzal, *JNES* 30 (1971), pp. 186—217, particularly 187—194. The bibliography of *špṭ* in the Semitic languages, p. 188, n.1, deserves special mention.

[22] It is immaterial for our concern whether "government" or "judgment" is the primary meaning of שפט, but it is gratuitous to opt for the second alternative without proof.

been king over Israel, and this by no means only of His own volition and intent but also because ... Israel accepted His kingship loyally ... Now, however, He has been dethroned, rejected as their ruler."[23]

An amazing answer, this seventh verse. Is God resigning? Is He, from now on, satisfied with the role of a *deus otiosus?* No. Vs. 9 restates vs. 7, "Grant their request!" (as vs. 22 will again repeat it)[24]—but it qualifies it: "yet [i.e., with the proviso that, as you give them a king] you shall make them witnesses against themselves [to bear testimony, whenever necessary, that kingship is granted on condition] and advise them of the rule of the king." What is the condition? It is "the rule of the king" (משפט המלך) here, or "the rule of the kingship" (משפט המלכה) in 10:25.[25] What is its content? Let us say first what it is not. It is not the immediately following paragraph which recounts the privileges and demeanor of a king as tyrant (8:11b—18). If there is in the Old Testament one substantial addition to a literary unit that twists and thwarts its intent, it is these seven and a half verses, as Buber has conclusively shown.[26] Not privileges but obligation and limitation are the substance of "the rule of the king" or "the rule of kingship" that is written down in a document and deposited before God (10:25). The limitation is that their king is not to be like the kings of all the nations (8:5), and, consequently, Israel is not to be a nation like all the nations (vs.20).[27] The authority of the king does not

---

[23] "Zunächst ... Du bist nicht dazu da, dich mit dir zu befassen, sondern meine Aufträge auszuführen. Sodann: Sie fordern nicht, dass dir, der du ja kein Melekh bist, sondern dass mir, ihrem Melekh, ein Nachfolger bestellt werde. Und endlich ... Es ist mein Wille, dass der Nachfolger bestellt werde." And, "Der Erzähler lässt hier, das ist gewiss, JHWH sagen, er sei bisher, nicht etwa bloss aus eignem Sinn und Willen, sondern durch die ... Untergebenheitshaltung Israels dessen König gewesen ... nun aber sei er entthront, sei aus dem Herrschertum 'verworfen' worden" (Buber [n.19], p. 733).

[24] שמע בקול means "to accede, grant, listen, obey."

[25] "Rule" is an attempt to cover both semantic areas of משפט present in this text: "standard, regulations" to which the king is subject, and "government" which he exercises.

[26] Buber, (n.19), pp. 735—738; see also H. Seebass, *ZAW* 77 (1965), p. 287.

[27] God responds favorably to the request of the people in part only (8:7,9), but He ignores the important detail that it be a king like the kings of all the nations. Weiser (n.3), pp. 37f., and M. Zer-kavod, כרמלית 6f. (1959/60), pp. 206—207, think that the omission is intentional and that, by indirection, it withholds divine consent from a form of kingship as all the nations know and practice it. In a review of Weiser's book S. Herrmann, *TLZ* 89

originate in him or the people but in God; he is God's deputy and vice-gerent. In 15:17f. Samuel says to Saul, "The Lord anointed you king over Israel, and now He has sent you on the campaign." Anointing and en-thronement are deputation and mission; the true king is not the succes-sor, the *homo novus* that the people demand, but the king of Israel from time immemorial, God.

Once more, in Ez 20:32, is the theme taken up of Israel's desire to imitate the peoples about them: "We want to be like the nations, the races of other lands."[28] Ezekiel's contemporaries, according to his accusation, had idolatry in mind, as the text continues, "and worship wood and stone." It was a bleak, ill-omened time; nothing seemed more remote than the possibility of theocratic rule as reflected in the Book of Judges. But how does God react to the desperate quest of the exiles? "As I live, says the Lord God, I will be king over you ruling with a strong hand, with arm outstretched and fury outpoured" (vs.33). In Ezekiel's as

---

(1964), col.821, criticizes the author: If Samuel objects only to a monarchy "in the man-ner of all the nations," but not to a different kind of monarchy, this qualification should not be missing in vs.6 which contains a full statement of Samuel's view. Herrmann is right. Weiser has unnecessarily laid himself open to stricture by his identification of the positions of God and Samuel ("die ablehnende Haltung des Samuel und die dahinterste-hende Ablehnung ... durch Jahwe"). This results from the confusion of the study of literature and the study of history. Weiser approaches his text as a historian (*Samuel; seine geschichtliche Aufgabe* ... is the name of his book) in an area where only the philo-logian and exegete should dare tread (infra, pp. 177—187, "Israelite History and the His-torical Books of the Old Testament").

The following is an attempt to improve the argument for the point of Weiser and Zer-kavod: As a piece of literature, the text is pellucid. It emphatically and sharply distin-guishes between the positions of God and Samuel. Samuel's opposition to the monarchy is absolute; any qualification, such as "like all the nations," would weaken it. But God disavows His spokesman. This does not mean, however, that He accedes to the wish of the people without subtraction or change. He qualifies it in various ways, one of them being His passing in silence over the "like all the nations" of their request. This is an argument from literary silence, which is incomparably stronger than one from historical silence, the common *argumentum e silentio*. (The author of literature is sovereign; he creates his texts. The historian receives his sources; he is at the mercy of their contin-gencies.) The point of Weiser and Zer-kavod is plausible, but certainty about this author's intention eludes us.

[28] "I wish to appoint a king over me like all the nations round about" (Deut 17:14) probably depends on our text (8:5), but it lacks the general and existential sweep of the continuation: "We, too, want to be like all the nations" (8:20).

in Samuel's age the two propositions, "We want to be like the nations" and the kingship of God, are polar opposites. When Israel reiterates its old desire four and a half centuries after Samuel, God forces His kingship upon it "with fury outpoured." It is significant that this is the only time that Ezekiel mentions the kingship of God;[29] the idea did not concern him as it concerned many other prophets. But to the quest "We want to be like the nations" there is only one answer: "I will be king over you."

In this biblical regime God is the king and the human ruler is His deputy in contrast to the regimes of "all the nations." This is the interpretation of the biblical texts as regards the political order of the nations, namely, that kingship is an attribute of earthly monarchs with the absence of a higher kingship of a deity. And, as far as we know, this may have been true in the days of Saul. But whatever the situation in his time, this was frequently not the case among the peoples of western Asia in earlier periods. On the contrary, we find in these lands a phenomenon that resembles the one that the Bible holds up as an ideal for Israel, a political order wherein the god is the king and the human head of the government his representative. Urukagina,[30] king of Lagash in southern Sumer (ca. 2355 B.C.[31]) says: "When Ningirsu (the god of Lagash) . . . gave the kingship of Lagash to Urukagina . . . he (Ningirsu) enjoined upon him the (divine) decrees of former days. He (Urukagina) held close to the word which his king (Ningirsu) spoke to him."[32] Rimuš, the suc-

---

[29] See W. Zimmerli in *Maqqel Shaqedh . . . Hommage à W. Vischer* (1960), p. 218.

[30] So read conventionally. Proposed pronunciation: uru.inim.gi.na (W.G. Lambert, *Orientalia* NS 39 [1970], p. 419).

[31] The middle chronology is employed throughout (its case is powerfully supported by J. D. Weir, *The Venus Tablets of Ammizaduga* 1972). The first three dates are from D. O. Edzard in *Fischer Weltgeschichte* 2 (1965), p. 59.

[32] ud ᵈnin-gír-su ...uru-KA-gi-na-ra nam-lugal lagaški ena-sum-ma-a ... nam-tar-ra ud-bi-ta e-šè-gar inim lugal-ni ᵈnin-gír-suke₄ e-na-dug₄-ga ba-díb. The above translation is S.N. Kramer's, *The Sumerians* (1963), p. 318; cf. p. 80, n.3. Another translation, together with transliteration and notes, is offered by M. Lambert, *RA* 50 (1956), pp. 176f. It reads: "Lorseque Ningirsu ... fit donner à Urukagina la royauté de Lagaš ... il fit placer comme périmées les décisions (existantes). Les paroles que son roi Ningirsu lui fit dire furent comprises." For the difference, see Lambert's note to 8:7–9, on p. 176. The idea of divine kingship and its reflection in society and government in pre-Sargonic southern Mesopotamia is discussed by B. Kienast, *Orientalia* N.S. 42 (1973), pp. 491–495.

cessor of Sargon of Akkad (ca. 2284–2275), declares: "Rimuš, king of Kish, to whom Enlil has given the whole land (of Akkad), holds the upper and the lower seas and all the mountains for Enlil"[33]; he is the "stadtholder" or "lieutenant"—with the literary meaning of the words—of his god. His second successor, Naramsin (ca. 2260–2223), curses the potential mutilator of his inscription with these words: "May he not hold the scepter for Enlil or kingship for Innin."[34] The Old Assyrian king Silulu (perhaps at the end of the twenty-first century) expresses the same idea thus: "(The god) Aššur is the king, and Silulu is the iššiakkum ("governor") of Aššur."[35] Another Old Assyrian king, Irišum (perhaps in the last third of the twentieth century), employs this formula to himself.[36] A text from Warum in eastern Mesopotamia, whose capital was Eshnunna (perhaps eighteenth century), reads: "(The god) Tišpak is a strong king, the king of the Land of Warum. Azuzum, the iššiakkum of Eshnunna, is his servant/minister."[37] In Mari (eighteenth century) the god Iturmer was called "King of Mari."[38] From another part of the ancient Near East, the land of the Hittites, we have this text: "The land is the 'storm-god's';[39]

---

[33] [rí]-mu-uś/š šar (LUGAL) kiš (KIŠI) [šu ^{d}en-líl mātam (KALAM.MA.KI)] kà-la-ma i-dí-šum ti-a-am-tám a-li-tám ù ša₁₀-pil-tám ù [ša₁₀]-dú-e kà-la-šu-nu-ma a-na ^{d}en-líl u-kà-al (H. Hirsch, AfO 20 [1963], pp. 65 f., 9b, lines 1-16).

[34] Sumerian correspondence of Ishtar. The text: ḫaṭṭam(PA) a-na ^{d}en-[l]íl šar-ru-tám a-na ^{d}INNIN a u-kí-il (id., p. 78, lines 9–13).

[35] a-šùr^{KI} šar(LUGAL) ṣi-lu-lu iššiak(PA.TE.SI) a-šùr^{KI} (Garelli [n.9], pp. 35f.). Aššur is the god and not the city; cf. M.J. Seux, RA 59 (1965), pp. 107f.

[36] Garelli, ibid., p. 36, n.2.

[37] ^{d}tišpak šarrum(LUGAL) da-núm šàr(LUGAL) ma-at wa-ri-im a-zu-zum iššak (PA.TE.SI) áš-nun^{KI} waras(IR)-sú ([H. Frankfort ... and] T. Jacobsen, The Gimilsin Temple ... [OIP 43, 1940], p. 148, No. 22).

[38] ^{d}i-túr-me-er šar(LUGAL) ma-ri^{KI} (ARM 10:63:16 for further possible occurrences, see W.H.P. Römer, Frauenbriefe ... in Mari [1971], p. 17). J.R. Kupper, JCS 21 (1967), pp. 123–125, provides additional information about Warum and Mari and a similar phenomenon in Der, a neighbor of Warum. As to Warum, the god Tišpak is called the king of the land; victory in war is credited to him, the king; the human ruler is called našparšu "his envoy." (Rulers of Warum were the first monarchs to apply this title to themselves.) See also H. Lewy, CAH, rev. ed., vol. 1, ch.25 (1966), p. 29.

[39] Storm god is a paraphrase, not a translation. The text contains a name, ^{d}U. Its reading is not ascertained, but it seems to be something like Tarḫus or Tarḫunts (cf. J. Friedrich, Hethitisches Wörterbuch, 2. Ergänzungsheft 1961, p. 31; H.G. Güterbock in G. Walser, ed., Neuere Hethiterforschung [1964], pp. 59f.; A. Kammenhuber in Altkleinasiatische Sprachen [Handbuch der Orientalistik 1:2:1-2:2, 1969], p. 285).

heaven and earth and man are the 'storm-god's.' But he has made Labar-
nas, the king, his deputy and has given him the whole land of Ḥattusas
(i.e., the Hittite state)."[40]

These citations do not exhaust possible documentation. Moreover,
the idea which they set forth explicitly is also implied in other material.[41]
All these sources combine forcefully to refute the assertions that the idea
of a state whose head is the chief god of its people and whose human
ruler is the god's representative is foreign to the ancient Orient, and that
in biblical Israel this idea is but the product of late theological speculation. Formally speaking, there is obvious similarity between Israel and
other peoples of the Near East, prior though the non-Israelite sources are
to Israelite history.

A caveat is the mandate, however, at this point. Formal resemblance
should not prompt us to draw further far-reaching and otherwise unsupported conclusions in the matter of substance. By substance I mean a
marked impact of divine kingship on the life and thought of a people.
Substantive similarity cannot be affirmed simply because documentation
in this matter for Israel's neighbors, close and distant, is virtually non-
existent. We know nothing about Akkad, Old Assyria, and Warum. Judging from the little we know about the Neo-Hittite empire and also early
Lagash, it is improbable that the concept of the supreme god being the

---

[40] KUR-e dU-aš-pát ne-pí-eš te-kán-na ERÍN.MEŠ-az (cf. F. Sommer ..., *HAB*
[1938], p. 30. Güterbock in J.A. Wilson, ed., *Authority and Law in the Ancient Near
East* [1954], p. 16, translates: "with the people") dU-aš-pát nu-za LÚla-ba-ar-na-an
LUGAL-un   LÚma-ni-ia-aḫ-ḫa-tal-la-an   i-ia-at   nu-uš-ši   URUKUBABBAR-aš
KUR-e ḫu-u-ma-an pa-iš (A. Goetze, *JCS* 1 [1947], pp. 90f.).

[41] It includes epithets or titles of Mesopotamian kings that designate their bearers as
appointed and dependent officials rather than independent monarchs. They are the following (the numbers refer to the pages in M. J. Seux, *Épithètes royales akkadiennes et
sumériennes* [1967], with concentration on pages important to our purpose): *iššiakku*/
ensí (111—113,115), *rābiṣu*/ maškim (233f.), *šakkanakku*/GÌR.NITÁ (279f.), *šaknu*/
gar (280), and *waklu*/ ugula (358; see further J. Lewy, *JAOS* 78 [1958], p. 100). It
would be pointless and possibly misleading to provide these vocables with English translations. Now it ought to be pointed out that not all these titles of deputation and dependence originated in the realm of religion (see W. W. Hallo, *Early Mesopotamian Royal
Titles* [1957], pp. 39—47 for ensí), although most did. Yet all of them, at least at one time,
meant that the ruler is but the agent of a god, usually the chief god of the land, who is the
true king; cf. the example of Ṣilulu. In later times the concept became more and more rari-
fied, with less and less political reality to correspond to it, but this inner-Mesopotamian
history need not be considered here.

king of the state generated standards of conduct and specific laws for the society and the individual that molded their thinking and prescribed their actions in an appreciable manner. Mari of the time when the god Iturmer was its acknowledged king is a little different. There is indeed a modicum of similarity with Israel regarding state, government, and religion; the theme of prophecy at Mari, which has attracted much attention, comes to mind. Having pointed out a certain commonality between Mari and Israel, it is in order to say that the commonality has of late been overrated; similarities have been overemphasized and dissimilarities neglected. The following two paragraphs, supported by the balance of this study, should make it clear, it is hoped, that, as far as we can judge, a comparison of the substance of the Israelite and non-Israelite concepts is largely a comparison of incomparables.

The meaning of the kingship of God, according to the Bible, is the denial to man of the concentration and permanence of power. Power in society is God's. He is the only source of might, authority, command, and ownership of the land; He is the author of morals, law, and judgment; He guarantees freedom and a measure of equality; He is the leader of journeys in the desert and campaigns in the sown. By the eighth century the consequences of the idea of divine kingship had been ever more ignored by the rulers of the people, and reality had come ever more into conflict with it. It was then that the great prophets rose to adjust the reality of their day to the standards of the idea. But conflicts had occurred before that. Indeed, they must have originated with the very birth of the idea, which was designed to reshape reality. In the eleventh century Samuel responded to such a conflict as a true forerunner to Hosea and Isaiah. Fittingly the Bible calls young Samuel "prophet" (1 Sam 3:20), as it were in anticipation of future events.

The request of the representatives ("elders") of Israel to give them a king upset Samuel grievously (8:6). It amounted to the intention of restructuring the body politic and a concomitant redefining of the faith. As regards society, power would be permanently institutionalized and invested in a man who ruled by the grace of the people. As to religion, the nature of the redefinition was to become manifest in Solomon's time, when it was expressed as follows:

Then the priests brought the ark of the covenant of the Lord to its place, the inner shrine of the temple, the Most Holy Place ... The poles [by

which the ark was carried on migrations and campaigns] jutted out, and
their ends could be seen from the Holy Place immediately in front of the
inner shrine, but from nowhere else outside; there they are to this day . . .
At this occasion Solomon said . . . "I have built You a princely house, a
place for You to stay forever" (1 Ki 8:6,8,12,13).

A portentious ceremony and grand design permanently to enclose God in
the fixed structure of the temple. His leadership was over; henceforth He
was only to be venerated. It goes without saying that the shift of
authority was liable to affect all other manifestations of power, mores,
standards, and beliefs. This Samuel opposed strenuously. God's response,
however, is different. It constitutes a device for maintaining what of the
old order was essential in the changed circumstances requested by the
people. This is the sum and substance of the story about the assembly of
Ramah. There is neither a definite no nor a definite yes but an expression
of disappointment, concern, warnings, and a new attempt.

Section A (8:4–22) delineates the new age; section B (9:1–10:16)
tells of its initiation. The story moves with measured speed and the style
is idyllic, but when it approaches the first peak, the meeting of Saul and
Samuel, the style turns to the programmatic language of salvation. God
says to Samuel, "At this time tomorrow I will send you a man from the
land of Benjamin. Anoint him regent over My people Israel; he shall
deliver My people from the Philistines. I have indeed seen 'the suffering
of'[42] My people; their cry has indeed reached Me" (9:16). The programmatic diction can be recognized, among other things, by three key expressions ("I will send; I have seen 'the suffering of' My people; their cry has
reached Me"[43]), which also occur in Ex 3f., the story of the commission
of Moses as the first act of the salvation theme. I employ "regent" to
render נגיד, one of the narrative's four terms for ruler,[44] as corresponding

---

[42] LXX.

[43] The expressions occur in Ex 3:10,12,15; 4:13. 3:7. 3:9 (see also Buber [n.19], pp.
758f.; and W. Richter, *Die sogennanten vorprophetischen Berufungsberichte* [1970], pp.
50f.). "Deliverance" is not listed as a fourth expression since the texts use different
words—Samuel הושיע, Exodus (3:8) הציל. (It is almost predictable that Exodus would not
use the Samuel expression. For the notion of deliverance from the Land of Egypt, Exodus
uses the second word 3:8; 5:23; 6:6 (12:27); the first, very rare before Deuteronomy, is
employed in the story of the Reed Sea [verb 14:30; noun 14:13; 15:2]).

[44] See p. 84.

to some or most of the expressions for viceroy or deputy in Sumerian and Akkadian.[45] The people want a מלך "king," but God gives them a נגיד "regent." With the possible exception of 1 Sam 15:1—16:1, the Book of Samuel denotes the nature of rulership by the choice of words: the ruler is called נגיד when his bond or subordination to God is preeminent, מלך when the origin of his position and the base of his power lie in the people.[46] The fourth term for "ruling," עצר, appears in vs. 17 and probably also in the Vorlage of the Septuagint to 10:1 (which is the preferred reading). Its rarity prevents us from discerning its special meaning, but the general semantic range is not in doubt. In 9:17 עצר refers to, and sums up, the meanings of נגיד "regent" and הושיע "to deliver" of the preceding verse (and similarly in 10:1 LXX), and in Isa 53:8 the noun עֹצֶר forms a hendiadys, or something close to it, with מִשְׁפָּט "rule."

The meeting between Saul and Samuel initiates a series of events, actions, and symbolic expressions which culminates in the anointing of Saul. Among them are the three signs that confront Saul on his way home (10:2—12). I do not understand their precise meanings, but their general sense is unmistakable: Saul has become another man, God is with him (10:7), and people recognize it. An ordinary stranger would not be presented with two loaves of bread (10:3f.), especially not bread designated for a sanctuary.[47] As to the recognition which goes with the third sign,

---

[45] See n. 41.

[46] One hesitates, however, to call 1 Sam 15 an exception to the rule. To be sure, Saul's relation to God is the issue, but מלך is used not inappropriately (vs., 11, 17, 23,26, [35]) because Saul acts as a ruler whose authority derives from the people (or lies in himself) and not from God. It is precisely this stance of his independence of God, leading to his undoing, which is the content of ch.15. 16:1 opens the cycle of the David stories by linking it (narratively and) linguistically to the preceding chapter; cf. על ישראל, מאסתיו, מתאבל, אשלחך and מלך. For the function of the נגיד, see W. Richter, *BZ*, NF 9 (1965), pp. 71—84, especially pp. 73,77,83. Of נגיד in 1 Ki 1:35, Richter rightly says that the text describes an "Eingriff [of David] in das Recht Gottes" (p. 77). C. Wilcke, *Das Lugalbandaepos* (1969), pp. (44-)48, makes a similar observation about the distribution of ancient titles in Sumerian epics: The rulers (at least those of Uruk and Aratta) are called e n "lord" when their relation to their city (and its goddess) is meant, l u g a l "king" when their relation to their subjects is intended.

[47] The sacred nature of the bread follows from narrative details and the expression שתי לחם, sing. fem. (10:4; similarly Lev 23:17 and 24 times in the Mishna referring to such loaves).

the text is explicit (10:10—12).[48] At this point the narrative pace relaxes. People see that Saul is an extraordinary man, but this is not to recognize him as regent or king. Kingship, sought in a convocation, will be made known and established in a convocation; until then, Saul's kingship is kept under wraps (10:16), and the section ends as it began—unpolitical and at home.

The promulgation of kingship takes place in the assembly at Mizpah, whose report comprises section C (10:17—27). Samuel calls the people "to the Lord" (10:17), as in the case of the next assembly, the one at Gilgal, he convokes them "before the Lord" (11:14f.; cf. 10:19, 25). He wants to pledge the monarchy to God. By contrast, the first assembly, which met at Ramah at the initiative of the people, was not summoned to (or before) the Lord; the narrative situation did not suggest, and the history of ideas was moving away from, implicating God in the affairs of the state.

Samuel opens the assembly of Mizpah with a report of the answer God gave him at Ramah to the effect that Israel rejected God (10:18—19a). Then he continues without any logical connection, yet in a manner not unlike the equally abrupt transition in the corresponding part of the speech of God (between 8:7 and 9[49]), "Now then, take a stand before the Lord." There is and can be no logical connection between Israel's rejection of God and God's accession to their request.[50] The core

---

[48] The event as told in 10:10 is clear and not in need of the explication of the following two verses. This is to say that the question of the literary priority of 10:11b or 19:24b can be bypassed here.

[49] As stated above, p. 83, 8:8 is not part of the original text, but this statement is immaterial for the present comment; the transition from vs.8 to vs.9 is hardly less abrupt than that from vs.7.

[50] ועתה "now then" is a general transitional indicator, meaning: Now comes the substance or the main point. It is alogical; such logical progression as is present lies in the context. Example: Nathan says to David in a long protasis, God was good to you, but you sinned dastardly (2 Sam 12:7b—9); ועתה, the inescapable conclusion is that you will be punished commensurately, "the sword shall never depart from your house" (vs.10a). Where the context shows no logical progression, ועתה cannot provide it. Example: Jehu writes letters to a number of high officials, "[Greetings omitted.] ועתה, when this letter reaches you, take the fittest of the princes and set him on the throne of his father" (2 Ki 10:2f.). The demand does not follow from the greetings (omitted by the narrator just as in 5:6; shortened elsewhere [Ezra 4:11]). 1 Sam 10:19b belongs to the class of the second

of this section is vss. 24 and 25. The former recounts God's designation of the king ("Do you see him that God has chosen?") and the people's acclamation ("the people shouted mightily, 'Long live the king!'").[51] The latter reports the promulgation of "the rule of kingship," its recording, and the deposition of the record "before the Lord."

As was the case in Ramah (section A), so also here and even more so: the assembly is the occasion for voicing, and vividly describing, the ambivalent estimation of kingship. On the one hand, the people's request for a king is called rejection of God. On the other hand, the men who follow the king whom they demanded so reprobately, are called "right-minded,[52] whose heart God has moved," whereas those who rebuff him are called "scoundrels" (vss.26f.).[53] Perhaps the presentation and acceptance of "the rule of kingship" (vs.25) has to do with this widening spectrum of attitudes; a political system that is based on the rule introduced here is not unequivocally and unredeemably bad.

The problems of section D (11:1—11) are well known. The first is that the emissaries of Jabesh-gilead do not make it their business to come before the recently appointed king and ask him for help. Gibeath-Shaul,

---

example. Vss.17—19a do not logically lead to vs.19b, and ועתה does not bridge the gap. 7 ועתה of 12:7 seems to be a similar case and to call for a similar evaluation, but contextual problems render the judgment uncertain.

[51] Designation and acclamation after A. Alt, *Kleine Schriften* 2 (1953), p. 23, and elsewhere.

[52] החיל "Men of valor" (RSV) was good in older English, when valor meant "worth;" but "courage," its present-day meaning, suggests the military, which understanding is excluded by (the following relative clause and) the antonym בני בליעל (vs.27).

[53] The different evaluations of the monarchy within section C are the reason that O. Eissfeldt divides it into two independent components, 10:17—21bα and 10:21bβ—27 (*Die Komposition der Samuelisbücher* [1931], pp. 7f.,10). This hypothesis has to cope with difficulties we cannot discuss here which, in my opinion, discredit it. Others declare vss. (26—)27 as an addition, mainly because these verses are friendly to the new king (R. de Vaux, *Les Livres de Samuel*[2] [1961], p. 61, note a; Weiser [n.3], p. 67; P.R. Ackroyd, *The First Book of* Samuel [1971], p. 88 ["may be"]). This amounts to the circular process of first taking the position that section C maintains an unbending hostility toward kingship and then proceeding to establish its truth by removing the contradictory evidence for hardly any other reason than that it contradicts that position. But even this dubious procedure does not help. It leaves premonarchical vs.24 untouched, because dislodging it would bring down the whole edifice.

Saul's home town where we meet them (11:4), is one stop on their circuit
through an apparently leaderless Israel (v.2), nothing more. The second
and third problems have to do with the person of Saul. He is engaged in
farming and not in kingly pursuits (vs.5). Also, his response is that of a
ruler of the Book of Judges, such as Jephtah. Wildberger and others[54]
resolve the difficulties by a historical approach. The event of Jabesh-
gilead, section D, occurred before those of sections A, B, and C. The action of Saul in Section D is the one-time action of a charismatic leader,
as the Book of Judges tells of its heroes. When Israel requested a king,
perhaps many years after, they seized upon the savior of Jabesh-gilead.
According to this opinion, the only one that solves the problems of this
section, the connection of the story in its original stage and sense with
the account of the foundation of the monarchy is most tenuous. In its
new status the connection is strengthened, but at the price of the difficulties created by its position after sections A—C, which I have mentioned.

   But Wildberger's answer generates a question: why this order which
is contrary to history and creates literary difficulties, to boot?[55] There
are, I think, three reasons for the position of D after A—C. The one is the
rondo form of the total account (assembly—action—assembly—
action—assembly), which can only be maintained by the present order.
The second is the literary nature of section B. It is a narrative of the first
appearance of a hero and does, therefore, not permit the author to tell of
an appearance that happened before the first appearance. The third reason is related to the second. Section B contains the motif that God
chooses for the great task and high office an undistinguished man (9:21).

---

[54] H. Wildberger, *TZ* 13 (1957), pp. 442—469. See also A. Biram in לדוד ז"ע [Jubilee
volume for D. Ben Gurion] (1964), pp. 218f. G. Wallis, *Geschichte und Überlieferung*
(1968), pp. 45—66 (= *Wissenschaftl. Zeitschr. Halle-Wittenberg.* Gesellsch.-sprw. Reihe
12 [1963], pp. 239—247), proposes a somewhat similar view but does not concern himself
with the literary aspect of the issue. Cf. the favorable view of G. Fohrer, *TLZ* 91 (1966),
col. 902.

[55] To Weiser (n.3), p. 72, this question is so troublesome that it makes him reject Wildberger's proposal. Weiser assumes implicitly that the author of 1 Sam 8—12 knew the
chronological order of the events and changed it. This assumption cannot be taken for
granted. If it is wrong, there is no reason for rejecting Wildberger. If it is right, the following proposal of reasons for the present order of the sections should lay Weiser's objection
to rest. Note, however, that the reasons are primarily of a literary nature; their disputative
effect or contributions to understanding history, if any, are incidental.

The motif is characteristic of stories about rulers and saviors (e.g., David, Basha, Gideon, and Jephtah), and the author, it seems, would not miss it in his account of the foundation of kingship. Had he followed the chronological order and, in consequence thereof, arranged the meeting in the gate (v.18) between the man of God and the famous commander of the Ammonite campaign, he would have demolished his motif and deadened the literary impact of much of chs.9 and 10.[56]

Section E (11:14–12:25)[57] opens with a festive scene at Gilgal. Into the festivity the stern voice of Samuel breaks with words of admonition. Irruptions like this are known not only from the literary prophets but also from psalms (50:7ff.; 81:6ff.; 95:7ff.). Certainly, the present example is no valid criterion for assigning 11:14f. and 12:1ff. to different sources. What is the nature of the celebration? The text says: "Samuel said to the people, 'Let us go to Gilgal and renew the kingship there'" (11:14). The mention of the renewal of kingship (vs.14) and enthronement (vs.15), with which commentators have so much difficulty, finds its explanation in either of the following ways: (1) It is a narrative representation of the annual ceremony of reenthronement of the Israelite and Judean kings.[58] (2) The installation of Saul was a one-time series of acts performed in different places. This explanation, which is the preferred one and which accords with Wallis's view,[59] is supported by the Mesopotamian custom of coronations, multiple and in different cities.[60]

[56] R. Smend, *Jahwekrieg und Stämmebund* (1963), p. 49, proposes yet another reason for the actual order of the sections but without following Wildberger.

[57] 11:12f., echoing the attitude of 10:26f., function together with them as a frame for section D. These two verses were added to the original story (11:1–11) perhaps with the particular intention of showing Saul's success in the growing acceptance of him by the people. An alternative reason is the desire to have a suitable end to the now fragmentary report about the campaign of Jabesh-gilead.

[58] The ceremony is not attested in Israel, but its historicity might perhaps be argued from the study of chronology. Certain chronological phenomena suggest that there were official days for the ascension to the throne of the kings of Israel and Judah; they were fixed and general, independent of the beginnings of government of the individual kings. Such days easily become festivals, embellished by ceremonies. J. Pedersen, *Israel . . .* 3–4 (1940), pp. 746–750, and S. Mowinckel, *The Psalms in Israel's Worship* (1962), pp. 60,62, have adduced other reasons for the historicity of this ceremony, but I find them unimpressive.

[59] See n.54.

[60] See W. W. Hallo, *JCS* 20 (1966), p. 136.

Chapter 12 contains the description of the convocation proper. Its text is impaired, and its literary quality must be judged as inferior to the other sections. It surpasses them in the number of corruptions and accretions. Buber has isolated the accretions and, in the process, reduced what is to him the original piece to ten verses out of the twenty-five of the chapter.[61] Yet if we examine that discarded bulk of the text, we find that it is a literary unit in its own right. Ch. 12 thus consists of two constituent parts of unequal length.[62] The first[63] includes vss.1—5, 13—15, 24f.; the second vss.6—12, 16—23. In the first component Samuel calls on the people to testify that he has conducted himself in office with scrupulous honesty. He asks for the testimony not because he intends to retire now but, on the contrary (as Weiser rightly says[64]), because he means to continue. To Weiser's argument, which is based on the interpretation of salient features of the chapter, one should add the argument from the corresponding case of Moses, whose words in his encounter with Korah (Nu 16:15) resemble Samuel's here (vs.3 with vs.4, its echo),[65] and who certainly did not mean to relinquish his position to Korah, Dathan, and Abiram. In the continuation Samuel places life and death before the partners under the new order, the people and the king, that is to say, he sets forth conditions for the existence of the monarchy, surely in the spirit of "the rule of kingship."[66] His words "both you and your king ... follow the Lord" (12:14) define the new body politic—people and king together, and this body, for whose success he is so passionately concerned, is to "follow the Lord," Who is, as it were, its third partner.[67]

The second unit paints a court scene.[68] There is the summons for the trial (vs.7), indictment (vss.8—12), proof (in the form of a miracle,

---

[61] Buber (n.19), pp. 792—797. Since Buber's core text absorbed glosses, it actually has less than ten verses.

[62] A detailed analysis is not presented here.

[63] It is Buber's original text.

[64] Weiser (n.3), pp. 81f.

[65] See Seebass (n.26), pp. 289f. Šuwardata, a ruler in the Hebron area in the 14th century, uses similar words ("... if I have taken a man or a single ox or an ass") to assure his suzerain, the king of Egypt, of his good behavior (EA 280:26—29). Again, the intention of such protestation is continuation, and not termination, of office.

[66] See Weiser (n.3), pp. 81f.

[67] Cf. Buber (n.19), pp. 797f.

[68] The nature of vs.6 and its connection with its environment are not clear, and the questionable integrity of the text adds to the confusion. The verse is perhaps a bracketing gloss.

vss.16—18), admission of guilt (vs.19), decision (vss.20—21 f.), and certain
sequels (vs.23) concerning the role of the prophet in the monarchy. The
literary form of this unit is well chosen. The description of a trial is a
natural form for the expression of the sense and purpose of this unit: a
pronouncement of Israel's guilt as the climax and conclusion of the whole
narrative; specifically, a declaration that the very request for kingship is
an "evil."[69] The prominence of this idea can escape no one. It is stated
three times (vss.17, 19f.). It is put forth with an authority which knows
nothing different having been said and nothing divergent having happened in the preceding sections and even in this section itself. The possibility of a monarch ruling as God's deputy occupies the entire composition's center of gravity; the extreme position of this unit is at a far
remove from it.

This is a conflict within the narration, so radical that it cannot be
resolved by literary interpretation. It can be accounted for, though, in this
manner: The original end of the composition, section E, unit 1, was not as
well constructed and convincingly told as the rest of the narrative, and its
slackness attracted alien material, expressions of absolute opposition to
the monarchy. Alternatively, it may be proposed that such material tends
to condense at the end of a story, a collection of laws or sayings, a book.
But whatever the reason, the result is that the aftergrowth of section E
has partially concealed and deformed its core. Unqualified and definitive
opposition to the monarchy, which is the burden of the court scene, sub-
verts the essence of the last section as well as of the totality of all the sections. Without that scene the account affirms and reformulates the
kingship of God over Israel: When circumstances change, the form of the
kingship changes, and thus it came about that in the days of Samuel the
office of regency was created in the process of refashioning the kingship
of God in a less immediate form.

The story explicates the events and implies a question. As it tells of
the stress and strain which surrounded the creation of the new office, it
casts a shadow of apprehension over the future: what chance has the
untried institution? Will it work, will it last? From 1 Sam 13 onward, the
"Book of Kingships"[70] stands under the sign of this disquieting question.

---

[69] רעה. This is an objective statement, quite different from the description how the initial request of the people first affected Samuel (וירע הדבר בעיני שמואל, 8:6).

[70] Βιβλίον βασιλειῶν = Samuel + Kings.

The Steadfast House

What Was David Promised in 2 Samuel 7?

A noticeable advance in the interpretation of 2 Sam 7 appears in M. Noth's discussion of the chapter in the André Robert jubilee volume.[1] David's ascent to power, Noth says, was unrelated to the tradition of Israel as a sacred people. He became king first over the southern tribes, then over the northern tribes (though his kingship did not merge the two kingdoms); later he made Jerusalem, a city which had played no role in the Israelite tradition, his royal residence, and he even integrated the Ammonite kingdom into his state. Against the background of these accomplishments 2 Sam 7 recounts the divine promise of a dynasty which, in the nature of things, cannot be related to any of these single and secular kingdoms but only to the confederacy of the tribes of Israel. The tangible object which symbolized the sacral league of the tribes was the ark, now kept in the Jerusalem sanctuary, to which it had been transferred (as told in the preceding chapter) by its patron David. The sanctuary together with the ark, figuring prominently in this chapter, constitute the basis of David's kingdom over the totality of Israel. In this chapter, pre-Solomoninic[2] except for a few later accretions, David's royal hegemony is recognized, sanctified, and projected as the beginning of a dynasty.

Thus David's kingship and that of his descendants is made an amphictyonic[3] institution. This means that the Davidic covenant, of which

[1] "David und Israel in 2 Samuel 7," in *Mélanges bibliques . . . A. Robert* (1957), pp.122—130; republished in his *Gesammelte Studien zum A.T.*[2] (1960), pp.334—345. The references are to the republication. This paragraph summarizes parts of pp. 339 and 341.

[2] The relative date follows from the rejection of David's wish to build the temple; cf. Noth, ibid., p.345; also A. Bentzen, *Introduction to the O.T.* I (1948), p.161.

[3] I am using "amphictyony, amphictyonic" for the confederacy of the Israelite tribes

this chapter speaks,[4] should be seen probably as incorporated in, but at least as derived from, the Israelite (that is, the Sinaitic) covenant. This conclusion, however, which appears both simple and incontestable, is not reflected in all parts of the chapter. In vss.13b—16 God speaks:

> "I will establish the throne of his [David's descendant's] kingship enduringly. [14]I will be a father to him, and he will be a son to Me, whom, when he commits iniquity, I will chasten with rods for the ordinary and scourges for the common,[5] but from whom My loyalty shall never be withdrawn as I did withdraw it from Saul whom I removed from your way. [16]Your house will be steadfast in My favor, your throne established enduringly."

The clear meaning of this passage is reinforced in Ps 89:29—38. Derived from the Samuel passage,[6] these verses reiterate this theme in detail. David is destined the founder of a dynasty whose unlimited duration is not contingent upon the conduct of his successor, the future king; the possibility of such contingency is explicitly anticipated and explicitly excluded.

This theme of the unconditionality of this covenant in the Samuel and Psalms passages is at variance with the idea of the conditionality in the Sinaitic covenant and thus, indirectly, with the concept of the amphictyony. Basic to the latter is the covenant with God. As regards Israel (preexilic Israel, at least), covenant assumes conditionality. To be sure, where the Bible speaks of God covenanting with individuals of early antiquity, e.g., Noah, Phinehas, the patriarchs, covenant means a one-sided commitment of God, and this one-sided commitment is sometimes

---

approximately in the sense of R. Smend, "Zur Frage der altisraelitischen Amphiktyonie," *Evangelische Theologie* 31 (11/12 [H. W. Wolff jubilee issue], 1971), pp.623—630. About the term, Smend says, "Auf den Ausdruck kommt es nicht an."

[4] "Covenant," translating ברית, is used as a convention. ברית itself does not occur in 2 Sam 7 but it is represented by the semantically related חסד (vs.15) and by the expression ודבר ... את הטובה הזאת (vs.28), a more distant relative; cf. M. Weinfeld לשוננו 36 (1971/72), pp.91 f.; id., *Theologisches Wörterbuch zum A.T.* I., col.787. ברית is found in Ps. 89 (which refers extensively to this chapter) in vss.29 and 35.

[5] Cf. A.B. Ehrlich, *Randglossen* ... III (1910), pp.288 f.

[6] See N. M. Sarna, "Psalm 89: a Study in Inner Biblical Exegesis," *Brandeis University* (P.W. Lown Instit.), *Studies and Texts* 1 (1963), pp.29—46, for a full discussion.

taken as an unconditional commitment.[7] Preeminent among these individuals is Abraham. Opinions to the contrary notwithstanding, however, the covenant with Abraham is conditional for all its frequent statement as a simple promise of God.[8] As time goes on, such covenant formulation, nothing more and nothing less than a one-sided divine commitment, is recorded ever more frequently and gains ever more in importance. The late preexilic and exilic prophets contributed notably to this development.[9] Yet even their prophecies, dissimilar though they may be to the Sinaitic covenant, do not share the blank-check feature of guaranteed, unqualified validity which is present in the covenant with the House of David and is the sense and purpose of 2 Sam 7:13b—16. The message here is unique; no matter what the dynast does, he cannot thereby endanger the dynasty. Remarkably, this unconditionality appears in a kind of text where it would be least expected, i.e., in an amphictyonic narrative, a genre where covenant is conditional.

If this consideration does not in itself raise a red flag, the appearance

[7] D. N. Freedman, *Interpretation* 18 (1964), pp.3—15; M. Weinfeld, *Deuteronomy and the Deuteronomic School* (1972), pp. 74—81; id., *JAOS* 90 (1970), pp.189—203; id., *Theologisches Wörterbuch zum A.T.* I, coll. 799—801.

[8] In Gen 18:18 f., a passage central to the Abraham stories in more than one respect, God first summarizes the blessing of 12:1—3 and then continues: "For I have singled him [Abraham] out so that he may charge his children and his posterity to keep the way of the Lord by doing what is just and right, so that the Lord may bring about to Abraham what He has promised him." Conditional אם "if" is not used, but the double למען "so that, in order that," introducing each half of vs.19, establishes a perfect balance between them. As the two halves tell, respectively, what Abraham and what God will do, the structure of the sentence emphasizes the two-sidedness of the relationship between Abraham and God and all that it entails. (I cite Gen 18:18 f. as proof although, as the narrative goes, the verses render only God's thought and do not make known its burden, the conditionality of the covenant, to Abraham, the partner of the covenant. My justification is that the author stated his idea and was satisfied to inform his audience but was unconcerned abut his actors. A literary flaw? Probably.)

Weinfeld, *Deuteronomy* (n.7), p.81, for all practical purposes misinterprets these verses: " ... the promise ... was ... unconditional, although it presupposed ... loyalty and the fulfillment of some obligations and duties (see Gen 18:19 ...)." But he apparently feels the insufficiency of this interpretation; he refers to p.74, n.2, citing a typical case where the commitment of the overlord is coterminous with the loyalty of the vassal. L. Perlitt, *Bundestheologie im AT* (1969), denies the existence of a predeuteronomic covenant altogether. About his position see D. J. McCarthy, *Biblica* 53 (1972), pp.110—121.

[9] See particularly Freedman (n.7).

of an anachronistic concept is enough to pose the question as to whether this passage is not an intrusion. This suspicion warrants a careful investigation. Our investigation will consist of two parts. (a) A comparison of the divine promise about the future of the Davidic dynasty of this chapter with other dynastic promises and similar statements elsewhere; (b) a study of a pertinent aspect of this chapter. The pre-Chronicles dynastic promises,[10] in addition to that of 2 Sam 7:11b—16, are: Ps 89:27—38; 2 Sam 23:5; 1 Ki 2:4; 8:25; 9:4 f.; Jer 33:17; Ps 132:11 f. We shall now consider them separately.

A (a) 2 Sam 7:11b—16.

A (b) God is quoted as having said: "He will call to Me, 'You are my father, my God, my saving Rock'; [28]and I will make him My first-born, superior to the kings of the earth. [29]I will maintain My loyalty to him enduringly, My covenant with him stands fast. [30]I will preserve his seed without end and his throne as long as the heaven endures. [31]If his children forsake My instruction, do not comport themselves according to My ordinances, [32]if they violate My laws, do not keep My commandments, [33]then I will punish their transgression with the rod and their sin with scourges, [34]but I will not renounce the loyalty I bear him, nor let My faithfulness prove false; [35]I will not violate My covenant or alter the promise of My lips. [36]Once for all I have sworn by My holiness: I will not be false to David," etc. (Ps 89:27—36 [ff.]).

B David responds to a word of God: "Does my dynasty not[11]

----

[10] Chronicles falls outside the scope of this article. Among the pre-Chronicles promises Labuschagne counts also 1 Ki 2:45; 8:16; Ps 61:7 f. (C. J. Labuschagne, in *Studies on the Books of Samuel. Papers Read at 3rd Meeting of Die O.T. Werkgemeenskap in Suid-Afrika* [1960], p.29, n.8). These references are not pertinent. The first and the last passages are prayers or expressions of hope, and the second passage is a brief recitation of history which includes a quote of an earlier statement of God that He chose David to be (regent) over Israel (cf. 2 Sam 7:8).

[11] This sentence can only be a rhetorical question. Naked כי introduces such a question in 1 Ki 18:34, וכי in 1 Sam 24:20; Isa 36:19; and very often in Middle Hebrew. See H. L. Ginsberg, *Proceedings of the American Academy for Jewish Research* 21 (1952), p.45, n.25; id., קהלת (1961), p.93.

stand fast[12] by[13] God? Verily, He has made with me an enduring covenant, drawn in every detail and (to be?) preserved"[14] (2 Sam 23:5).

C (a) David quotes a divine promise to Solomon: "If your sons look to their ways and walk faithfully in My sight with all their heart and all their soul, then . . .[15] never shall you fail of a descendant to the throne of Israel" (1 Ki 2:4).

C (b) Solomon quotes God's promise to David: "Never shall you fail of a descendant by My favor seated on the throne of Israel if only your sons look to their ways and walk in My sight as you have walked in My sight" (1 Ki 8:25).

C (c) God to Solomon: "As for you, if you walk in My sight, as did your father David, with integrity of heart and uprightly doing exactly as I have commanded you keeping My laws and ordinances, [5]then I will make your royal throne endure over Israel even as I promised David your father, 'Never shall you fail a descendant on the throne of Israel'" (1 Ki 9:4 f.).

C (d) God speaks: "Never shall David fail of a descendant seated on the throne of the house of Israel" (Jer 33:17).[16]

D The psalmist tells: 'The Lord gave to David a firm oath on which He will not go back, "Through your own body's issue will I guarantee the throne for you. [12]If your sons keep the stipulations of the covenant[17] which I shall teach them, their sons will in unending succession sit on your throne"' (Ps 132:11 f.).

---

[12] כן; qal part. of בון. Only the participle is attested in the qal, as is the case with עוד, ברך, and דבר (? Ps 51:6). Alternatively but similarly, כן is the adjective "firm." The corresponding prose passage uses the more frequent nif'al: ובית עבדך דוד יהיה נכון לפניך (7:26).

[13] עם corresponds to לפני in 7:26, quoted in the preceding note. with √כון it occurs in Ps 78:37 in another covenant text.

[14] Is this the figure of speech שמר הברית "to keep (the terms of) a covenant," or is it a reference to a copy of the covenant text deposited and kept at a sacred place? For such deposition, cf., in general, G. E. Mendenhall, *The Biblical Archaeologist* 17 (1954), pp.60,64; and M. Haran, *IEJ* 9 (1959), pp.89 f., with bibliographical references in n.11.

[15] Delete the second לאמר as a vertical dittography. (About vertical dittography, see H. M. Orlinsky, *HUCA* 33 [1962], p.139.)

[16] Vss.21 and 26 vary this statement.

[17] Translated as a hendiadys. For עדתי see n.60.

What can be ascertained from these dynastic promises that bears on 2 Sam 7:13b—16?

A (b), Ps 89:27—38, as said before,[18] is derived from 2 Sam 7 and contains no independent information.

B, 2 Sam 23:5. It might be argued that כי ברית עולם שם לי "Verily, He has made with me an enduring covenant," from David's Last Words,[19] suggests an unconditional covenant. Unconditionality, however, could only be guaranteed by a concessive clause, such as "even if (my) sons commit iniquity." The translation of עולם as eternity, taken as connoting in itsef immutability and unconditionality, is untenable. The assumption that לאלף דור, לעד, לעולם or similar expressions, to which secondarily נאמן could be joined, are always to be translated by "eternity" or equivalent words will not bear scrutiny. The word עולם or some of the others appear in passages of permanent duration of covenants in general or covenants promising indefinite dynastic stability where the context specifically rules out unconditionality. Aside from instances in the texts cited above, which are being interpreted as we proceed, there is, for example, 1 Sam 2:30. Concerning the priestly office at the central sanctuary long held by the Elides, God announces to Eli: "I had indeed formerly promised/ intended that your house and the house of your father should serve before Me עד עולם; but now [i.e., under the changed circumstances wrought by your unfaithfulness] it is the Lord's pronouncement: Far be it from Me (חלילה לי). For those who honor Me I will honor, but those who despise Me will be slighted." In plain words: The end of the time designated by עד עולם has arrived. Another passage (1 Ki 11:38) has God speaking to Jeroboam, the very person who is to supplant the Davidic line in kingship over the larger part of the united kingdom: "If you obey all My charge ... I will be with you and build you a steadfast house (בית נאמן), as I built for David." Can it be clearer that the "steadfast house" which God promised David and which elsewhere has the temporal term עד עולם could be steadfast for all of two generations at the most?[20] Evidently, if Jeroboam is steadfast with God, his house will be steadfast; it is all conditional. By the same token, since the steadfastness of Jeroboam's

---

[18] P.102 with n.6.

[19] Preexilic; not amenable to more exact dating.

[20] Davidic rule over Judah alone, envisaged in vs.36, is not the continued fulfillment of the "steadfast house" mentioned in vs.38, but rather a bitter caricature.

dynasty is compared with that of David, the latter's steadfastness is also conditional. In yet a different passage (Deut. 7:9 f.), Yhwh is called "the steadfast God (האל הנאמן) Who to a thousand generations (לאלף דור) keeps covenant loyalty with those that love Him and keep His commandments, [10]but Who without delay requites those that reject Him by destroying them." These texts leave no doubt as to what is meant by עד עולם, לאלף דור or בית נאמן; modern readers and interpreters would be well advised not to fasten modern concepts upon biblical texts. Hebrew words for "enduring/permanent," or "steadfast" and the like do not by and in themselves connote either infinitude or absoluteness. The sense of עולם in ברית עולם, which we render as "enduring," is no more emblematic of eternity or absoluteness of a covenant than in its appearances as a qualifier for a slave whose servitude ends with his death. Surely eternal life is not held out to a man whom the Bible calls עבד עולם (Deut. 15:17; 1 Sam 27:12; Job 40:28; cf. Ex 21:6 ועבדו לעולם).[21] This expression and others of its kind qualify a thing within its natural limits: temporal limits in the instances just cited—the span of a human life; in other instances religious, legal, or social limits—the intrinsic suppositions of the covenant. The notion that absoluteness can be attributed to anything (even time and duration) other than to God and His set norms is alien to the Bible. The words חלילה לי "Far be it from Me" (1 Sam 2:30), spoken by God, say it all.

C (a)—(c), 1 Ki 2:4; 8:25; 9:4 f. The conditionality of the dynasty is unequivocally expressed; רק "only" of (b) underscores it. Common to the passages of the C group, including (d), is על כסא (בית) ישראל. It occurs in the Solomon narratives (1 Ki 2:4; 8:20,25[22]; 9:5; 10:9), in Jer 33:17 (d), which is a citation from the Kings passages,[23] and in 2 Ki 10:30, which is

---

[21] E. Jenni's interpretation that the duration of עולם in this phrase transcends a man's lifetime in that servitude is extended to include the offspring of the slave (*ZAW* 64, [1953], p.236; but cf. p.233) may perhaps be right for Deut 15:17 (Job 40:28 is poetic imagery) but it is less suitable, even in a modified form, for 1 Sam 27:12. Vassalage was a personal relation with the oath binding only the man who swore it. The Hittite suzerains found it necessary to make new treaties with the sons of their deceased vassals, although some treaties would envisage the continuation of vassalage during the following generation(s); cf. J. Pirenne, *ArOr* 18:1–2 (1950), p.381; A. Götze, *Kleinasien²* (1957), p.101.

[22] Parallels 2 Chr 6:10,16.

[23] The expression על כסא ישראל of Kings is in Jer 33 expanded to על כסא בית ישראל in adaptation of this late paragraph to the style of the prophet Jeremiah. Jeremiah and those

quoted in 15:12. The occurrences in Second Kings can be disregarded in-asmuch as they refer to the throne of the Northern Kingdom. Outside of the five Solomon passages (and their citation in Jeremiah), the Davidic throne is never called "the throne of (the house of) Israel."[24] What conclu-sions can be derived from the fact that among the dynastic promises to David all the C passages, and only the C passages, feature (בית) על כסא ישראל? Their clear literary affinity with the Solomonic tradition[24a] points to their belonging to that tradition and their relative independence of 2 Sam 7 or other (Davidic) dynastic promise texts. Thus not only על כסא (בית) ישראל but also the main clause לא יכרת לך איש מעל כסא ישראל, in which it is imbedded, can only have originated at the court of Solomon.[25] The condition (belonging to a later time, as we shall see momentarily) is absent in (d), as befits the spirit and intention of this context; in (the second half) of Jer 33 the conditional aspect of the prediction of (a)–(c) has been removed.

D, Ps 132:11 f. The condition is present and clear.

The foregoing survey confirms our earlier suspicion that A (a) (2 Sam 7:11b–16) is a gloss. It does so, first, by bringing into relief the vir-tual isolation of A (a), an isolation which extends to its derivative A (b). Only group A and section (d), the latest section of group C, are uncondi-tional. B says nothing about conditionality; C (a)–(c) and D are condi-tional. But this isolation should be seen in perspective. What matters is not the quantity of the various pronouncements on the issue but rather their relative weight. C (a)–(c) has in recent years been taken to be of exilic origin, a group of *vaticinia ex eventu*[26] in the service of theodicy; it

---

who continued his tradition have a predilection for בית ישראל; the phrase occurs in his book 20 times (contrast the Book of Isaiah with its three times).

[24] Where the texts qualify the throne by a genitive, it is usually "David's" or a word referring to him, sometimes "kingdom."

[24a] This means tradition and its history, origin, etc., and not the literary record of the tradition.

[25] That the phrase is deuteronomistic (M. Noth, *Könige*. 1. Teilband [1968], p. 183) is a statement about the history of literature and not about the history told in that literature. Cf. the preceding note.

[26] O. Eissfeldt in E. Kautzsch (-A. Bertholet), *Die Heilige Schrift des AT* I[4] (1922), pp. 497, 514, 516; id., *Einleitung in das AT*[2] (1956), p. 362; M. Noth, *Überlieferungsgeschicht-liche Studien* (1943), pp. [66, 70f.]; A. Jepsen *Die Quellen des Königsbuches* (1953), p. 94,

can shed no light on A (a), which is much older for one thing and certainly not *ex eventu* for another. (The contrary view, viz., C (a)–(c) is preexilic, is encumbered with difficulties,[27] and we shall not consider it here.)

It is the conditionality of D (Ps 132:11 f.), however, which is important. The passage is part of an early[28] (though post-Davidic[29]) psalm that belonged to the liturgy of the Jerusalem temple and it is unabashedly royalist. These considerations render it a suitable instrument for testing our emerging conclusions that A (a) is a gloss. Let us assume for the purpose of the test that the conclusion is wrong, that is to say, that the unconditional verses 13b–16 are a genuine part of the pre-Solomonic[30] seventh chapter of Second Samuel; in other words, that unconditional A (a) is older than conditional D. This would mean that at a time when unconditional A (a) was a matter of record and sanctioned doctrine (it would not have been less than that), a conditional rider, a gloss (vs.12), was attached to a psalm (Ps 132) that had been silent about the issue of conditionality, and that this was done under the very nose of the royal patron and head of that temple to whose liturgy the psalm belonged. The effect, perhaps even the purpose, of the rider would have constituted a considerable diminution of the dynastic benefit that A (a) bestowed on the person who was the head of the state and the patron of the temple.[31]

---

with the table at the end of the book. (J. A. Montgomery, *A Critical . . . Commentary on . . . Kings* [1951], p. 193, says about 1 Ki 8:22–26, of which C (b) is a part, that these verses are "of preexilic character without question." In context, this statement seems to apply to the main clause of C (b), allowing exilic origin for the dependent conditional clause which expresses the theodicy.) It is consonant with the interpretation of history of the deuteronomists to qualify the dynastic premise of the Solomonic tradition by an explicit condition. Since the House of David did not fulfill the condition, its downfall is sufficiently explained, and God is justified.

[27] See the references of the preceding note.

[28] See M. Tsevat, *HUCA* 33 (1962), p.110.

[29] Because of vs.10; thus H. Gunkel, *Die Psalmen* (1926), p.567, and other commentators. (M. Dahood, *Psalms III* . . . [1970,] p.246, disagrees.)

[30] See p.101

[31] A variation of this argument would be that the whole psalm and not just one verse, vs.12, is conditional, and that consequently that verse is not a rider. The net result of this alternative is the same as that of the main line of reasoning, but it is even more unlikely that a complete psalm stipulating the condition, and not just one verse, was composed and accepted for the liturgy of the temple under these circumstances.

The unlikelihood, if not the absurdity, of such a scenario virtually guarantees that A (a) is a gloss.[32] With the confutation of the consequent, the premise that 2 Sam 7:13b—16 is genuine is refuted. Inescapably, A (a) is a gloss.

Let us now turn to the internal evidence of 2 Sam 7, the second part of the examination of our original suspicion that vss.13b—16 are an intrusion in that chapter. The chapter consists of an introduction (vss. 1—3) and two main parts (along with their connecting passages): the divine message delivered by Nathan (vss. 4—17) and David's response to it (vss. 18—29). The latter is a well constructed prayer consisting of two components of about equal length. The first is composed of thanks and praise, the second is a petition.[33] David begins with an expression of modesty; he is not worthy of God's action which made him king (vs. 18b, corresponding to vss. 8 f. of God's message); and yet, God is now transcending this favor in His promise for the future (למרחוק), i.e., an enduring kingship for his house (vs. 19, referring to vss. 11b—12 of the first part). Is such common in human affairs, he asks. Has such a grace ever been bestowed upon mortals?[34] The former rulers[35] as indeed the king, his

---

[32] Linguistic considerations also counsel against taking D as a gloss. The short vs.12 contains two (or probably three) elements of psalm language (cf. M. Tsevat, *A Study of the Language of the Biblical Psalms* [1955], p.7), viz., (עדתי [pp.18,94f.].), זו (p.24), and ישבו לכסא (p.15; cf. id., *HUCA* 29 [1958], p.131). Not only would the hypothetical glossator have to be credited with the successful handling of this type of biblical Hebrew but also with the skillful stylistic integration of ישבו לכסא לך (vs.12) into the preceding אשית לכסא לך (vs.11), as well as into the following אוה למושב לו (vs.13) and אשב כי אויתיה (vs.14), thus achieving a fine poetical balance between Jerusalem, the seat of the king, and Jerusalem, the seat of God; and if this had not been dexterity enough, he would have enhanced this effect by shaping בניהם עדי עד—ישבו (vs.12) after פה אשב—עדי עד (vs.14). Is this credible?

[33] For requests following thanks and praise, see H. Gunkel and J. Begrich, *Einleitung in die Psalmen* (1933), pp.58,275; H. J. Kraus, *Psalmen* (1960), p.XLII.

[34] The medieval commentators Rashi, Redaq, and R. Yeshaya of Trani have prepared the understanding of the passage. (1) It is a rhetorical question, the interrogative nature of which is retained in writing by the ו of וזאת; cf. Gesenius-Kautzsch §150a. (2) תורת with the meaning "nature, essence, manner of" is fairly frequent in Middle Hebrew. Ben-Yehuda lists in his dictionary, p.7704: תורת כלי, תורת פיקדון, תורת קידושין, תורת רגל, תורת שוחד "nature of an implement," etc. W. Gesenius noted this meaning of the word, but not of the sentence, in his dictionary of 1817, quoting 18th century authorities; cf. O. Eissfeldt, *Kleine Schriften* V (1973), pp.142 f.,146. The support of Middle Hebrew was not sought.

[35] שפטי(ם), vss.7 (emended), 11.

predecessor, were chosen each in his own right and person; rulership for
their sons was not considered.[36] Confessing the inadequacy and super-
fluousness of anything he might add (vs. 20; cf. Ps. 139:4; Isa 65:24),
David nonetheless continues with gratitude for the divine message (vs.
21)[37] culminating in praise of God's greatness as it manifests itself in His
ways with Israel (vss.22—24). He then, in a reference to vss. 10—11a of
the divine address, continues:[38] "Is there[39] on earth a single nation
comparable to Your people Israel in that a god 'proceeded'[40] to redeem it
to be his own people, to make a name for it, to perform for 'it'[41]
great'[42] and terrible things? 'Yet You for Your part did drive out'[43]
nations and '(their) gods'[44] in the van of Your people whom You
redeemed from Egypt to be Your own, You did establish Your people
Israel to be enduringly Your very own people, as You, Lord, did become
their God."

That vs.25 begins a distinct unit, the second component of David's
response, is clear from the following: (1) It opens with ועתה (vs.25), a
word which, like its equivalents in cognate languages (וכען ,וכענת, *inanna*
(+) *anumma*, etc.), introduces a new section or summarizes, or draws

---

[36] Saul's attempt to secure kingship for his family (cf. p. 113) was a private and unsuc-
cessful venture.

[37] Read at the beginning 'עַבְדְּךָ וְכַלְבְּךָ בעבור' "for the sake of Your 'slave' and Your
'dog'" with N. H. Tur-Sinai, הלשון והספר II (1950 f.), pp.415f., after 1 Chr 17:19 and 2 Ki
8:13, Lachish Ostraca, and numerous other texts in the ancient Near Eastern court style.
The problem is not so much reading or restoring the text as to assess correctly, here and
elsewhere, the emotional connotations and social—or religious—intentions of the words
for "dog." King Anum-Ḥirbi (Asia Minor, 19th cent. B.C.) refers to his and his royal correspondent's vassals as *kalbū* "dogs" (K. Balkan, *Letter of King Anum-Ḥirbi . . . to King
Warshama . . .* [1957], lines 9,13). See also E. von Schuler, *Die Kaškäer* (1965), p.150, for
the lowly position but loyal nature of the dog in ancient Oriental imagery.

[38] Use is made for the reconstruction of the text by H. W. Hertzberg, *Die Samuel-
bücher* (1956), p.227.

[39] מי is an interrogative particle, not an interrogative pronoun, as in Gen 33:8; Amos
7:2,5; and elsewhere. It also occurs in Middle Hebrew and Aramaic. B. Hartmann,
ZDMG 110 (1961), p.232, parses the word differently but achieves a similar effect; see
also E. Wagner, *MIO* 10 (1964), pp. 267f.

[40] 'הָלַךְ'; MT הלכו.

[41] 'לוֹ', or 'לָהֶם' 'them'; MT לכם.

[42] 'גְּדֻלּוֹת'; MT הגדולה.

[43] 'וַתְּגָרֶשׁ'; MT גוראות לארצך.

[44] 'וֵאלֹהִים' (perhaps 'וֵאלֹהֵיהֶם'); MT ואלהיו.

conclusions from, a preceding statement.[45] (2) The operative verbs of this unit are imperatives and optatives, whereas those of the previous one are indicatives (preterites): the first half is a thankful narration of events, the second a petition. (3) Only the second half can properly be called תפלה. Only to it can the sentence "Your servant has found courage (את . . . מצא לבבו) to utter this תפלה to You" (vs.27) refer, for no courage is required to restate facts, as David does in the first half, that were originally set forth in Nathan's prophecy (vss.10—12). It is the petition, or better put, the content of the petition, that is daring and momentous: permanency for the promised dynasty. Three times David asks this explicitly (vss.25,29) and a fourth time implicitly (vs.26) as he says עד עולם or לעולם. The expressions relate to עד עולם of the limitless future of Israel of which he spoke in the first part of his reply (vs.24), venturing that his house is to rule over Israel as long as Israel is the people of God.[46] In vs.26 he supports his request with a special argument: The greatness of the name of God[47] rests not only on His Godhood over Israel but also, so he subtly suggests, on the stability of the royal house. The summary of his petition is heralded by a repeated ועתה (vss.28 f.): May God bless his descendants with continuous kingship.

The conclusion from this analysis is inescapable. One thanks for what one has received in fact or in promise, and divine promise is equal to fact; one petitions for what he lacks. David offers thanks for kingship which he has received in his own person (vs.18) and which he has been promised for his house (vs.19); his petition is for that which he has not been promised: the permanency of his dynasty (vss.25—29). We would impute confusion to the narrative, if not impiety to its author, if we understand David to be praying (vs.27) for what, according to the present reading of the chapter (including vss.13b—16), God has just committed Himself to do.[48] It follows that the man who wrote

[45] Cf. A. Laurentin, *Biblica* 45 (1964), pp.168—197; H.A. Brongers, *VT* 15 (1965), pp.289—299.

[46] It is true that, while Nathan does not use the expression עד עולם with respect to Israel, he does paraphrase it in vs.10.

[47] Concern for the divine reputation is not a sign of a late text; cf. J. Harvey, *Biblica* 43 (1962), p.190, n.8.

[48] A. Schulz, *Die Bücher Samuel* II (1920), p.85, takes note of some incongruence and then moves on.

vss.25—29, i.e., the author of the chapter, could not have written
vss.13b—16.[49]

Several separate and independent lines of reasoning[50] thus converge
upon one conclusion: An insertion was made into 2 Sam 7 which materially changed its original intent. The unglossed chapter conceived of
David as king in a manner which was compatible with the idea of the
Israelite confederacy. The gloss precludes this possibility—and it does
much more. The concept of kingship within an amphictyonic framework
does not represent a self-contradiction, albeit Samuel questions its prop-
riety and viability (1 Sam 8:4 ff.)[51]; and indeed the lease of life of this
kingship was short. The king was at first "the head of the tribes of
Israel," whom "the Lord sent on a mission" when the need arose
(15:17 f.).[52] Hereditariness of the throne, while sought from the beginning (20:31), could only have placed the amphictyony under a new and
greater stress, for in limiting the recipient of the divine charisma, it

---

[49] F.M. Cross, *Canaanite Myth and Hebrew Epic*, 1973, p.247, n.118, rejects this part
of my reasoning as too rationalistic. He writes, "A traditionally pious man prays daily
that the divine promise, be it the throne of Israel, the kingdom of God, or the (new)
temple of Jerusalem (all the same promise), be fulfilled." My response to this criticism is
that the examples he proceeds to adduce are eschatological. What characterizes eschatological prayers, to the extent that they are petitions, is not the request for an event, a state,
or a thing as such but that the event come soon; it is, as it were, a request for a speed-up
of history. Often this is stated explicitly, e.g., "Yes, I am coming soon.—Amen, come
Lord Jesus!" (Revel 22:20); similarly, " ... in your lifetime and your days ... speedily
and in good season" (Kaddish, a Jewish messianic prayer in Aramaic). Even when not so
explicit, e.g., "Your kingdom come!" (Matth 6:10), the element of urgency cannot be dis-
missed. In 2 Sam 7:27, by contrast, the proximity of fulfilment is not the issue, for
David's request is, by its nature, only capable of realization in the course of ongoing history, in generation after generation; the petition does not admit of acceleration or retarda-
tion. The content of his request can therefore not relate to an attendant circumstance but
only to the substance. And this substance of the request, an uninterrupted dynasty, turns
out to be the substance of the preceding promise (vss.13b—16).

[50] The last argument is also independent of the two premises, argued by Noth (see p.
101), of the amphictyonic nature and pre-Solomonic date of 2 Sam 7, premises, which I
accept. But I stress the independence of the third argument because it constitutes a line of
reasoning unencumbered by any premises and, therefore, by any need to vindicate
premises.

[51] See supra, pp. 83, 86, for the distorting additions to 1 Sam 8:4 ff.

[52] Cf. H. Wildberger, *TZ* 13 (1957), p.468.

would inevitably impair its religio-political character.[53] But even this
might not have been considered a complete break with the past; the new
might still lend itself to an understanding in the spirit of the old. While
the throne was reserved for a descendant of the king, any king, whatever
his origin and social background, would be measured by the same canons
that apply to every Israelite, and whatever the king did was bound to
have inexorable and possibly fatal consequences for him and his house.
To this stage had the idea developed in unglossed 2 Sam 7, which spelled
out this possibility of dynastic kingship over the historical entity of the
twelve tribes. With the absolutization of the dynasty as expressed in the
gloss—the line is secure whatever an incumbent may do—the critical
limit of kingship within the amphictyony was passed. The gloss may well
be an early one. Under Solomon the confederacy, already declining
rapidly, was less and less a factor with which the monarch had to reckon;
all the while the demands of the new, complex political structures were
steadily growing. As it had now become less necessary, so it was still less
possible for a ruler to unite in his person the office of the amphictyonic
kingship and sovereignty over a double kingdom and even an incipient
empire.[54]

The political changes were accompanied by cultic developments of
equal gravity. David's amphictyonic position was based on his relation to
the ark.[55] It accords well with this that in his time the ark was still the
palladium that went with the army into battle (2 Sam 11:11). He re-
frained from constructing for it a "house of cedars" but continued to
keep it in a tent, the symbol of its mobility and of the immediate leadership of God (7:5—7). This, too, changed under Solomon. The ark became
enshrined and fixed in a permanent abode, its God, Whose throne it was,
was now solemnly ensconsed in a "princely house" but, be it noted, as a
political *deus otiosus* (1 Ki 8:6—9,12 f.).[56] Solomon was too shrewd to
scrap the empty shell of amphictyonic life. The Jerusalem sanctuary, now

---

[53] Cf. M. Buber, *Königtum Gottes* [2](1936), pp.146 f.; [3](1956), pp.120—122. For the
problem of the freedom of the charisma, cf. A. Alt, *Kleine Schriften* ... II (1953),
pp.121 f.; and, on the other hand, J.A. Soggin, *ZAW* 75 (1963), pp.54—65.

[54] Cf. Alt, ibid., pp.62 f.

[55] See p. 101.

[56] M. Buber, *The Prophetic Faith* (1949), p.71.

a magnificent temple housing the ark, was assiduously cultivated as the center for all Israel's worship (1 Ki 8; 12:27), diminished though the former significance of the ark had become.

From the vantage point of these political and religious developments the following may be discerned: Just as Solomon changed the role and the meaning of the sanctuary to serve his ends, so is it likely that he reformulated the original prophecy of Nathan, that charter of the House of David, to rid it of potential danger to the dynasty—conditionality. Plausible as this suggestion is in itself, its probability is heightened by the consideration I raised earlier. The expression (לא יכרת לך איש מ(על כסא ישראל "(Never shall you fail a descendant) on the throne of Israel," peculiar to the texts about Solomon, would hardly have originated anywhere but at his court.[57] This statement witnesses Solomon's preoccupation with the divine guarantee of a permanent dynasty. A divine pronouncement in favor of the dynasty was already on record, Nathan's prophecy of 2 Sam 7. Its only lack could be supplied by a slight amendment or expansion. Two passages in the chapter supply that lack. The one, vs. 13a, is the prediction or commandment—in stark contradiction to vss. 5—7—that David's immediate successor build the temple; the other, vss. 13b—16, the unconditional dynastic promise. While it is convenient to speak of these passages as two separate glosses, they are, in fact, one continuous text; indeed, it is difficult to decide whether vs. 13b belongs to the first or to the second gloss, and the delimitation of the second gloss as vss. 13b—16 is accepted in this article merely as the preferrred alternative. Be that as it may, the clear outlines of Solomon's policy point to the conclusion that the two glosses are indeed one, not only textually but also in origin and intent, providing an old and hallowed jar for the heady wine of his own ideas about monarch, state, and religion. I cannot fix a degree of probability for the Solomonic date of vss. 13b—16 nor for the concomitant proposition that vss. 13a and 13b—16 are one gloss. It should be clear, however, that the closer to Solomon's time one dates the glosses, the easier it becomes to support that date. With the break-up of the state under Rehoboam the basis for an amphictyonic kingdom disintegrated, and after a short and sobering interval the Davidic dynasty could hardly

[57] See p. 108 with n.24a.

have had reason to link their kingship to the amphictyony. (On the northern side of the border it was an act of a rebellious individual [1 Ki 18:17]
to emphasize the amphictyony vis-à-vis the state [vss.30 f.].)

Confed‗racies may fall apart, tribal authorities give way to monarchy,
and monarchical claims and prerogatives may change. Texts may be fabricated, and inherited texts may be altered. But the old often remains
alive in the new and may reemerge in later circumstances. For all the
transparency of the literary history of 2 Sam 7 it would be amiss not to
recognize that the idea of Davidic kingship in the spirit of the original
seventh chapter of Second Samuel did not die with the gloss. Let us trace
briefly the history of that idea down to the end of the Babylonian exile.
The idea survived in D (Ps 132:12) and in all probability was periodically
proclaimed in the liturgical recitation of that psalm. Centuries later it
reappeared in the Solomon narratives, C (a)—(c), but was again oblit-
erated in the Book of Jeremiah, C (d). It asserted itself, furthermore, in
prophecy. Our reference is to Isa 7:9 אם לא תאמינו כי לא תאמנו "If you do
not hold fast, surely you shall not stand fast."[58] Explicitly addressed to
the "House of David" (vss.2,13),[59] its meaning can only be that the entire
royal house is in danger; it will be no longer a בית נאמן "a steadfast house"
in the sense that the dynasty, which could look back over a rule of two
and a half centuries, would have understood the expression. The cherished theologoumenon of unconditionality is either ignored or put aside
by the prophet as the royal house is again placed on probation.

Another prophetic passage is Isa 55:3—5: "Lend me your ears and
draw near to Me, harken that you may live, that I may make with you an
enduring covenant of My steadfast loyalty/goodness (חסדים) for David:
⁴As I invested him with office[60] over peoples, verily a regent and com-

---

[58] Translation of A. R. Gordon in *The Complete Bible: an American Translation*
(University of Chicago Press). The interpretation follows E. Würthwein (from J. J.
Stamm, *TZ* 16 [1960], p.442). See further O. Kaiser, *Der Prophet Jesaja. Kap. 1–12* ...
(1960), p.65, n.4.; H. W. Wolff, *Frieden ohne Ende* (1962), pp.22,(24); but also G. Fohrer,
TLZ 87 (1962), col.747.

[59] I refer to both verses, but they are not equally significant. It is unlikely that vs.2 is
Isaianic, but it is likely that vss.3–9 and 10–17 form one authentic unit of progression
and purpose.

[60] עד (נתתיו) . . . . As the parallelism and the tenor of the passage show, עד denotes ruler.

mander over nations, ⁵so will you beckon a nation you do not yet know, and a nation that does not acknowledge you will run at your bidding by reason of the Lord your God ... " Deutero-Isaiah's vision of the future includes no place for a Davidic king. The prophet's silence on so important an institution is significant in this programmatic book; that Davidic kingship was not omitted by accident or oversight is indicated by his insistence on the kingship of God, an exclusive kingship which admits no human king.⁶¹ Furthermore, there is the consideration of this prophet's disillusion with the people's leaders in the past, be they patriarchs, magistrates, or kings.⁶² When loyalty/goodness (חסד) withered like the flower of the field (40:6), these proved no better than the common lot. Therefore, the place of favor which had been occupied by the king, now reverts to the nation.⁶³ The Davidic covenant has lapsed; it will be discarded in favor of the exclusive Sinaitic covenant—on this condition: Harken that you may live and the covenant of David be given to you.⁶⁴ This covenant of David enriched the history and thought of Israel; the concepts ברית עולם "enduring covenant" and חסדים נאמנים "steadfast loyalty/goodness" will not be lost. But they will henceforth serve different purposes.

This is substantiated by עדות, an emblem of kingship (2 Ki 11:12; see G. von Rad, *Gesammelte Studien* . . .[1958], pp.207–211, and M. Tsevat, *JBL* 96 [1977], p.277). Its relation to Aramaic עדיא and Akkadian *adū* "sworn political agreement" has often been discussed; see, e.g., J.A. Fitzmyer, *CBQ* 20 (1958), p.456; K. Deller, *WZKM* 57 (1961), pp.31–33. But in Deutero-Isaiah the word also connotes "witness for God" (Isa 43:10; 44:8).

⁶¹ Buber (n.56), p.221; O. Eissfeldt, in *Israel's Prophetic Heritage; Essays in Honor of J. Muilenburg*, ed. by B.W. Anderson ... (1962), pp.203 f.

⁶² 43:27 f.; see Redaq, a.l.; W. Gesenius (-F. Buhl), ... *Handwörterbuch*¹⁷, p.386; K. Budde, in Kautzsch (-Bertholet, n.26), p. 667.

⁶³ M. Haller, in *Die Schriften des A.T. in Auswahl* ... II 3 (1914), p.61; P. Volz, *Jesaja II* (1932), p.139.

⁶⁴ Vs.3aβ-b is final in form but conditional in meaning, a stylistic feature that can be studied to advantage in the Book of Deuteronomy.

*Yhwh Ṣeba'ot**

The divine name יהוה צבאות (YS)[1] occurs 285 times in the Hebrew Bible,[2] of these, 11 times in the Book of Samuel.[3] But it arouses the interest of the commentator of this book to a greater degree than is warranted by the comparatively small figure. There are two reasons for this. In the order of the biblical books, it is in Samuel that the name occurs first,[4] and it is seriously to be considered whether the liter-

---

* The main study on the subject is B. N. Wambacq *L'épithète divine Jahvé Seba'ôt* (1947); hereafter referred to as Wambacq.

[1] The interpretation of the name YS that is given here was proposed *in nuce* long ago by A. B. Ehrlich, מקרא כפשוטו 1 (1899), p. 256, n. 1, and *Randglossen zur hebräischen Bibel* 2 (1909), pp. 144 f., and 3 (1910), pp. 164 f., but has been virtually overlooked ever since. P. Joüon, *Grammaire de l'hébreu biblique* (1923), p. 399, mentions it with approval; Wambacq. p. 99, n. 4, referring to Joüon, also mentions it but withholds approval. Both leave unrecorded those of its elements which lend it strength and substance. A renewed and firmer presentation of the interpretation together with an examination of some attendant problems is therefore in place.

[2] In Samuel-Jeremiah, Hosea, Amos, Micah-Psalms (Chronicles). For details the reader is referred to Wambacq, pp. 50—55. All figures are taken from that basic book. Lists and groupings are found also in a number of encyclopedias and dictionaries as well as in W. Kessler, "Aus welchen Gründen wird die Bezeichnung 'Jahwe Zebaoth' in der späteren Zeit gemieden?", *Wissenschaftl. Zeitschr. der M.-Luther-Univers. Halle . . .*, *Gesellsch.-u. sprachwiss. Reihe* 7:3 (1957/1958), pp. 767 f. Kessler, pp. 768 f., gives a useful survey of the discussion in the decade after Wambacq.

[3] 1:1:3, 11; 4:4; 15:2; 17:45; 2:5:10; 6:2, 18; 7:8, 26, 27. (The resulting ratio 11:274 is to be adjusted to 11:271 by the deduction of the 3 Chronicles occurrences as these are found in passages identical with their Samuel parallels.) Regarding word counts, the present study is concerned with the masoretic text. Differences between it and the texts of the Septuagint deserve attention in individual cases but do not affect the course and the result of this investigation.

[4] For ליהוה . . . והיתה העיר חרם (Jos. 6:17) the LXX has καὶ ἔσται ἡ πόλις ἀνάθεμα . . . κυρίῳ (σαβαωϑ/ var. τῶν δυνάμεων). Very suspicious! It would be the only occurrence of YS in the pre-Samuel books and the only occurrence of ליהוה צבאות חֶרֶם (or חֲרָמִים) in the Bible.

ary first is not representative of a historical first, i.e., whether the name
did not originate in the later part of the period of the judges. The other
reason is the association of YS with (one or very probably) two entities
which figure prominently in Samuel, to wit, the temple of Shiloh (1:1:3,
11, (also 20 LXX)[5] and, probably, the ark (1:4:4; 2:6:2, 18; indirectly
7:8, 26, 27).[6] The significance of the twofold association is accentuated
by the fact that the God, venerated at the amphictyonic[6a] sanctuary of
Shiloh, is called YS in 1 Sam. 1:3, 11 and אלהי ישראל in vs. 17, the latter
name being the formal appellation of the God of the tribal league, as
Beyerlin,[7] following Noth,[8] has shown. As regards the combination of
the two names into one compound, יהוה צבאות אלהי ישראל,[9] it is achieved in
2 Sam. 7:27 (prepared in the preceding verse) in an amphictyonic
chapter[10] that grew out of a concern for the ark.

As one sets out to interpret the name YS, he is embarrased by the
duplication of the compounds in which it appears, יהוה צבאות and יהוה אלהי
צבאות (YES). To which of the two shall he give priority? He inventories
his material and is rewarded with eloquent statistics: YS occurs 261
times, YES 18 times.[11] Considering the frequency of occurrence, the

---

[5] That the name YS originated at Shiloh (O. Eissfeldt, "Jahwe Zebaoth," *Miscellanea
Academica Berolinensia* 2:2 [1950], pp. 139 ff., 148; reprinted in his *Kleine Schriften* 3
[1966], pp. 113 ff., 121) transcends the information of, and safe inference from, the
sources.

[6] YS does not occur in the actual LXX text of 1:4:4 and in the reconstructed LXX text
of 2:6:2; cf. Wambacq, pp. 62–67. (It is otherwise in 2:6:18 LXX because of Lucianic
κυρίου σαβαωϑ.) In favor of MT which has the full form of the name (ישב יהוה צבאות
הכרבים) at the beginning of the two narratives of 1:4 and 2:6 is the occurrence of YS also
at the beginnings of other stories, proclamations, and the like (1:1:3; 15:2; 2:7:8) and its
subsequent reduction to single יהוה in the sequels.

[6a] Cf. "The Steadfast House," pp. 101 f., n. 3.

[7] W. Beyerlin, *Herkunft und Geschichte der ältesten Sinaitraditionen* (1961), pp.
34–36.

[8] M. Noth, *Das System der zwöf Stämme Israels* (1930), pp. 94 f.

[9] Frequent in the Hebrew (but lacking in the Greek) Jeremiah in introductory כה אמר
יהוה צבאות אלהי ישראל; rare otherwise.

[10] Cf. n. 6a.

[11] A third compound, אלהים צבאות (Ps. 80:8, 15) and surprisingly יהוה אלהים צבאות (59:6;
80:5, 20; 84:9), occurs 6 times. It is difficult to explain. It is probably not a scribal mis-
take in everyone of these passages since it occurs four times in one Psalm. H. D. Hum-
mel, *JBL* 76 (1957), p. 97, takes the final consonant of אלהים in these cases as an enclitic *m*

interpreter opts for YS. He assumes that the three-word name is an expansion of the two-word name rather than that the two-word name is a contraction of the three-word name. Statistics is not unanswerable but neither is it a matter of indifference. Conclusions based on it should not be rejected but for better arguments. In their absence, the philologian proceeds to support his statistical judgment by two additional considerations. The first is one of the relative chronology of the contexts. YS prevails in Samuel, an early book, over YES by the ration of 10:1. The second regards the *Sitz im Leben*. As was mentioned before, the two-word form is in Samuel connected with the sacral institutions of the Shiloh temple and, probably, the ark. Conservatism that marks such institutions and everything that is connected with them does not favor the assumption that an author changed at will the name of the deity of these institutions. This must be stressed in view of the fact that an early witness, Amos, has YS once and YES 8 times. For the question is one of author and *Gattung*. Stated appropriately in terms of probability, it reads like this: Who is likely to put a personal stamp on style and innovate expressions, Amos or the author of Samuel? There is no doubt as to the answer: Amos. Cultic prophet or not, compared with the narrators of stories about sacral institutions Amos was free and spontaneous and individualistic. And however late one dates the Book of Samuel, no one denies that the older parts, with which we are mainly concerned here, are at the latest contemporary with Amos. The upshot of this reasoning is that frequency of occurrence, chronology, and specific usage of language converge on the preference of YS to YES.

This conclusion would probably have enjoyed universal acceptance, were it not for the difficulty felt by a number of scholars to account for the syntax of the two-word name. The explanation "Yhwh of Hosts" is objectionable, they say, because it makes a proper name, Yahweh,

---

common in Ugaritic, which is appended to the putative construct אלהי-*. Two considerations speak against this explanation. First, the formulaic nature of (יהוה) אלהי צבאות, occurring 18 times, would probably have protected the standard expression from veering into irregular formations. Second, in two of these verses the same words were not affected by the putative mimation; there the regular construct אלהי appears in other phrases, namely, אלהי ישראל (59:6) and אלהי יעקב (84:9). When, in the following, the difference between the compounds is not the issue, the name will be referred to as YS irrespective of its actual form.

govern a genitive. It is clear that the objection is not rendered less valid by calling the genitive adjectival.[12] Some time ago, however, G. R. Driver seemed to have removed the obstacle when he asserted that the proper-name-genitive construction is grammatically unexceptionable. He presented a fairly long and representative list of Hebrew and cognate-language phrases to demonstrate the possibility, which was apparently meant to be tantamount with the probability, of correctly rendering "Yhwh of Hosts."[13] In the following examination of the matter it is indicated that attention be paid to questions of language as well as of the history of relgion.

It is soon noted that Driver rests his argument on the disproof of a rule which does not exist and in so doing fails to see the actual linguistic situation. The rule is stated thus: "Proper names as such cannot stand in the construct state."[14] This may be an acceptable formulation for first orientation but it is too inaccurate for scholarly study. The following is proposed instead: Hebrew and other ancient Semitic languages avoid certain kinds of overdetermination of substantives.[15] Hebrew does not overdetermine personal pronouns, nouns with articles and, apparently,

---

[12] W. R. Arnold, *Ephod and Ark* (1917), p. 142. M. Buber, *Königtum Gottes*[2] (1936), p. 233, and Wambacq, pp. 146—51, have no difficulty in refuting Arnold's hypothesis.

[13] *JBL* 73 (1954), pp. 125—28.

[14] Ibid., p. 125.

[15] Overdetermination (Schwyzer speaks of hypercharacterization, which is of somewhat wider scope) is a phenomenon not unknown to linguists; cf. E. Sapir, *Language; an Introduction to the Story of Speech* (1940) [paperback; first published 1921], pp. 95—97; E. Schwyzer, *Sprachliche Hypercharakterisierung* (Abhandl. d. Preuss. Akad. d. Wissensch. [1941], Philos.-hist. Kl., No. 9); E. Locker, "Tendenzen des Denkrhythmus ...," *Corolla Linguistica, Festschr. F. Sommer* (1955), pp. 163—67. In the above statement the qualifying "certain" is important. In Hebrew, overdetermination may be required, permitted, or forbidden. Required, as in בתים מלאים (Deut. 6:11; Neh. 9:25)—plural twice expressed, contrasting with English "full houses"—plural once expressed. Permitted in various degrees [including the negative degree of underdetermination], as in חרבתיהם (Mic. 4:3)—plural twice expressed, contrasting with חרבותם (Isa. 2:4)—plural once expressed; or as in שבע הפרות הרקות (Gen. 41:27), contrasting with שבע פרת הטבת (vs. 26); [or as in יום השׁשׁי (Gen. 1:31), contrasting with יום חמישי (vs. 23)]—article twice expressed, once expressed, [not expressed] (very many examples of article once expressed in GK § 126 w-aa; in rabbinic Hebrew this is standard, but the fact is blurred in the deteriorated texts of the ordinary editions). Forbidden, as in the cases mentioned in the immediate continuation.

proper names; they are determined and are not further to be determined by a genitive (construct state). There are, however, proper names which, in the course of time, have lost their determination, in part or in full, oftentimes for discernable extralinguistic reasons. In ancient Semitic languages, among them Hebrew, these are chiefly geographical and divine names, and it is from these groups that Driver draws most of his examples.

As for geographical names, matters are obvious. There are two towns in Palestine named Bethlehem. If the speaker wants to make clear that he means the southern one, he says בית לחם יהודה. A town by the name of צען may lie outside the listener's ken or experience and thus be to him vague, ill-defined. The genitive מצרים provides the desired determination.

Considering the other group, the divine names, it must be stated at the outset that many members of Oriental pantheons were in frequent danger of losing their identity. This needs no demonstration for those deities whose names are also used in the plural, e.g., (*ištar*) *ištarātu* ("Ishtar, [goddess]") "goddesses, [Ishtars]" in Akkadian. Examples from the Bible are Astarte, Baal, and perhaps Anat (see GN ענתות), from Egypt the Canaanite immigrant Reshef.[16] These words oscillate between proper and common nouns. Indeed, some (Baal, El) may sink back to the common clay from which they once rose. Such pluralization reflects in language what happens in religion. In like manner, genitives governed by divine "names" are the linguistic aspect of the religious process of stabilizing or restoring the vanishing identity of the bearers of these names. Naturally, not every phenomenon in language is the imprint of an event in the extralinguistic world. Possibilities in a language once established often set in motion new and autonomous developments within the language, and their influence may reach beyond it. Thus the determination of a divine name by a genitive may, at times, be the result, at other times, the cause of the disintegration of the divine personality. As for the genitive words, they appear in a wide variety of classes:[17] geographical names

---

[16] Cf. S. A. Cook, *The Religion of Ancient Palestine* (1930), p. 112; R. Stadelmann, *Syro-palästinensische Gottheiten in Ägypten* (1967), p. 50. It is similar in Ugarit; see Ch. Virolleaud, *PRU* V (1965), p .8.

[17] Driver (n. 13), pp. 126 f.

(as in ^{d}sin āl̮arrān),[18] other divine names (as in 'štr kmš),[19] or nouns
denoting tangible, visible, or imaginable things (as in b'l ṣmd "Baal of the
Team [of Horses?]" or "of the Mace" or in b'l šmm "Baal of the
Heaven").[20]

A third group of Driver's examples, proper nouns with pronominal
suffixes, is culled from non-Hebrew languages; its treatment will be
short. The fallacy of the approach of Driver and others[21] lies in the exclusively syntactical interpretation ("pronominal suffixes, which imply the
construct state").[22] The syntactical indentity of suffixed nouns with construct phrases does not connote other identities of the two kinds of
nominal expressions, such as identity of emphasis, value, or emotional
content; this means that the two classes of expressions are only of limited
comparability. Driver's examples illustrate the point. They are personal
names with 1st pers. suffixes, expressive of the speaker's own relation to
those personages (Ishullanu, Krt?).[23] This is clear in certain Akkadian
prayers where Nabu is the darling of the people: ^{d}na-bi-ia-nu-u-a "our
dear Nabu,"[24] ^{d}na-bi-ia-a-ni "our Nabu,"[25] ^{d}taš-me-tu₄-ia "my
Tashmetu."[25a] These cases have nothing to do with determination and

---

[18] In some cases involving geographical nouns the loss of the personality of the god is
not at stake; the genitive is just the simplest device for distinguishing the Sin of Ḥarran
from the Sin of Ur.

[19] Not all compounds of this group are construct states. Compounds may, for instance, be appositional phrases reflecting autochthonous divine growth, enhanced person-
alization and invigorated absorbency, or syncretistic coalescence. A study of pre-
Hellenistic Near Eastern gods in the manner of H. Usener, *Götternamen* (1896), pp.
218—220 and elsewhere, (on Greek gods) is desirable.

[20] About ršp ṣbi (UT 2004:15) nothing certain can be said. The genitive ṣbi may
qualify adjacent ršp or more distant (b.)ġb or it may be part of the compound ršp ṣbi, the
whole of which being a genitive (pace M. Liverani, *Annali. Istituto Orient. di Napoli* N.S.
17 [1967], pp. 331—34).

[21] E.g. C. Brockelmann, *Grundriss* II, § 176, to whom Driver refers.

[22] Driver, (n. 13), p. 125.

[23] A transfer in speech of this personal relation to the grammatical 2nd or 3rd person,
i.e., in an address or a report, is conceivable, but I know no examples.

[24] *KB* VI 2, p. 34. line 20.

[25] *JSS* 4 (1959), p. 2, col. A, line 16; W. G. Lambert's translation p. 11.

[25a] KAR 122 = E. Ebeling, *Quellen zur Kenntnis der babylonischen Religion* I (1918),
p. 81, lines 12, 14; a prayer of King Assurbanipal. The supplicant's close personal relation
to the deity is vividly expressed by ḥi-ir-ti-i na-ra-am-te at-ti "you are my bride, my
sweetheart."

overdetermination and are therefore not pertinent to the interpretation of
the compound YS where possible overdetermination is the issue.[26]

There is no onomatological need whatsoever to determine the name
Yhwh in the manner and for the reasons that the above names are determined. The linguist is therefore restrained from setting aside his rule,
the rule of overdetermination, and he concludes that YS is not a construct
state. The remaining alternatives are that it is a compound of a noun and
an apposition[27] or a nominal clause.[28] Since our knowledge of biblical
Hebrew is solely based on written sources which do not record secondary
phonemes (transition, stress, etc.), an isolated appositional phrase יהוה
צבאות is for us indistinguishable from, and therefore identical with, a
nominal sentence of the same notation in which יהוה is the subject and

---

[26] From the Hebrew Bible Driver quotes one example which falls outside the groups
here discussed (p. 127): (sic) גוג ארץ המגוג (Ezek. 38:2). This is very probably a case of a
wrong word division, viz., of postulated original גוג 'ארצה מגוג' and is shaky ground for
the demonstration of a rule. He also cites Ps. 38:23, but this is an example from the Septuagint, rarely distinguished by a sensitive understanding of the Hebrew language: κύριε
τῆς σωτηρίας μου. Of six major Psalms commentaries of the last forty years none finds
this "translation" of אדני תשועתי worth mention. GK §125h also has ציון קדוש ישראל (Isa.
60:14). This is a poetic license to achieve parallelism with עיר יהוה of the first stich.

[27] The appositional interpretation is that of Ehrlich and of Joüon (n. 1). Eissfeldt, who
calls it "attributive," considers it as a possibility ([n. 5], pp. 130 f. 138, and pp. 105 f.,
112 f., respectively). His understanding of the plural צבאות, however, is questionable; cf. C.
Brockelmann, Hebräische Syntax (1956), p. 16, n. 1; W. Eichrodt, Theologie des A.T. I⁵
(1957), p. 121, n. 71; Theology of the O.T. I (1961), p. 193, n. 2. See also H.-J. Kraus,
Psalmen² (1961), p. 201.

[28] A further alternative is a verbal sentence whose subject-predicate is יהוה in its pre-
sumed original form and meaning of a causative of הוה/היה and whose direct object is
צבאות: "He (who) creates the (heavenly) armies" (Cross); "...the hosts of Israel" (Freedman; cf. W. A. Albright, JBL 67 [1948], pp. 379–81; D. N. Freedman, JBL 79 [1960], p.
156; F. M. Cross, HTR 55 [1962] p. 256), The extrinsic advantage of all other interpretations of YS over the verbal-sentence interpretation is that they can be discussed and
accepted irrespective of a particular exposition of the name יהוה, an issue which is still very
much sub judice. Their intrinsic superiority lies in a chronological difficulty of the verbal-
sentence alternative. Given (Schrader's and) Albright's above mentioned explanation of
the tetragrammaton, it is very unlikely that this putative early meaning—the extant Hebrew language does not have the hifʻil of היה/הוה—of יהוה was still sufficiently free and
alive at the probably much later time of the origin of YS to attract generic words and use
them as direct objects. A further objection has been raised by W. von Soden, WdO 3
(1966), p. 182; see also pp. 178f.

צבאות is the predicate. According to the latter alternative, YS is a sentence name of a common Semitic type. The meaning of the name is materially the same for both interpretations: "יהוה, (the) צבאות" or "יהוה (is) צבאות." It states for the two components an identity of general validity or, at least, of momentary concern.[29]

What, then, are the צבאות with whom Yhwh is identified or by whom He is strongly characterized? Scholars who see a construct state in the name explain them variously as the Israelite army (better: the totality of the able-bodied men of Israel) or the heavenly bodies or the demons or the whole world.[30] None of these solutions is compatible with the appositional or the nominal-sentence interpretation as Yhwh cannot possibly be identical with any of these entities. Only one answer remains: צבאות in the divine name has the common and general denotation "armies." What this means is shown by a very similar cognomen bestowed on a *homo religiosus*. Joash, king of Israel, calls Elisha אבי אבי רכב ישראל ופרשיו "My father, my father, Israel's Corps of Chariots and Its Horses" (2 Kings 13:14).[31] In the ninth century, when chariotry had become a prominent weapon in Israel, one so designated a man in whom one trusted for help and delivery. In an earlier period, when Israel's military strength lay in its levy in mass, the people called its God "Armies" (plural of extension and importance as in Elisha's cognomen). The word, which denotes infantry,[32] at least in early times, is an expression of trust in "Yhwh, the man of war" (Exod. 15:3; cf. Isa. 42:13; Ps. 24:8).

The same idea is expressed in Num. 10:36: שובה יהוה רבבות אלפי ישראל

---

[29] This is not only true of the sentence, where it is obvious, but also of the apposition which is of the order מים לחץ "water (which—is so scarce that it—amounts to) affliction" (1 Kings 22:17; Isa. 30:20; in both passages it is a clear appositional phrase, the direct object of its respective sentences).

[30] Cf. Wambacq, pp. 4–45; briefly, e.g. Eichrodt (n. 27), pp. 120 f. and 192 f. This variety of meanings is also available to the verbal-sentence with object interpretation; cf. the quotations at the beginning of n. 28.

[31] The name was then transferred to Elijah (2 Kings 2:12). Cf. K. Galling, "Der Ehrenname Elisas und die Entrückung Elias," *ZTK* 53 (1956), pp. 129–48 (on the transfer of the name, pp. 138–42).

[32] Cf. Galling, ibid., p. 144.

"Rest,[33] O Yhwh, Israel's Myriads of Thousands!"[34] We note that it is again an expression for army which is the apposition of Yhwh and it describes the army to its greatest extent, the total arrière-ban of Israel.[35] We further note that, just as its synonym YS, so is this evocation connected with the ark.[36] The God of the ark is the God of martial might. Both יהוה צבאות and יהוה רבבות אלפי ישראל originated in the period of Israel's preoccupation with the wars about and in Canaan, which the Book of Joshua initiates with a revelation relating to an army (Josh. 5:13—15). These names and the related expression מחנה "troop"[37] (and the distinguished names of Elisha and Elijah) are of the same kind as divine epithets stemming from other aspects of warfare, such as חרב "sword" (Deut. 33:29), various words for "shield" (ibid.; Gen 15:1; and frequently) and, on the other hand, חומה "wall" (Zech. 2:9), מגדל "tower" (Ps. 61:4; and elsewhere), and בית מצודות "fortified house" (31:3). Some refer to attack or mobile tactics, others to defense or static fighting; some are preferred in texts of national concern (and are frequent in the prophets), others in those solicitous for the individual (and are relatively frequent in Psalms); some are early ("army"), others late ("fortress").[38]

---

[33] This meaning of שוב, which is in keeping with the introductory ובנחה of this verse and in proper contrast to ויהי בנסע הארן with its קומה of the preceding verse, is not necessarily based on the frequently proposed change of vocalization 'שְׁבָה'. The oscillation between שוב and ישב is also observed elsewhere; cf. S. D. Luzzatto, ספר ישעיה (1855—1867), p.45; to the passages quoted there, 2 Sam. 15:8; 19:33 may be added.

[34] Thus, in essence, the Jewish Publication Society of America translation of 1962. "... Myriads of Israel's Clans" is also possible.

[35] The fullness of the name evocation, of the same rhythmic form as רכב ישראל ופרשיו, provides some balance with the longer evocation and prayer of the preceding verse, קומה יהוה ויפצו איביך וינסו משנאיך מפניך.

[36] Cf. above, p. 120.

[37] Cf. the following note.

[38] In an early narrative, a group of divine representatives encounters Jacob (ויפגעו בו מלאכי אלהים), who recognizes them as a מחנה אלהים "divine troop" (Gen. 32:2f.). A later psalm says that one representative is encamped (חֹנֶה) around the pious (Ps. 34:8). The linguistic incongruity of the Psalms passage shows an incomplete semantic adaptation of the older expression, where מחנה (from √חנה) is a mobile (פגע) "troop," to the newer concept of static protection, which uses חנה with the meaning "to encamp" around (סביב) people.

But these differences must not blind us to the typological identity of the names, metaphors, and parables. To him who sees the identity, the name YS will not longer remain in near isolation, and the line of military epithets, etc., of God will not show a void created by the apparent absence of the word for the most important instrument of warfare, the army. That the void has not been noticed—for a void it is to the interpreter as long as he understands YS differently—is probably due to an ever more forceful tendency in religion, arising in late biblical times and culminating in modern western civilization, which may easily deflect the awareness of readers of the Bible from other types of religion. I mean the tendency in the development of religions toward preoccupation with shelter and submission, preponderance of the individual and dominance of prayer. But in early Israel, this tendency was yet little noticeable; in those days there was room and need for "Yhwh (Is) Armies."

It is remembered that in Samuel the name YS is linked largely to institutions, the Shiloh sanctuary (2 times) and the ark (3 [+3] times);[39] only three occurrences are unconnected with either. It stands to reason that in the protection of these institutions its meaning was exposed to but scant and slow extension and change. Nothing specific can be said about Shiloh other than that it was the place where the ark was stationed. Yet as regards the latter, the inference is forced upon us that the role it still played in war in that period (1 Sam. 4; 2 Sam. 11:11)[40] further tended to retard extension and change of the meaning of the divine name whose origin was in war. The continuous combative involvements of early Israel down to the time of David likewise inhibited a semantic change during that period.

The extensions and changes become apparent in the age of the prophets.[41] It is in the literary Prophets that the name YS is found pre-

[39] Cf. above, p. 120.

[40] 1 Sam. 14:18 is not an additional source, although (הָאֱלֹהִים) אֲרוֹן is certainly to be maintained against the Septuagint.

[41] YS occurs in the Psalter 15 times. It would be a futile attempt to date the eight psalms which use it (24;46;48;59;69;80;84;89) relative to the prophets. Parenthetically, two of them (24;80) probably refer to the ark indirectly. In general, it must be borne in mind that the comparable paucity and accidentality of the sources caution against overconfidence and rigidity of periodization.

dominantly, 251 times out of a total of 285 in the Bible.[42] No longer is it connected with the old institutions. Shiloh had been lying in ruins for centuries, and the ark had disappeard, at least not very long after the beginning of the prophetic era.[43] The Shilonian tradition of the name was resumed and continued on Zion, as can be gathered from some Psalms and prophetic passages,[44] but this aspect plays a very minor role in the words of the prophets. The prophetic use of YS, whose detailed study is not assayed here, is many-faceted, and this has contributed to the diversity of interpretations of צבאות by scholars who parse the word as a genitive or accusative of יהוה.[45] The appositional or nominal-sentence understanding leaves no room for these interpretations. Throughout biblical times, צבא was and remained a common noun, clear, live and exciting. Everyone knew what it meant and therefore everyone also knew what YS meant. The prophets, who used it so often, knew it better than anyone. More than anyone were they sensitive to God's might and overwhelmed by His power, often a militant power against the nations, against Israel, against themselves.

---

[42] We note with interest that also in the Book of Kings YS occurs exclusively in prophetic speech (1 Kings 18:15; 19:10, 14; 2 Kings 3:14 as well as 1:19:10 and 14 are identical, and since 2:19:31Q is only an alternative text (the Ketiv does not have צבאות) and is, moreover, from a section which seems to have been taken from a collection of Isaiah legends (cf. O. Eissfeldt, *Einleitung in das AT*² [1956], p. 356), the importance of Kings for the study of YS is very small.

[43] Cf. מ. הרן, ידיעות החברה לחקירת א"י ועתיקותיה, 25 (1961), pp. 211—23.

[44] Cf. Wambacq, pp. 268 f.

[45] Cf. above, pp. 121 f., 125, n. 28.

God and the Gods
in Assembly

An Interpretation of Psalm 82*

A ncient Israel was committed to montheism but constantly challenged by polytheism. How does the Old Testament, the document of the committed, respond to the challenge? The best
known answer is that propagated by Deutero-Isaiah and many other
authors: The gods of polytheism, the "other gods," often equated with
the gods of the nations, are nonthings. This answer is known best
because it is recorded most frequently, argued most vigorously, and
comprehended most easily; it is water-clear monotheism.

Another, and differing answer is less prominent: Yhwh, the god of
Israel, is the supreme god, but the "other gods" are also real gods; He
maintains their reality even as He has ordained their subordination.
Moreover, He has assigned them functions in the scheme of the universe.
Deut. 4:19 puts it as clearly as one could wish (and 29:25 refers to it):
"When you look up to the heavens and behold the sun and the moon and
the stars, the whole heavenly host, you must not be lured into bowing
down to them and serving them. These Yhwh your god has alloted to the
other peoples everywhere under the heaven."[1] In keeping with this,
David, persecuted by King Saul and, fearing that he would be forced to
leave his people, says that wicked men may have enticed the king to drive
him out of the land so that he would no longer "be part of Yhwh's pro-

---

*References in these notes to (M.) Buttenwieser, (M.) Dahood, (F.) Delitzsch, (H.) Gun-
kel, and (E. J.) Kissane are to their commentaries on Psalms (a.l.). H. W. Jüngling has
devoted a monograph to this psalm: *Der Tod der Götter; eine Untersuchung zu Psalm 82*
(Stuttgarter Bibelstudien 38), 1969.

[1] After the *New Jewish Publication Society Translation; The Torah* (1962).

perty (נחלת ה', i.e., Israel), saying (to him in effect), 'Go, serve other gods!'" (1 Sam. 26:19). If he takes refuge in another country with an alien people. he will have to serve the god(s) of that domain.

Y. Kaufmann shows some awareness of this concept in his treatment of the religion of the Pentateuch and the historical books (Former Prophets),[2] but its significance eludes him, as indeed it must, if he is to remain consistent with one of his central theses: the Bible does not allow to the gods of pagandom the attribute of reality. This thesis is unfortunate, as the issue under discussion shows. For one thing, it is bad philology in that it disregards unequivocal literary attestations, such as the Deuteronomy passage just quoted. For another, it obstructs our view of the scope and the thrust of biblical faith (and is bad philology on that account also). It would have been easy for Israel to recognize Yhwh as its only god once it was convinced that there were no other gods in existence. It was another thing altogether to be faithful to Him in the face of a plethora of gods from among whom they might choose their deity. The above Deuteronomy passage continues: "(. . . These Yhwh your God has allotted to the other peoples . . .) But you Yhwh took and brought out of Egypt . . . to be the people of His own property" (נחלה). Israel is to hold fast to Yhwh because of the special relationship between them, which relationship, formed in the past and reaching into the present, is nevertheless capable of being disregarded by Israel. Joshua puts it to them succinctly: "If you do not wish to serve Yhwh, choose now whom you do wish to serve—the gods whom your fathers in Transeuphratia served or the gods of the Amorites in whose land you live" (Josh. 24:15).[3] Choose they must because no people can be without a god, but they have their pick from a sizable number, and the objects are neither pagan figments nor "fetishes." The Old Testament records the many centuries of Israelite history as a succession of challenges, real challenges, emanating from real sources. The record does not read like a psychiatric case history with the subject chasing after illusions.[4]

---

[2] תולדות האמונה הישראלית I (1938 ff.), pp. 40 (ff.), 615 f., and elsewhere; *The Religion of Israel* . . . Abridged by M. Greenberg (1960), pp. 127 f.

[3] For the understanding of the passage, as well as the whole story and its historical background, I recommend to the reader V. Maag's contribution to *Hebräische Wortforschung; Festschrift . . . W. Baumgartner*, VT Supplem. 16 (1967), pp. 205–218.

[4] Nota bene: The object (indirect) of עשה שפטים "to mete out punishments" is man in

Analogous to the foregoing is the biblical attitude regarding various forms of magic, occult science and practice. The Bible prohibits necromancy, soothsaying, and the like. It does so not because they are ineffective but precisely because they are efficacious. Scripture shows the general view of its time that the ideas behind these practices are sound and, if these techniques are correctly and auspiciously performed, they may well achieve their purpose, but—they are not for Israel.[5] In most of the nonprophetic books of the Bible, we have actuality pitted against actuality and not actuality against nonactuality. If the modern reader is disillusioned with the polytheism[6] and occultism of some parts of the Bible, let him consider that it is the aspect of actuality (reality) against actuality that makes the Bible a living book; where the issue is actuality against nonactuality, interest flags because battle with a strawman is no battle at all.

Actuality and nonactuality are the pair of categories under which the Old Testament sees the "other gods," with the chronological and literary progression moving from the first to the second. For the theologian there is no middle ground between the two; a thing either exists or does not exist. But for the historian who is interested in beliefs as they were held and in their formation and transformations, in the appearance and disappearance of concepts in the flow of time, there is a middle ground; it is the phase of transition in the mind of man, the event of change of concepts from that of the actuality of the gods to their nonactuality. The study of history begins with the assembling of sources and their interpretation. In what follows I translate and interpret a document revealing this transition, psalm 82.

I   A Psalm of Asaph

'Yhwh' stands in the divine assembly,
He gives judgment in the midst of the gods.

Ezekiel (9[11] times) and in late Chronicles (once); in preprophetic Exodus (12:12) and Numbers (33:4) it is the Egyptian gods, who (pace Kaufmann) are every bit as real as man and beast preceding them in the same verse of Exodus.

   [5] Cf. Kaufmann (supra, n. 2), pp. 462–465, 467 f., and elsewhere (English abridgment, pp. 78–80).

   [6] To call the phenomenon henotheism—less accurately, monolatry—is only to reaffirm its essential polytheism.

2   "How long will you judge unjustly
    and show partiality to the wicked?[7] (Selah).

3   "Give judgment to the poor and the orphan,
    vindicate the wretched and the destitute;

4   "rescue the poor and the needy,
    deliver them from the hand of the wicked!—

5   "Without knowledge, without understanding
    they walk in darkness;
    the very foundations of the earth are shaken.—

6   "Once I had thought you to be gods,
    all of you sons of the Most High;

7   "verily, however, you are now mortal like man,
    you will fall like any minister."

8   Arise, O 'Yhwh', judge the earth,
    for all the nations are indeed Your property!

The psalm offers no textual or linguistic difficulties. The only question is whether the first אלהים in vs. 1 and its recurrence in vs. 8 have
supplanted an original יהוה. The shrewd suspicion that אלהים is not original rests upon two considerations. (1) The psalm belongs to the elohistic
group (chs. 42—83), which as an entity is characterized by a rather late
change of most occurrences of יהוה to אלהים. (2) It corrects the defect of
the poem in having אלהים twice but with different meanings in the same
verse (vs. 1), which is both stylistically gauche and likely to confuse the
listener or reader.

Vs. 1. The meaning of עדת אל "divine assembly" is so well known
today that it no longer needs broad documentation.[8] Similar phrases
occur in Sumerian, Akkadian, Ugaritic, and Phoenician literatures. The
expression referred originally to the political organ of a primitive demo-
cracy, a phenomenon which can be discerned in the pantheons of various
non-Israelite cultures. In Israel this image has given way to that of an

---

[7] Or "guilty." רשע has both an ethical and a juridical sense.
[8] F. M. Cross, *Journ. of N.E. Stud.* 12 (1953), p. 274, n. 1, gives an instructive and still
quite useful survey.

absolute monarchy (see Ps. 95:3), and the "divine assembly" is a body of counsellors and (/or) administrators. We encounter this body in 1 Kings 22:19—22; Isa. 6; Job 1:6—12, 2:1—7; and elsewhere. In this psalm, its members are called אלהים "gods" (vss. 1, 6; also in 95:3) and בני עליון "sons of the Most High" (vs. 6). In Job they are בני אלהים "sons of God/of the gods"; in Ps. 29:1 (though not functioning as counsellors or administrators) בני אלים "sons of the gods," an appelation closely resembling עדת אל of the verse under discussion.[9] As will be seen, in Ps. 82 they function as largely independent executives; "vassals" would be a; term loosely in keeping with the time. What brings them together to the assembly of which this verse speaks is presumably one or more of its normal functions: report (Job 1 f.), deliberation, or execution (1 Kings 22).

In this assembly Yhwh "stands"—in order to judge the assembled, as the text goes on to state. From various occurrences in the Bible, and as far as their limited number permits generalization, we know that a judge in Israel was normally seated (1 Kings 7:7; Isa. 16:5; 28:6; Ps. 122:5; Pr.

---

[9] It is likely that the component "sons of" in some of these phrases points to an earlier conception of the minor gods as sons of the supreme god, El, or of major gods. While this is full-bodied mythology, its employment as a linguistic fossil was not necessarily offensive to later generations of a different faith. Hebrew "son of A," as is well known, often has the meaning of "member of group or category A," e.g., בן־נביא "member of the class (sometimes guild) of prophets," i.e., "prophet"; בן־בקר "bovine." In this connection בן־ המלך, literally and often actually "son of the king," is an expression of special pertinence. As was first observed by Ch. Clermont-Ganneau in 1888 and recently fully demonstrated for Israel and some other ancient Oriental peoples by G. Brin (לשוננו 31 [1966 f.], pp. 5—20, 85—96), בן־המלך and its correspondences in other languages not infrequently mean one in the service of the king, usually in an administrative role. (A. F. Rainey has challenged Brin's interpretation [לשוננו 33 (1968 f.), pp. 304—308]—successfully, in my opinion, in respect to some of his examples—unsuccessfully, in respect to the phenomenon in general.) In view of the correspondence between earthly and heavenly courts, בן־אלהים* (the singular does not occur in the Hebrew Bible but is found in the Aramaic part, viz., בר־ אלהין, Dan. 3:25) may well mean one belonging to the divine sphere. This observation can both be amplified and sharpened. While בן־ "son of" and איש־ "man of" are usually interchangeable in the sense discussed here (cf. Brin, pp. 93—95), this is not the case in regard to the divine. Here the classification is clear-cut: בר־אלהין/בן־אלהים* is a supernatural being belonging to the sphere of God, whereas איש־אלהים is a human being belonging to this sphere, a prophet or a man considered particularly close to God. (This understanding of the compound is at variance with that of W. Herrmann; see his "Die Göttersöhne," Zeitschr. für Rel.-und Geistesgesch. 12 [1960], pp. 242—251. I cannot accept Herrmann's interpretation of a number of texts, particularly those from Ugarit.)

20:8—a king; Exod. 18:13 f.— Moses: Judg. 4:5—Deborah; Ruth
4:2—a multijudge court). God, on the other hand, when He judges is
commonly spoken of as standing[10] (נצב nifal [also עמד], Isa. 3:13; Ps. 82:1)
or standing up (קום, Ps. 76:10; 82:8).[11] The employment of one of the
verbs, קם, is particularly instructive in that it indicates the suddenness
and dynamism of the action (cf. Isa. 33:10; Ps. 12:6); God's judgment
has many meanings for man, but it is first and most immediately experienced as His intervention. Accordingly the other verbs (עמד, נצב) express
the resultant stance (cf. Isa. 3:13 f.). Whereas it is the normal posture of
God, in conception or vision, to be seated as He is surrounded by His
servants and ministers (I Kings 22:19–22; Isa. 6; Ezek. 1:26 ff.), standing is a sign of an extraordinary event. The meaning, then, of the psalm's
opening is that what might normally be a routine assembly, where the
gods report or participate in deliberations, has unexpectedly turned into a
tribunal; God has stood up to judge the assembled.[12]

Vs. 2. The speaker is God—He speaks throughout most of the psalm
and He opens with the accusation. A prosecutor, separate and apart from
the magistrate, is not a normal feature in Israelite court procedure.[13]
Furthermore, God, the author and guarantor of the norms of justice, is
the aggrieved party; He acts as plaintiff and lodges the accusation.
(Where God is a party, there is no distinction between criminal and civil
cases.) Literarily this fact is put to effective use: Placing the accusation in
the mouth of God lends it special force and authority.

"How long will you practice injustice?" Although the gods act individually and each one is responsible in his realm, they are addressed collec-
tively, because it is as a group that they constitute the opposition: "the
gods" against "God."

Vss. 3–4. The English translation does not adequately convey the
force of these lines which the Hebrew poetic mechanisms held for the

---

[10] Cf. H. L. Ginsberg, *Journ. of the Am. Or. Soc.* 88 (1968), p. 51, n. 24.

[11] The exception is an occurrence in Daniel (7:9), a book which shows many foreign
influences to normal Old Testament style and ancient Israelite mores and ideas. On the
other hand, the substantial reason, in this passage, for God being seated may be that the
procedure has not yet begun and in the continuation it is only fragmentarily described.

[12] Cf. "Yhwh in heaven will call to account (יפקד) the heavenly host" (Isa. 24:21).

[13] Exceptions are Ps. 109:6 (denied by G. Fohrer, *Das Buch Hiob* [1963], p. 83) and,
on a different plain, Zech. 3:1.

Israelite audience. The lines form two distichs which, while expressing the same content with different words, are yet of great formal similarity.[14] The duplication of the content, possibly a mere play with poetic devices, serves here to retard the progress of action and urge on the hearer the consideration of what these rulers of the world ought to have done but have not. With this admonition, which, for all its force, is no longer than twelve words, the accusation, first part of God's speech, concludes.

Vs. 5. The failure of the gods, however, is not only a thing of the past and it is not accidental. Not that they are unwilling to do what they are bidden—if that were the case, there would be hope that they would change their minds—but they are inherently incapable of grasping the issue, of walking in the light. As long as they are in office there is no hope for the world; the whole present order is corrupt, and the corruption affects the foundations of the earth.[15]

The speaker here may possibly be the psalmist, a reflection interrupting the account of events. But it is much more likely that it is still God Who is speaking. Realizing the futility of His exhortation, He ponders the issue. The verse, the second part of God's speech, is not an address or a proclamation but the deliberation of the judge in camera in preparation of the verdict.

Vss. 6–7. This is rendered in vss. 6 f. While some interpreters have understood this to be the psalmist's aside rather than the Deity's decree, this construction possesses little merit. A trial typically ends with the

---

[14] The similarity is manifest in three areas: corresponding sounds—quantity (word lengths) and quality (alliteration, assonance, etc.); corresponding verb forms—shape, type and function; and in the structure of corresponding word groups (including identical chiasmi). This similarity in phonetics, morphology and syntax, going far beyond the normal parallelism, is a noteworthy poetic element and lends weight to the exhortation.

[15] The idea that the earth is founded upon justice shines through the Isaian passage: "I am laying a stone for a foundation in Zion ... and I shall make justice the line and righteousness the plummet" (Isa. 28:16 f.). In Ps. 89:15 and 97:2 justice is even the foundation of God's throne and, similarly, in Prov. 16:12 of a king's throne. (Therefore, contrary to F. I. Anderson's opinion [*Biblica* 50 (1969), p. 393], the idea that ימוטו refers to the shaking of the foundations of the world is not "incongruous in the context," and the strained linguistic interpretations of the verse which he, in consequence of this opinion, is forced to make are unnecessary.) For the embellishment of the theme in rabbinic thought see, e.g., Yoma 38b on 1 Sam. 2:8 and Prov. 10:25. See also 1Q Isa^a9:6.

pronouncement of a judgment. Our construction has this pronouncement made, as one would naturally expect, by the judge. One might resort to the alternative of the psalmist's expressing his reflections, if there were anything in the text which would make a juridical proclamation by God a forced interpretation. As the matter stands, however, to encroach upon the prerogative of the judge and place a judgement-like utterance in the mouth of an onlooker is clearly to weaken an already weak case. To have the psalmist say, "I thought you were gods, but now I know better," is, furthermore, to credit him with a rather trivial statement; for this merely amounts to the admission of a mistaken opinion, a misinterpretation of the facts. But of far greater moment is God's recognition of a fault in the order of the world as He established it (see to vs. 8).[16] Now the purport of God's words, expressing this recognition, is not to deny that the accused have ever been gods—were this so, there would have been no assembly or court scene to begin with—but rather to declare that their status is not immutable. Because the gods have not fulfilled their function, they will be deposed, will cease to be gods.[17] This is expressed by "you are mortal like man."

Immortality is the hallmark of the divine, mortality that of the human. Gen. 3:22 reads: "Yhwh God said, 'Now that man has become like one of us (i.e., a divine being) in that he knows good and bad, what if he should stretch out his hand and take also from the tree of life and eat and live forever!'" Knowing good and bad is one characteristic of the divine, living forever is another.[18] In a passage from a Ugaritic epic the goddness Anat offers immortality to Prince Aqht:

> "Ask for life, O hero Aqht,
> ask for life, and I shall give it to you,
> for immortality, and I shall bestow it on you,"

[16] For this meaning of אכן . . . אני אמרתי "Formerly I thought . . . but now circumstances make me reconsider" see Gunkel, pp. 134, 363.

[17] The very same words אלהים אתם appear to epitomize the unlikely result of another test of divinity to which Yhwh puts the "other gods" in the equally dramatic passage of Isa. 41:21–24.

[18] There would be a symmetry as logically apt as poetically forceful if the psalmist has in mind that the failure of the gods to exercise the divine attribute of knowing good and bad in acts of judgement is here balanced by their being deprived of that other divine attribute—immortality.

and goes on to describe with words which clearly point to immortality as an attribute of the divine:

"I shall make you count years with Baal,
you will count months with the son(s) of El."

In Aqht's answer, however, in rejection of the offer there is expressed, with equal clarity, the converse, namely, that decline that comes with old age[19] is the characteristic fate of man:

"I shall die the death of all (men),
I, too, shall certainly die" (2 Aqht:VI:26—38).

The Old Babylonian version of the Gilgamesh epic has it very succinctly:

When the gods created mankind,
they set apart death for mankind,
but retained life in their own hands (X:3:3—5).

The decree, then, that the gods are to die spells their demotion: deprived of divinity they will fall like אחד השרים, that is to say, they will be deposed from office.

What is represented by אחד השרים, the class with whom, or which, the gods in their fall are compared?[20] Interpretations that go beyond the myth clearly present in this psalm, invoking extraneous myths for the explanation of this phrase, are beset with difficulties.[21] We are, therefore,

---

[19] This is the likely interpretation.

[20] Ewald was the first to interpret the passage: "O princes, you will fall together," taking כְּאַחַד, repointed 'כְּאֶחָד', as an adverbial phrase meaning "all at the same time," a meaning it has half a dozen times in the Hebrew Bible, e.g., Ezra 2:64 (H. Ewald, *Die poetischen Bücher des Alten Bundes* II [1840 (since this, second ed.)], p. 260). The following arguments militate against this proposal: (1) כאחד "together" is probably translated from Aramaic כחדה ([L. Köhler-] W. Baumgartner, *Lex. Vet. Test. Lib.* [1953], p. 1073b; *Supplementum* [1957], p. 200b). Its acceptance for this verse would require a later date of the psalm than its content suggests. (The weakness of Baumgartner's claim for Akkadian origin [*Heb. u. aram. Lex* ... (1967), p. 29b] is clear from the rarity of the Akkadian expression; *CAD, I/J*, has one entry [p. 227b], and *AHw* none.) (2) It destroys the obvious parallelism כאדם ‖ כאחד השרים. Kissane, vol. 2, p. 58, bases his translation "suddenly" upon the same revocalization ('וּכְאֶחָד'), but כאחד does not have this meaning.

[21] J. Morgenstern has given the most elaborate one (*Heb. Un. Coll. Ann.* 14 [1939], pp. 73—126, especially pp. 73—75, 117). He translates the stich: ". . . as one of the leaders of the host of heaven shall ye fall (to earth)" (p. 117) and identifies the leader with Helel

well advised to reject these alternatives in favor of the common interpretation of אחד השרים as "any minister" or the like. The allusion may be to
the ignominious end[22] of governors, princes, ministers, or generals, to
which the Bible makes occasional reference (Isa. 43:28; Jer. 49:38; Hos.
7:16; 13:10 f.). Or it is possible that "minister" in juxtaposition to "man"
constitutes a merismus, "commoner and prince," implying the whole of
humankind.[23]

With vs. 7 the court scene ends. Pure dramatic description that the
poem is up to this point, its inclusion in the Psalter would be an ano-
maly.[24] What makes this poem a psalm, i.e., an address in poetic form by
man to God, is the last verse: "Arise, O 'Yhwh'. . . . " This verse has an
importance, moreover, which goes beyond even the function of constituting the poem as a psalm. For it plays a key role in the answer to the question, What specific genre confronts us in the psalm? Vss. 1–7 may present a free story like Job 1 f. or a report of a vision like 1 Kings 22 or Isa.
6. Now Job 1 f. or 1 Kings 22 and Isa. 6 are easily classified because their
openings contain specific information (Job 1:1, 6; 2:1; 1 Kings 22:19;
Isa. 6:1). Such information, however, is lacking in Ps. 82. It is this difference which thrusts upon us the task of interpretation, and it is vs. 8
which yields the answer to the interpreter. A free story is not normally
interrupted with a call to God; a vision not infrequently is (Isa. 6:8; Ezek.
9:8; 11:13; Amos 7:2, etc.). This consideration alone would point
strongly to the conclusion that the verses in question are the report of a
vision. In support of this we add the following: The verses betray no sign
whatsoever of either narrative or narrative style. Beyond the short rubric

---

ben Šaḥar of Isa. 14:12. The psalm text hardly bears the weight of this complicated
exegesis, and the anonymity in the frame of reference is disturbing, as Morgenstern himself admits; "'Like one of the *sarim* . . .' is a bit vague and weak" (pp. 117 f., n. 167). If Ps.
82 in its mythology makes reference to another myth the name of whose chief protagonist
(be it Helel ben Šaḥar or another) was generally known, this name could hardly remain
unmentioned in our psalm passage because its bearer is to serve as an example (cf. Isa.
65:15); anonymous examples are not likely to be exemplars. Morgenstern would emend
the text to read 'וכהילל בן שחר' as against וכאחד השרים. This proposal reveals Morgenstern's
awareness of the problem but is not, by that token, any the less self-serving. H. S.
Nyberg's efforts in *Studien zum Hoseabuche* (1935), pp. 46 f., 124, need not detain us.

[22] נפל means "to experience disaster" as in Prov. 11:28; cf. 13:17+ברע; 17:20,
28:14+ברעה; 11:5+ברשעה. The meaning may also apply in Ps. 5:11.

[23] So Dahood.

[24] There are, to be sure, some compositions in the Psalter, viz., wisdom poems, that
are not psalms; cf. G. Fohrer, *Einleitung in das A.T.* (1965), p. 283.

of the opening verse there is no description of events or situations, no introduction of speaker or speakers and, notably, no use of waw consecutive.[25] Indeed, absent is the rhythm of narrative, that elusive quality which every fine author attempts to realize as he spins the sequence of events.

Vs. 8. We begin with the second part of this verse: "For all the nations are indeed Your property!" The passage is reminiscent of Deut. 32:8 f.:[26]

> When the Most High apportioned the nation,
> when He set up the divisions of mankind,
>
> He fixed the boundaries of the peoples
> according to the number of sons of 'gods' (or 'God').[27]
>
> But[28] Yhwh's own allotment is His people,
> Jacob His apportioned property.[29]

[25] The existence of narrative features in reports of a visionary serving, as they do, to transmit his experience does not invalidate this observation. Nor is the isolation and analysis of simple forms put into question by the existence of mixed ones (e.g., Zech. 1:7—6:8).

[26] The relation has been commented on before, most elaborately by S. E. Loewenstamm in פרסומי החברה לחקר המקרא בישראל. ספר ה' לזכר ש' דים (1957/58), pp. (120—123), 124; and in his מסורת יציאת מצרים בהשתלשלותה (1965), p. 50, n. 53. In this lengthy note, Loewenstamm anticipates the position expressed in the present study and refutes explicitly an earlier opinion of Y. M. Grintz and implicitly a later one by J. Jeremias, *Kultprophetie und Gerichtsverkündigung* ... (1970), pp. 120—125, especially p. 123, n. 1.

[27] The received text has ישראל "Israel." The above translation follows the Hebrew Qumran fragment (P. W. Skehan, *Bull of the Amer. Schools of Or. Res.* 136 [1954], p. 12) and the LXX (paraphrastic but nontheless clearly reflecting the *Vorlage;* see also the Armenian daughter translation and part of the Aquila tradition, both rendered in Brooke and McLean's edition) in postulating אלהים (with אל as a less likely alternative) as the original text. The passage has been discussed by R. Meyer in *Verbannung und Heimkehr ... W. Rudolph zum 70. Geburtstage*, ed. A. Kuschke (1961), pp. 197—209.

[28] Adversative כי that is not in opposition to a preceding negation; so also in Isa. 28:28; Jer. 23:18; Ps. 44:23; (141:8?). This interpretation presupposes, for this text at least, the identity of עליון with יהוה, i.e., the former is a nominalized adjective and an epithet of the latter, and not the name of a separate and distinct deity. The second alternative is that of O. Eissfeldt (who, further, identifies עליון with אל; *Journ. of Semit. Stud.* 1 [1956], pp. 28 f. [English = *Kleine Schriften* 3 (1966), pp. 389 f., German]); but he seems to modify his opinion, granting that at the time of Deut. 32 concepts were in flux and that in vs. 43, at any rate, it is Yhwh to Whom the homage of all gods is due. This, however, is the same as saying that Yhwh is the "Most High."

[29] "Allotment" and "His apportioned property" are attempts to render חלק and חבל

In the distant past, Yhwh, the Most High, divided mankind into nations, whose number He determined by the number of sons of 'gods/ God', i.e., the minor gods; each of these gods received a nation as his portion (and, conversely, each nation received its tutelary deity [Deut. 4:19[30]]). Only one nation was not given over to these gods—Israel; that people Yhwh retained for Himself.[31]

Ps. 82 shares with Deut. 32 this myth as background, even to the point of using the same significant vocabulary.[32] Like the rest of the psalm, the last verse, too, is grounded in the myth, but it goes beyond it, for it asks the consummation of the decree. The visionary, having witnessed the judgment against the gods, realizes that the implementation of the decree is not immediately effective; it is a thing of the future ("you will fall," vs. 7). At this moment, the unpredictable happens. Overwhelmed by his fear of a delay of unknown duration[33] he, the bystander, calls into the court: "Arise, O 'Yhwh,' judge the earth!" This is not that personal call for help on the part of the psalmists we meet so frequently in the psalms,[34] but an imploring of God to take over the regiment of an

---

נחלתו. The roots גורל, חבל, חלק, and נחל (all four occur in Micah 2:1—5, while the Deuteronomy passage has the last three but not the first root) belong to the same semantic field of vested property (cf. F. Horst in *Verbannung und Heimkehr* [cf. supra, n. 27], pp. 135—152; A. Malamat, *Journ. of the Amer. Or. Soc.* 82 [1962], pp. 147—150).

[30] Cf. Supra, p. 131.

[31] This concept presented no difficulties to ancient Israel. At various times and places in the Near East, there were large or medium-size states, of which Assyria is the best-known example, into which smaller states had been merged. The head of the empire, the Great King, was at the same time, in a particular sense, the king of that political unit with which he or his dynasty had had the longest and most intimate relation, a fact which is sometimes reflected in his titles.

[32] "Sons" or "assembly of" בני; אל "of 'gods/God'" or "the Most High"; גוים: עליון; נחל. The feature of identical words and phrases becomes even more noteworthy when a quantitative analysis is made, comparing a total of only six distichs (Deut. 32:8 f.; Ps. 82:1, 6, 8) which contain 19 words in Deuteronomy and 23 in Psalms.

[33] M. Buber in his essay on this psalm says: "God pronounces sentence upon them, i.e., the gods, and ... with God there is no division between sentence and execution" (*Good and Evil* [1953], p. 29; in the original: *Recht und Unrecht* ... [1952], p. 37). This apodictic statement does not hold true; for example, God rejected Saul (1 Sam. 15), but the latter continued to rule for quite some time (to 1 Sam. 31).

[34] קומה has this meaning eight of the ten times it occurs in the Psalter; the exceptions are this passage and 132:8.

unfragmented world—now; an entreaty that He administer justice undiluted and without delay, "for all the nations are indeed [His] property." When God established the existing order, He turned over to others[35] part of what was His. It never ceased to be His; may He, then, today reenter into His own.[36] The present order of the divided world, governed by deputies wielding delegated power, is disintegrating because of inner contradictions: O God, why do You delay? Sweep away the phantasms! Assert Yourself as the one and immediate ruler and judge.

Ps. 82 must be seen as a historic psalm, historic in the sense that, whatever its date, the thought expressed in it represents a watershed in the history of ideas. The poem presents two views of the gods, an earlier one and a later one, the former and prevailing one yielding dramatically to the new and true one. What is remarkable is that the conclusion expressed in this psalm's poetic imagery, particularly in the epitome of the heavenly verdict, sets the course for future religious development, true though it be that a charting of that course would reveal not a straight line but a tortuous curve.[37] The psalm, then, is historic not for its recording of history but because of the importance of its contribution to the making of history. The psalmist, as he prays for the speedy realization of the verdict, sets history in motion, at the same time that his uttered prayer—this psalm—becomes a document and as such acts itself as a historiogonic kerygma.

It would hardly be productive to attempt here to determine whether the idea represented in Ps. 82 owes its inspiration to prophecy or itself constituted a source of prophetic thought; the psalm's prophetic features are nonetheless impressive. It centers on a vision of the divine council, the visionary responds to the judgement made in that council, and judgment and response together herald the end of paganism.

---

[35] "Apportioned," causative of נחל (Deut. 32:8).

[36] Simple stem of נחל (Ps. 82:8).

[37] Cf. Dan. 10:13 and for the vast postbiblical literature L. Ginzberg, *The Legends of the Jews* V (1925), p. 205, as well as the many references in VII (1938), p. 197b, to "Guardian angel(s) of . . ."; E. E. Urbach, אמונות ודעות; חז"ל: פרקי (1969), p. 118.

Addendum

Modern biblical exegesis frequently links Ps. 82 with 58, a link made possible by changing the pointing of incongruous אֵלֶם (58:2) to 'אֵלִם', a defective spelling for אֵלִים "gods." Sometimes, though, the connection is only superficial. Formerly it was often said that this word, so revocalized, might be a reference to rulers, priests, and the like, but this is now generally recognized as unsupportable.[38] G. R. Driver, therefore, assumes a doubly defective spelling, viz., 'אֵלִם' for אֵילִים "rams," but occasionally designating "chiefs, nobles," e.g., Exod. 15:15.[39] By either reading the psalmist is understood as rebuking the nobles, from whose ranks the judges come, for perverting justice. Ps. 58 so interpreted would share two features with Ps. 82: a concern for justice and the conclusion with a prayer for its establishment on earth.

But this gain of the change of vocalization is insignificant. The two psalms remain unrelated in any particular and characteristic way. Moreover, Driver's interpretation of 58:2 is not fully satisfactory. While it makes sense in its immediate context, that is hardly the case when the verse is seen as part of the whole psalm. The verse in question, the opening of the poem, corresponds with vs. 12, the closing verse, at least in the matter of the judgement of man. Now the second half of the latter, "Verily, there is a God Who judges on earth," ceases to be a pallid generality (which it would be in isolation) once it is seen as serving as a contrast to the question raised in the first distich, "Do you really . . . judge man equitably?" The end of the psalm asserts the existence of a God Who judges equitably in specific reply to the doubting of the reality of divine justice at its beginning. This doubt, to be sure, arises because of "the gods," who are not properly performing the function of judges;[40] but this is the case only if 'אֵלִם' "gods" is the reading and rendering in vs. 2.

As likely as the latter change of pointing and the translation are, however, and, by consequence, as easy as it is to note an essential similarity in the two psalms (i.e., the common feature of the gods' failure to judge),

---

[38] Cf. Gunkel.

[39] *Journ. of Theol. Stud.* 43 (1942), p. 157. Dahood, vol. 2, p. 57, seeks to support this interpretation with additional revocalization.

[40] So approximately Gunkel.

it is advisable to interpret Ps. 82 independently and without any appeal to a psalm whose particular interpretation hangs, in the last analysis, by the slender thread of one revocalized word. Now that we have done just that, however, we proceed to a comparison of the two psalms in order to bring into higher relief what is characteristic of, and intended by, Ps. 82.

Psalm 58

1   To the Musicmaster. (According to) "Do Not Destroy."
         A Mikhtam of David.

2   Do you really pronounce just verdicts, you 'gods'?[41]
     Do you judge men equitably?

3   Quite the contrary![42] In your heart you devise wrongs,
     (and) in the world[43] you gloat[44] over the violence you wreak.

4   From the womb the wicked are estranged,[45]
     from their birth the peddlers of lies do err.

5   Like the (very) serpent's venom is their venom,
     as that[46] of a deaf adder that stops up its ear

6   so that it may not hear the charmers' voice,
     nor even that of the enchanter most cunning.

---

[41] 'אֵלִם'; cf. supra.

[42] אַף; cf. 44:10: "yet" (cf. L. Köhler-[W. Baumgartner], *Lex. Vet. Test. Lib.* [1953], p. 74b, no. 4).

[43] I.e., in actuality. First the gods devise the evil in their minds and then sit content to observe its realization in the world. It is the same sequence as in the preceding verse: first conception (תדברון), then actualization (תשפטו).

[44] תְּפַלֵּסוּן. The root, meaning "to behold," is frequent in Akkadian. It is commonly used in the N-stem, which, if followed for Hebrew, would yield 'תִּפָּלֵסוּן', but the basic stem also occurs in Akkadian, and speculation about the proper conjugation of the Hebrew form is pointless. What the stich says of the gods is the opposite of what Habbakuk says of Yhwh: You are "too pure of eye to gaze with equanimity upon evil and You cannot bear to look on wrong" (1:13).

[45] זרו. Frequently emended to 'נֹזְרוּ' (e.g., Gunkel), but unnecessarily so (cf. Delitzsch[5]). The nifal form in Isa. 1:4 and Ezek. 14:5 is of similar intent. Cf. W. Zimmerli, *Ezechiel* (1958 ff.), p. 301, for a somewhat different meaning.

[46] Cf. Dahood.

7   O God, break off the teeth in their mouth,
        smash the lions' fangs, O Yhwh!

8   Let them dissolve (becoming) like water that runs off,
        'like trodden grass'[47] let them wither.

9—10 ...[48]

11   The just will rejoice because he sees vengeance,
        he will bathe his feet in the blood of the wicked.

12   And people will say, "Verily, there is a reward for the just;[49]
        verily, there is a God Who judges on earth."

In spite of its textual perplexities, the psalm as a whole is not difficult. The three divisions are easily recognized. The first (vss. 2—3) is an
address to the gods; the second (vss. 4—6) describes the world as their
bailiwick; the third (vss. 7—12) is a prayer to God to crush the wicked
and make justice of divinity believable on earth.

(1) The address to the gods is scornful to the point of being sardonic:
How can justice ever come from you, who perpetrate wickedness?
(vss. 2—3). (2) Indeed, the world as it is, is testimony to the rule of the
gods—the wicked flourish (vss. 4—6). These latter, having the gods as
their patrons, seem proof against ordinary countermeasures. This is
expressed in the simile of protection against the snake.[50] Normally one
can counter poisonous snakes by recourse to a magic spell, but if a snake
knows how to stop its ears against the spell, both the spell and the one
who casts it are impotent[51] (vss. 5—6). (3) In this seemingly hopeless
situation the psalmist turns to God. He does not ask for an antidote; God
is no technician, possibly to be outwitted by a still cleverer manipulator.
Only the breaking of the poisonous teeth of the liars will end their
menace. Once deprived of the source of their power, they will disintegrate

---

[47] Read with Buttenwieser 'כְּמוֹ חָצֵר יִדְרֹךְ'.

[48] Unexplained. The verses seem to continue the imprecation of vs. 8, mainly by
adding further similes.

[49] פְּרִי לַצַּדִּיק. Cf. Isa. 3:10 f. (גמולו); Prov. 11:30 f. (attracting וְיֻשַּׁלָּם).

[50] The snake is an old symbol of evil speaking. In the Hittite-Akkadian bilingual political testament of Ḫattusilis I (middle of the 17th century) the queen, who instigated
rebellion, i.e., faithlessness, is called "serpent" (I:10,20).

[51] Cf. Eccl. 10:11; Jer. 8:17; Akkad. ṣēru lā šipti "spell-immune snake" (see CAD, Ṣ,
p. 148b).

(vss. 7 f.[−10]. When this will come about, man, who has become uncertain of God's responsibility and competence, will again experience the presence of God, the judge and ruler (vss. 11 f.).

This interpretation makes clear the similarity of Ps. 58 to Ps. 82. Hardly less clear is the difference between the two. Ps. 58 is concerned in theme and intention solely with the contemporaneous. The order of the author's aeon is disturbed but is capable of being adjusted, and it is for this adjustment that the psalmist prays. He implores God to secure justice in the world and thereby to remove the temptation to faithlessness.[52] The author of Ps. 82, by contrast, has despaired of his present; justice cannot be secured in it. And for all that the very limitation of God's government is part of the divine plan, he is impatient with this limitation and entreats God to remove it, to end the present order with dispatch, and to establish a new one in its place, His own kingdom.

[52] The gods are not mentioned again after the beginning. Presumably, they are left in their positions and will have to be rebuked again when corruption becomes unbearable.

The Death of the Sons of Eli

Eli ... heard all that his sons were doing ... [23]and said to them: "Why do you do these things, the evil things, which I hear about you? ... [24]Do not (do such), my sons ... [25]But they would not listen to their father because the Lord wished to kill them (1 Sam. 2:22–25).

In the last sentence of this quotation one easily recognizes the concept that God may harden the hearts of men.[1] Indeed, it is probable that nowhere in the Hebrew Bible is it stated more pointedly and more disturbingly.[2] That God hardens Pharaoh's heart[3] is the more famous case, but there the problem is seemingly rendered less acute by the particular circumstances: God does what he does in order to bring about the miraculous rescue of Israel, and for this purpose a non-Israelite, a person of lesser responsibility and, presumably, lesser responsiveness, is used. The same is true in the similar case of the Canaanites.[3] Here, however, Israelites, the sons of Eli, are sent to their death[4] without forewarning or rather, the forewarning of their father is neutralized as soon as it is ut-

---

[1] The problem received competent treatment by F. Hesse, *Das Verstockungsproblem im AT*, 1955, especially III 2, "Jahwe als Urheber der Verstockung" (pp. 40 ff.). The present attempt will explore a different approach, complementary rather than disputatious.

[2] Isa. 6:10 and 29:10 are not to be grouped with 1 Sam. 2:22 ff. and the other passages discussed here; cf. "The Throne Vision of Isaiah," pp. 155–176.

[3] For references see below, n. 5.

[4] The fact that here and elsewhere Israel or Israelites are the object of God's *opus alienum* renders this difference more apparent than real. But this distinction remains: the particular accountability of Israel (cf., e.g., Amos 3:2) makes their position a particularly delicate one. Passages referring to Israel are (1 Sam. 26:19); 2 Sam. 24:1; 1 Kings 18:37; Isa. 63:17; Ez. 14:9. On the other hand, in Ju. 9:23 God's action is the normal response to man's action; it does not cause it but is caused by it.

tered. God gives Eli's sons no chance to repent and improve; He "wishes to kill them."

This problem has always weighed heavily on the minds of readers of the Bible. More important than the tribulations of their creed, however, is the complication it creates in the Old Testament itself. If history in the biblical view is the march of mankind, and specifically of Israel, through time that is set and kept in motion by divine call and human response, then at these junctures biblical history ceases, for the response is forestalled. The resulting inconsistency goes to the root of biblical philosophy; the reason, the *raison d'être* of the Bible is in doubt. The question is thrown into even sharper relief when we observe that nowhere is the divinely-inspired hardening of the heart a narrative necessity employed to solve hopeless complications or stagnations. In none of the scenes that are our concern does Yahweh appear as a *deus ex machina*.

Now it may appear that these conceptual difficulties are overdrawn here, that the inconsistencies that this interpretation purports to bring out in certain Old Testament writings merely follow from the view of the biblical idea of history that is presented here, and that that view is faulty. Or it may be argued that these inconsistencies were unnoticed by the authors or that they did not disturb them. I think, however, that the above view of biblical history is too broadly established to be discarded at the first difficulty, and that the inconsistencies are too frequent and too glaring to be accidental, have remained unnoticed, or been taken lightly. Rather, they are structural to one way of biblical thinking and point to an inherent dilemma.

Israel's view of the world was by and large rational and optimistic. It is incomprehensible that, holding this view, man chooses freely that which leads to his ruin. Deut. 30:19 says: " . . . I have set before you life and death, blessing and curse, ובחרת בחיים—"therefore choose life!" or "and you will choose life." The form ובחרת is adhortative or indicative, or rather it is both: Israel should and will choose life, for how can it be otherwise? Yet experience shows that man does not always behave as rationally as one would expect. Strangely, he misbehaves and thus brings destruction upon himself. Comparatively minor transgressions pose no problem, nor do unforeseeable catastrophes. But there are grave sins, persistent obduracy, and they weigh all the more heavily when the inescapable catastrophic consequences have been predicted or the perpetrator has been warned; they defy explanation in human terms, common-sense, rational explanation. If one nevertheless wants to account for them, he can trace them only to one cause: God. For wherever one meets trans-human phenomena in the physical or psychic world, there Power manifests itself. And for Israel, Power and all the powers are incarnate in Yahweh. He is the power that, now and then, shakes the image of man that common experience has fashioned; he is the *fons et origo* of all behavior that is contrary to common sense. A passage in the first Book of Samuel has it very clearly (26:18f.). David blames Saul for wronging him; he does not deserve to be chased over the mountains as an outlaw. How can the king do such an unconscionable thing? The answer is obvious: It was either Yahweh or men who instigated the king. Men, that is court intrigue, personal enmity; if not men, then Yahweh—a third possibility, namely, that it was Saul's own idea and free decision, is not considered at all. A man who is master of his faculties does not act so senselessly. It should be kept in mind, however, that there are standards by which man is measured. They do not necessarily apply to God. God eludes our explanation. Even so plain, shall one say, so vapid a book as Proverbs says: "It is the glory of God to conceal things" (25:2).

A balanced view will note that this explanation of what seems to be otherwise inexplicable phenomena is not entirely a mechanistic construction, a convenience of philosophers. Man knows that God touches the heart. The Bible that lets one man pray: "Create me a clean heart, O God, and renew a steadfast spirit within me" (Ps. 51:12), lets another man, Elijah, ask God: "May this people know that you have turned their hearts back" (1 Kings 18:37). The latter is an ejaculation in despair, but so is Psalm 51 with its cherished and seemingly innocuous request of the clean heart. From here there are only a few short steps to the statement about the fate of the Elides. What is first experienced in the immediacy of tribulation is later generalized in the respite of detached retrospect, of transmitting tradition and of story telling. It has become the foundation of the view that God hardens the heart.

But the idea of divine coercion is not wide-spread in the Bible. We find it here and there in the narratives; later it all but disappears. What takes its place? Nothing! If this answer sounds casual, a few condensed quotations from the second chapter of Jeremiah will correct this impression. "[10]Cross to the coasts of Cyprus and see . . .: Has there been such a thing? [11]Has a nation changed its gods even though they are no gods? But My people have changed their glory for a useless thing. [12]Be appalled, O heavens, at this ... [13]For My people have committed two harmful things: they have forsaken Me, the fountain of living water, to hew out cisterns for themselves, broken cisterns, that can hold no water." Or this: "[21]I planted you a choice vine ... but how have you turned degenerate...?" Further: "[31]Have I been a wilderness to Israel...? Why then do My people say: We are roaming aimlessly, we will come no more to you?" The chapter abounds in questions; there are over twenty interrogative particles, but all questions remain unanswered. They are not rhetorical; Jeremiah torments himself to find an answer—he knows none.

These are the alternatives of the Bible. One is a rational explanation of human behavior. A chain of causality is traced back from an observed act of folly and sin, sometimes through mounting entanglement, to the first cause and origin, God. It satisfies man's search for a rational explanation of the world and himself. It relieves him of oppressive and bewildering irrationality. The gain is great, but the price is high. It is the disruption of the most essential thing the Bible has to say about man and history: that he is responsible because he can at any moment be responsive, and that history is the progression of moments of expected responsiveness.

Where the price is not paid and the Bible does not spend itself into near-bankruptcy, where the basic concepts of God and man are upheld even under the stress of inscrutable human behavior, the unanswered question stares into the faces of speakers and listeners. God is exonerated, man is charged instead, but reason is sorely taxed, and the intelligibility of the world is lost.

These are the bitter alternatives in the Old Testament, religious, moral, and intellectual. The trend of the inner-biblical development in dealing with the problem is clear: it is from the first alternative—divine coercion—to the second one—no explanation. The first is the position taken, to my awareness, in five clear cases in the narratives from Exodus through Kings,[5] to which two additional, but less clear, instances in the

---

[5] Pharaoh (Exod. 4:21; 7:3; 9:12; 10:1, 20, 27; 11:10; 14:4, 8, 17); Sihon (Deut. 2:30); Canaanites (Josh. 11:20); Elides (1 Sam. 2:25); Israel (1 Kings 18:37).

same books are added;[6] in the Prophets, it occurs fairly clearly twice,[7] there is probably one instance in the Hagiographa[8] and, of course, none in the laws. But even in the time and literature in which the second alternative prevails, the first has not disintegrated into archaeological debris. Jeremiah and Ezekiel do not attempt to explain the inexplicable behavior of the historical people of Israel by the divine hardening of the human heart.[9] But when God will act in the eschatological future, he will act also on the minds of the people, writing his teaching on their hearts (Jer. 31:32),[10] or giving it a new heart and a new spirit (Ezek. 11:19; 36:26 [f.]).[11] This is a clear mark of the new age, radically different from the historical age of man's unrelieved and unshared responsibility and full mastery of his fate. The prophets were sent into the historical age and towards it their endeavors were directed. Also the golden age of which they spoke was but an extension of the historical age. It would bring peace, prosperity, justice, and knowledge of God; a fundamentally different man was usually not envisaged. In the unique cases of the Jeremiah and Ezekiel verses, where a new and contrary concept of man appears, where his mind and deeds would not be his exclusive responsibility, one feels that one is at the outer reaches of historical time and prophetic literature. The passages are as strange in their particular books as is the Samuel passage about the sons of Eli in the Bible as a whole; indeed, these prophecies are *eschata,* "extremes," positions at the border of an inexplicable world or beyond it.

---

[6] Saul (1 Sam. 26:19); David (2 Sam. 24:1).

[7] Israel (Isa. 63:17); a prophet (Ezek. 14:9).

[8] Ps. 105:25. It has no independent standing as it is derived from Exod. 4:21, etc. But some commentators, e.g. Duhm and Gunkel, would not admit this example at all. They take הפך as intransitive: "Es wandelte sich (ihr Herz)" (Gunkel, *ad loc.*).

[9] For a qualified exception in Ezekiel see n. 7. It is to be remembered that a prophet is never fully his own free agent.

[10] The question of the authenticity of the passage is not of great importance in this connection.

[11] The expression is similar to Ps. 51:12, quoted above, p. 151.

The Throne Vision of Isaiah*

It is a near consensus of the commentators of Isaiah[1] that chapter 6 is the prophet's report of his consecration to prophecy.[2] There is, in my opinion, very little to support this general view[3] and much to favor the contrary position of a small minority,[4] to wit, that Isaiah had been a prophet before he had the experience reported in this chapter. This position is best put forth by Milgrom.[5] The argument of this paper, however,

---

* These observations were presented first in a considerably condensed form at the meeting of the Society of Biblical Literature in New York in 1970.

[1] The following abbreviations are used: Fohrer, *Jesaja*—G. Fohrer, *Das Buch Jesaja* I²-II² (1966 f.); Jenni—E. Jenni, "Jesajas Berufung in der neueren Forschung," *Theologische Zeitschrift* 15 (1959), pp. 321–339; Knierim—R. Knierim, "The Vocation of Isaiah," *VT* 18 (1968), pp. 47–68; Schmidt—J.M. Schmidt, "Gedanken zum Verstokkungsauftrag Jesajas," *VT* 21 (1971), pp. 68–90; Wildberger—H. Wildberger, *Jesaja* (1968 f.), pp. 230-261. Jenni, Knierim, and particularly Wildberger, pp. 230 f., 261, contain ample bibliographies. A good deal of secondary literature, especially of the Jewish tradition, is cited and discussed by B. Uffenheimer, הקדשת ישעיהו וגלגולה במסורת חז"ל in המקרא ותולדות ישראל (1972), pp. 18–50.

[2] The opinion goes back to late antiquity. It is recorded in Mekhilta to Ex 15:9.

[3] Jenni, who accepts it with such finality that he calls his study "The Call of Isaiah . . .," nevertheless admits "dass ein eigentlicher Berufungsakt garnicht berichtet wird" (p. 336).

[4] Wildberger, pp. 239 f., mentions five to six interpreters who reject the view of the majority. Add H. L. Ginsberg in ע"ז לדוד (D. Ben Gurion Jubilee Volume, 1964), pp. 335 f.; and Schmidt.

[5] J. Milgrom, *VT* 14 (1964), pp. 164–182; בית מקרא 15 [41] (1969/70), pp. 125–140. Wildberger mentions Milgrom but does not address himself to him. Instead, he deals with M. M. Kaplan, *JBL* 45 [1926], pp. 251–259), whom he apparently takes as the representative of the minority, and has no difficulty refuting him. Though I have a certain reserve about some of Milgrom's arguments (in part prompted by the underlying Near Eastern chronology, which is still a bit uncertain), I yet view his case as fundamentally sound. Milgrom reasons thusly: In the first five chapters of Isaiah, excluding the opening nine verses of the book, there are indications of sufficient number and strength for dating these chapters before the death of King Uzziah/Azariah; the event reported in chapter 6 dates

is compatible with either position. The import of the chapter transcends the discussion between the majority and the minority, and its substance is not affected by it. We shall, therefore, proceed without further paying attention to this issue.

Text, Language, Composition

(a) Text. Vss. 1,8,11,12. The question of the divine names—אדני "Lord, Sire"[6] and יהוה—remains unresolved.[7] Vs. 13 bα. For בשלכת and בם (sebir בה) 1QIsaᵃ has משלכת and במה. Speculations, in part based on error of fact, that this reading reveals something of the original text, are quite unconvincing.[8] The *receptus*, uncertain as it is, is hesitatingly accepted and translated "like an oak or a terebinth, whose trunk [or: stump] stands [remains] when the leaves [perhaps: flowers[9]] fall off . . . " or perhaps "like an oak or a terebinth, which, when felled, brings forth new shoots."[10] Vs. 13bβ. קדש, 1QIsaᵃ הקודש. The question of the authenticity of the last three words of the chapter has wrongly been considered a matter of textual criticism. It is exegetical, and its answer depends on the interpretation of the chapter as a whole and on the interpreter's view of Isaiah and his ministry.[11] Judged by the canons of textual criticism, the words are beyond reproach.[12]

---

from the year of this king's death (vs. 1); hence, 1:10—5:39 precedes that event, i.e., Isaiah's vision of God enthroned. In other words, the vision is not the first prophetic experience of Isaiah.

[6] Not "My Lord." See O. Eissfeldt, *Theologisches Wörterbuch zum Alten Testament* I, ed. G. J. Botterweck and H. Ringgren (1970 ff.), coll. 74 f. Eissfeldt renders it "der Allherr."

[7] In vs. 11 the major Qumran text (1QIsaᵃ) has יהוה instead of אדני of the *receptus*. Postmasoretic variants are not considered.

[8] See Wildberger, pp. 233 f.

[9] Cf. Job 15:33 and Joel 1:7.

[10] Approximately following H. Torczyner (N. H. Tur-Sinai) in his German translation *Die Heilige Schrift* . . . III (1936), p. 14, based on the meaning of *nṣb* in Aramaic. T. later relinguished this interpretation; see נ"ה טור־סיני, פשוטו של מקרא ג(א) (1967), pp. 22f.

[11] See below, pp. 167—171.

[12] After 1923 nobody should have claimed that the words had been missing in the Vorlage of the Septuagint, because in that year K. Budde demonstrated that they had been there (*ZAW* 41, p. 167). Budde later restated the matter, as have many others in detail or in summary, including I. Engnell (well argued!), O. Kaiser, R. Kittel (in so common a book as the BH³), J. Lindbloom, I. P. Seierstadt, D. W. Thomas, and H. Wildberger. Yet

(b) Language. Vs. 4. The meaning of אמות, an architectural word, is unknown. Vs. 13. The uncertainties surrounding שלכת and מצבת ("trunk/stump/shoots") were mentioned in (a), and a translation of the second part of the verse was proposed. The first part translates: "When there is yet a mere tenth[13] therein and it, too, is about to turn into herbage [or: land] for grazing [or: turn into ruin], then like the oak ..."[14]

(c) Composition. Many interpreters say that only vss. 1—11 constitute the original prophecy; the last two verses are part(s) of another prophecy (or other prophecies) of Isaiah or are post-Isaianic additions.[15] Their reasons are: (α) The change of the grammatical person in the speech of God from the first (vs.8) to the third (vs.12). (β) The repetition of the content of vs. 11 in vs. 12. (γ) The opposition between prose (vss. 1—11) and poetry (vs. 12). (δ) The mixture of literary genres: vss. 1—11 is a report of a call to prophecy, whereas vs. 12 (f.) is an announcement of punishment of the people.[16]

None of these arguments stands up under scrutiny: (α) The change of the grammatical person, especially in divine speech, is a well established stylistic feature[17]; it is no criterion for sorting out sources

---

the assertion that these words have no Septuagint support reappears, with no attempt to refute the demonstration of the contrary position, in as recent a publication as U. Stegemann, *BZ* N.F. 13 (1969), p. 169.

[13] עשיריה, being the smallest one-word fraction in the Bible, denotes the extreme.

[14] The structure of the verse is set down in nn. 43f. It follows the German translation of M. Buber and F. Rosenzweig; see also Buber, תורת הנביאים (1942), p. 123/*The Prophetic Faith* (1949), p. 133. For ושבה והיתה ל see 29:17; for לבער, 3:14.

[15] The last three words are considered post-Isaianic by a majority of authors; see the surveys of Jenni, p. 330, and Wildberger, p. 241. This is also the opinion of Knierim, p. 61.

[16] The last argument is, of course, not shared by those who deny that chapter 6 is the report of Isaiah's inauguration.

[17] The following list is limited to references to divine speech: Gen 18:14, 19; Ex 23:20—25 (ff.); Nu 11:23; Deut 28:68; 2 Sa 7:11 (the text is corrupt, but the corruption probably does not extend to the change of person); Isa 11:9; 44:24 f.; Hos 1:7. The inverse change, from the third to the first person with God as the grammatical subject, is found at least three times in the environs of our chapter (Isa 3:1—4; 10:12; 22:17—19 ff.). In the just mentioned Exodus passages the grammatical person switches back (23:20—25) and forth (vss. 26—33); similarly Isa 44:24 f. and 26:28; consider also 58:13 f. and Mal 2:17—3:1 (ff.).

and glosses. (β) It could scarcely be maintained that vs. 12 substantially repeats vs. 11. Whereas vs. 11 speaks about the destruction of the land, vs. 12 predicts the exile of the people[18] and illustrates it by the consequent desolation of the country. But whether or not we minimize the difference between vss. 11 and 12, the critical situation would hardly be affected. Repetition of small units of content in biblical poetry and even narrative constitutes no proper argument of source criticism; 1:13a stands unchallenged beside similar 1:11, and 1:14 beside almost identical 1:13b. (γ) The admissibility of a critical claim based on the opposition between prose (here purportedly vss. 1—11) and poetry (purportedly vs. 12) is debatable even in principle; in this case, such claim seems altogether subjective since there is a gaping disagreement as to what is prose and what is poetry in the chapter, as one may realize easily by considering the stichometric layout presented in recent text editions, original or translated.[19] (δ) The question of the literary genre of the chapter was touched upon at the beginning and will later be dealt with more fully.[20] As said before, it is very unlikely that chapter 6 is a report of Isaiah's inauguration (and this is also true of any part of the chapter), but the contrary opinion does not affect the interpretation of the text to be presented here. I shall, therefore, assume for the sake of the argument that the content of part of the chapter is Isaiah's consecration to prophecy. On this assumption and because of the incontrovertible observation that the punishment of the people is announced at the end of the chapter, some scholars distinguish two literary genres in the text. The decisive element of the argument, however, is the rule that mixed genres in prophecy indicate that the text in question is composite. This rule is insufficiently established, to say the least; it cannot be used as a criterion of criticism. With the elimination of this element, the argument falls to the ground.

The difficulties in the understanding of the chapter come to the fore in vss. 9 f. The reader of a hitherto simple story is here arrested by the

---

[18] Compare the similar expression in Ez 11:16.

[19] *Biblia Hebraica Stuttgartensia* (1968); *The New English Bible* (1970); commentaries with translations by O. Kaiser (1960); G. Fohrer, *Jesaja* (1966); H. Wildberger (1969).

[20] See below, p. 163.

divine order, given to Isaiah, to go and say to the people, "Listen as you
may, you will never understand; watch as you may, you will never recognize," followed by the directive, intended only for the prophet, "Make the
mind of this people gross, their ears heavy, their eyes bedaubed, lest they
see with their eyes, hear with their ears, their mind understands, and they
repent and be healed."[21] Bible readers are uneasy about statements that
God hardened the heart of Pharaoh, Sihon and others[22]; they are dis-
mayed by the notion that God appointed Isaiah to do just this to a whole
nation in order—this is the assumption—that they become guilty and
consequently be punished. This flies in the face of theology, of the common concept of prophecy, and of the exegesis of Isaiah. It was a theological maxim of biblical antiquity, and has been in vogue ever since, that
God desires not the death of the wicked but rather their repentance and
survival (Ez 18:23 and elsewhere); the prevalent notion is that the task of
the prophet is to exhort the people to repent and, most assuredly, not to
prevent repentance; and, accordingly, the predominant opinion among
scholars is that Isaiah did the expected: he urged repentance on the
nation.[23]

Confronted with what seems to border on a philological aporia, many
modern scholars have taken recourse to either of two nonphilological
solutions; they may be dubbed the psychological solution and the theological solution.[24] According to the first, behind the highly literary
expression of vss. 9 f. there resides a case of habit turning second nature.
Continuous rejection of God's word gradually closes the mind to perceiv-

---

[21] Alternatively, though somewhat less likely, "and it will again be hale." Where this
interpretation is accepted, it is usually based on the revocalization 'וְשָׁב', but masoretic וָשָׁב
may sustain this meaning; see G. Sauer, in *Wort-Gebot-Glaube . . . W. Eichrodt zum 80.
Geburtstag* (ed. H. J. Stoebe, 1970, pp. 277—296), pp. 282 f.

[22] See "The Death of the Sons of Eli," above, pp. 149 f.

[23] On repentance in Isaiah, see below, n. 33.

[24] See G. von Rad, *Theologie des Alten Testaments* II (1960), pp. 162—164. His
approach is refreshing and his critique justified. Yet he makes a concession. He admits
recourse to the criticized solutions if the exegete has exhausted all means of understanding
the text philologically, i.e., on its own terms (p. 164). It is a regrettable concession. The
student who has recourse to it ceases to be an exegete. He engages in an activity which
ought to be left to others. It would be more salubrious to say plainly and not in effect that
he cannot explain the passage.

ing it; unwillingness becomes inability. It is the automatic punishment of refusal.

The theological solution eliminates the element of divine command from the vision, the prophet's primary experience, and explains the bulk of vss. 9 f. as a record of his subsequent reflection. When Isaiah reviewed his career in later years, he found that the mind of the people was more closed at its end than at its beginning. He concluded that it was his activity which had produced this close-mindedness, and since he had been ministering at God's behest and for God's sake, it was natural for him to say that God had told him to close the people's mind. The command to dull the senses of the people was never an early, primary reality, and its report in our text is the consequence of a different circumstance—the prophet's interpretation of a later, secondary reality, the indifference of the people, in terms of an imagined past event, the divine injunction to create that indifference.[25]

Both solutions must be rejected.

(a) Both are psychologistic. Their protagonists do not undertake to interpret the text according to its own norms and intentions but rather to uncover and describe psychological mechanisms believed to have played a major part in its composition. Having performed this, they consider their work done. The tacit presupposition, expressed in its purest form, is that a text, a religious act, a work of art do not contain concepts and values that cannot be described in the language of psychology, usually by way of a genetic definition, and that such description is all that matters.

(b) Psychologism, consistently applied, drains the humanities, as well as other areas of endeavor, of their essence. But, at least, it has the virtue of consistency and it presents us, in the humanities as elsewhere, with a system embodying a recurrent theme of philosophy since Greek antiquity. These attributes fade, however, in the special instance of Old Testament study. Here psychologistic solutions seem to manifest them-

---

[25] Some adherents of the first view are mentioned by von Rad, ibid. As to the second view, G. B. Gray wrote as early as 1912 (*A Critical . . . Commentary on Isaiah* I, p. 101) that a few scholars assumed the influence of Isaiah's later experience in his report of the earlier vision, and that the experience may be reflected in the terms of the divine commission. Since then this view has gained considerable acceptance.

selves only when the going is rough and an exegetical answer unavailable. In the process, philology is surrendered; moreover, psychologism is itself abused since it is employed only as a mere convenience.

(c) In our case, the psychologistic solutions do not fulfill even what little they promise. According to the first solution, the inability to understand is the result of a natural, inexorable process. Now a natural, inexorable process does not need prophetic intervention. And should one argue that Isaiah's function is merely to work with the natural process, to strengthen and accelerate it, then the supposed philological aporia, which has given rise to the proposed solution, remains and the proposition has solved nothing: supportive prophetic occluding of the mind is occluding of the mind, and the concern of the reader is not lessened when he is told that the prophet only accelerated what was happening anyway. What disturbs him is the principle that occluding of the mind is a legitimate device of a prophet.

(d) The second solution is so patently apologetic that one marvels at the favor it has found in this century. As usual, apologetics is poor exegetics. In this case, its champions reject the notion that God directs His prophet to make the people unreceptive of His word and incapable of repentance, yet they accept it a moment later when it is presented as the result of the prophet's retrospection, reflection, and interpretation. This differentiation is theologically useless and literarily damaging. Theologically, i.e., in the light of the ordered totality of beliefs and views culled from the words of Isaiah, it makes no difference whether 6:10 tells about Isaiah's primary experience (the vision) or secondary experience (the interpretation of his frustration); in both the cases the verse contains his belief, and it is the same belief in both. In fine, the offence to theology is not removed, the text is tortured in the attempt to extract a conventionally acceptable meaning, and its literary substance is fatally damaged. If, indeed, vss. 9 f. are an interpretation in retrospect, the question "How long, O Lord?" of vs. 11 has a hollow ring. Still, there may be some to whom this solution affords the comfort of a God concept more sublime than that of Isaiah. I feel this is cold comfort.

An important contribution toward resolving the enigma of the chapter is Knierim's article of 1968. His solution is based on the comparison of Isa 6 with 1 Ki 22:19—22 (f.), the story of Micaiah ben Imlah.[26] A juxtaposition of the pertinent excerpts of the two texts will be useful.[27]

1 Kings 22	Isaiah 6
(19) I saw the Lord sitting on his throne	(1) I saw the Lord sitting on a throne high and exalted.
with all the host of heaven in attendance on His right and on His left.	(2) Seraphim were in attendance on Him. . .
(20) The Lord said, "Who is to beguile Ahab. . .?"	(8) I heard the Lord saying, "Whom shall I send? Who is to go for Us?"
(21) The *ruaḥ*[28] stepped forth and said, "None but I will beguile him."[29]	I said, "Send none but me."[29]
(22) He said, "Go forth and do it."	(9) He said, "Go and say. . ."

[26] Knierim, pp. 54 f., 57—59. He is not the first to compare the texts, but nobody has done it as well as he. Indeed, he is unduly modest, crediting others with good observations (see p. 55, n. 1) that they have never made. (He has been preceded by M. M. Kaplan, *JBL* 45 [1926], pp. 255—258; W. Zimmerli, *Ezechiel* [1959—1969], pp. 18—21; and Wildberger, pp. 234—236. Still others are mentioned by Zimmerli. M.-L. Henry, *Prophet und Tradition* [1969], pp. 22—27 [f.], emphasizes the dependence of Isa 6 on 1 Ki 22:19 ff., but draws conclusions which go far beyond anything warranted by similarity, dependence, or the like.)

[27] Here linguistic details and simple narrative elements are set down; emerging similarities will provide a basis for subsequent more elaborate comparisons. At the end the structures of the texts will be compared in a similar manner.

[28] Like Greek *pneuma* and Latin *spiritus, ruaḥ* means "wind" and "spirit," occasionally both at the same time. The second meaning is the usual translation in this verse, and for good reasons. Yet the first, impressively propounded by A. Klostermann (*Die Bücher Samuelis und der Könige* [1887], p. 389, nn. q and r), is no less present; compare: (Yhwh "Who takes clouds for His chariot, Who rides on the wings of a *ruaḥ,* Who makes *ruaḥ*s His messengers, flames of fire His ministers" (Ps. 104: 3—4; cf. further 147:18).

[29] אני אפתנו (1 Ki 22:21) and הנני שלחני (Isa 6:8) achieve the same end—emphasis on the speaker as the ready agent—by the same means, the duplication of the pronoun: אני (אפתנו), free form plus bound form in the casus rectus: (שלחני) הנני, bound form (attached to the deictic basis הנה) plus bound form in the casus obliquus. This means that אני and הנני have the same function and that, in consequence, the frequent two-clause translation of Isa 6:8: "Here I am, send me" is incorrect.

The similarity of the excerpts leaps to the eye; it enjoins us from dealing with the second passage, Isaiah 6, without considering the first, 1 Kings 22.[30] Nor would we say that the author of the second utilized the form of the first with no intention about its content because a close look reveals a similarity that transcends style and genre. The Kings narrative depicts a session of the heavenly court of law and administration. The verdict, Ahab's condemnation, has just been reached, and the question, the first words of the record, is how to implement it: "Who is to beguile Ahab to march to Ramoth-gilead and fall there?" The Isaiah scene, also portraying a session of the heavenly law court, is identical in substance to that of Kings. This conclusion is warranted by the accumulated similarities of circumstances: the heavenly ceremony, the verdict (which is the condemnation of the people: "lest ... they be healed" and "cities without inhabitants"), and the search for an executioner ("Who is to go?"). This is to say that also in Isaiah the verdict has been rendered, and that the report begins immediately thereafter. Both passages, then, are reports of visions of judgment.

Further common elements are the willingness of the executioners to volunteer and, especially, the manner of the execution: the impairment of the mind of the condemned parties so that they would run inexorably into their ruin; פתה "beguiling" says 1 Ki 22, השמן לב "fattening the heart" Isa 6. It follows that dulling the mind of the people, which Isaiah is bidden to do, is not a device to make them guilty and thus provide God with a reason for punishment, as is the case in the stories of Pharaoh, Sihon, and others,[31] but is the first phase of punishment. Unlike the case of hardening Pharaoh's heart, the fattening of the people's heart does not precede their guilt and cause it but follows it and is caused by it. Their guilt issues from the sinfulness of Judah (and Israel), accruing over the decades and centuries before Uzziah's death. The vision, prominently dated,[32] marks the end of an era; no more delay, the time of punishment

---

[30] "First" and "second" are used with chronological implications, i.e., earlier and later. But this, too, is not a necessary presupposition of the argument. If a reversal of the relative dating of the texts is preferrred, 1 Ki 22 becomes a very early and inestimable commentary on Isa 6.

[31] See above, p. 159.

[32] See Knierim, p. 49.

has come! Isaiah's commission is similar to that of Amos, who tells the people that time and again God gave them a chance, five chances in all, but they let them pass (Amos 4:6–11); now they have no further chance (vss. 12 f.), and God will delay no longer (7:8; 8:2).

Isaiah is unique in that he is commissioned not only to announce the punishment but also, and mainly, to bring it about. This is the sense of "Daube their eyes, lest they see and be saved." When this sense is recognized for what it is: an extension of the sense and purpose of the prophecies of Amos and other prophets, then there is no reason for being offended, turning apologetic, or casting about for psychological or theological, i.e., nonphilological interpretations. Not only are they unacceptable and inadequate to the task; they are also unnecessary.

This interpretation elicits new questions, which join some old ones, yet unanswered.

(1) Have we plumbed the exegetical potential of the comparison of Isa 6 and 1 Ki 22? Probably not; at any rate, where there is so much similarity, it may be rewarding to consider dissimilarities. (2) How is Isaiah to dull the mind of the people? (3) The problems that the end of the chapter raises (vss. 11–13) have received but scant attention. (4) Why does Isaiah, charged to make the ears of the people heavy, continue his ministry for decades in a manner that is inconsonant with his charge? Commissioned to foreclose repentance, what is his authority to call for it?[33]

---

[33] H. W. Wolff says that Isaiah never urged repentance (*Zeitschrift für Theologie und Kirche* 48 [1951], p. 137 f.; reprinted in his *Gesammelte Studien zum Alten Testament* [1964], pp. 138 f.), but he does not refer to 1:16 f.; 31:6; and the less explicit verse 2:5 (if he thinks that it is genuine). To be sure, of the explicit calls for repentence only 31:6 is later than the death of Uzziah, but in effect the totality of Isaiah's activity did amount to this urge, and it will be difficult to maintain that he was naive or unconcerned about this. (Wolff's attempt to draw conclusions from the name שאר ישוב is blunted by the uncertainty surrounding its meaning.) Also Sauer (n. 21), pp. 291–293, denies that the idea of repentance is, even implicitly (1:16 f.), contained in the genuine Isaianic passages. Against this understanding of Isaiah or Amos see G. Fohrer, *JBL* 80 (1961), p. 312; G. F. Hasel, *The Remnant* ... (1972), p. 231, n. 71; and especially O. Keel, "Rechttun oder Annahme des drohenden Gerichts?," *BZ* N.F. 21 (1977), pp. 200–218, an excellent statement, cogently argued. (It is obvious that I do not follow Keel's interpretation of Isa 6, p. 209, n. 37.) As

(1) The comparison with First Kings, far from having run its useful course, will permeate much of the examination of the other questions. At this point only one major difference shall be pointed out: In Micaiah's prophecy there are four protagonists, in Isaiah's three. Micaiah's four are God, the judge, and His court; the *ruaḥ* ("wind-spirit"), who carries out one part of the mission; Micaiah, who carries out the other part; and Ahab, the condemned party. Isaiah's three are God and His court; Isaiah, who carries out the total mission; and the people, the condemned party. Correlative with the reduction in the number of the protagonists in Isaiah is a reduction in mythological substance and a corresponding strengthening of the human element.[34] This is to say that the essential change from Kings to Isaiah is not one of literary economy or regrouping of concepts but of the function of a prophet: Participation in the deliberation of the court, announcement of the judgment, and execution of the judgment are in Isaiah's report not allotted to different beings but united in his person.[35]

(2) With regard to the manner of executing the punishment, we find both similarity and dissimilarity between the Isaiah and the Micaiah reports. The similarity is one of substance: depriving the condemned of a clear insight into their situations, undertaken by the four hundred prophets in Kings, by the one prophet in Isaiah. The dissimilarity is one of form: 1 Ki 22 tells us the essentials of the story, the command and the performance, in a simple and concrete way; a *ruaḥ* of lie speaks through Ahab's prophets. The Isaiah report, on the other hand, is limited to the

---

to Milgrom, he overlooks no pertinent passage but he, too, is handicapped by a hypothesis. After justifiedly removing from consideration 28:12 and 30:15 as having nothing to do with repentance, he disposes of 31:6 by emending the text, claiming linguistic and contextual reasons (see above [n. 5], p. 169, n.4/p.130, n. 24). Since the linguistic reason is, in my opinion, not applicable (the discussion would be too detailed for this note), and the contextual reason is wrong (cf. 2:2–4,5), there remains only one rationale for the emendation, the wish to satisfy the hypothesis that Isaiah did not call for repentance after the throne vision. For 31:6, see Fohrer, *Jesaja* II, p. 122.

[34] Kaplan (n. 26), p. 256, sees this and comments on it in his own way.

[35] See also below, p. 173. Prophets carry out their mission because they participated in the deliberations where the decisions were reached; see Jer 23:21 f.; Amos 3:7 f.; 7:1–9; 8:1–3. The idea is also reflected in Isa 44:26; cf. A. Rofé, האמונה במלאכים בישראל . . . (1969), p. 117 [dissertation, Jerusalem].

command; moreover, it couches it in metaphorical language whose precise meaning is not self-evident: "Make the mind of the people gross . . .
lest they understand." What does this mean realistically, and how shall
Isaiah do it? Specifically, since he is a prophet and works through his
prophecy, which of his prophecies tend to dull the mind? Buber asks this
question and answers, no doubt, rightly: prophecies of salvation that
quiet the frightened souls of the people and confirm their illusions.[36]
This interpretation, at which Buber arrives by internal reasoning, is
squarely supported by the Micaiah story. A prognosis of salvation is what
Ahab wants to hear and what he is given, and this prognosis becomes his
undoing (1 Ki 22:6, 11 f., [15]). Postponing for the moment the problem
of a more precise identification of the corresponding prophecies in
Isaiah,[37] we note that what we have is not dissimilarity—false prophecy
(in Kings), true prophecy (in Isaiah)—but rather a point of similarity,
indeed identity, of both reports—euphoria tending to obfuscate the mind
and its antidote, the respective statements of Micaiah and Isaiah that
obfuscating is being, or is going to be, induced (1 Ki 22:20—23; Isa 6:10).

(3) From the vantage point of modern exegesis of Isa 6 one would
think that the problems of the end of the chapter reside in vs. 13 or perhaps vss. 12—13; but with an eye to the comparison with 1 Ki 22 one is
prompted to give vs. 11 equal attention. Vs. 11a represents the second
major difference between the two reports of revelation. Isaiah's question
"How long, O Lord?" has no counterpart in Micaiah's account; struc-
turally the end of that account corresponds to the end of Isa 6:10. It has
been suggested that we look to the laments of the Psalter, in particular to
the national laments, where the call "How long, O God?" is a common
feature (e.g., Ps 74:10).[38] This suggestion is perhaps motivated by the
hope of gaining insight into the meaning of Isaiah's utterance. The

---

[36] M. Buber, תורת הנביאים (1942), p. 122/*The Prophetic Faith* (1949), p. 131. Schmidt
rejects Buber's view (pp. 70—73). He is certainly right that chapter 7 supports this view
neither by content nor position in the book. He is also justified in taking exception to
Buber's remark that chapter 6 is the work of the "mature" prophet. As to his further
argument (the main argument, although it appears as a brief appendix to the others) that
the "betr(effenden) Texte," i.e., the extant prophecies, do not uphold Buber's position, see
the reference of the following note.

[37] See below, p. 171.

[38] Wildberger, p. 257.

respective literary situations, however, have nothing in common. There is, however, a fairly close analogue, and it is in the prophets: "The angel of the Lord said, 'Ah, Lord Hosts, how long will you not have mercy on Jerusalem and the cities of Judah with which you have been angry now for seventy years?'" (Zech 1:12). The two passages are identical or similar in language (עד מתי), literary genre (vision report), content (a vision of the heavenly council[39]), intent, (eliciting from God a limitation of punishment), and the station of the speaker: When Isaiah, his lips cleansed (vss. 5—7), says, "Send none but me," he assumes his place among the other members of the council, the Seraphim, who, in turn, correspond to the angels of Zechariah's vision.

The intent of the question of Isaiah, the member of the court, is the limitation of punishment decreed in court. It is the same question as in Zechariah's report, whereas the Micaiah story presents no parallel. There the *ruah* volunteers and is commissioned, and with this the scene ends. On the other hand, the angel of Zechariah does not have a punitive or, for that matter, any executive task,[40] nor does Zechariah himself. Isaiah stands in the middle between Micaiah and Zechariah; again we see him combining two roles in his person.[41] God's initial response to Isaiah's intercession is not encouraging. The destruction will go on and on. But when the point of complete annihilation is almost reached with only a small remnant left in the land, events will take a turn, and this remnant will be spared.

Comparable interpretations of vs. 13 have been rejected for textual, linguistic, or literary reasons, but none of these reasons has merit. The argument from text, viz., that the end of vs. 13b is a late addition (as evidenced by its—alleged—absence in the Vorlage of the Septuagint), has been dealt with above.[42] The linguistic argument says that, in view of the admitted dubiety surrounding בשלכת מצבת בם, vs. 13b is too uncertain

---

[39] In Zecharaiah, the scene takes place at the entrance of the court of law; thus E. Sellin, *Das Zwölfprophetenbuch*[2] [3] (1929), p. 494; (T. Robinson-) F. Horst, *Die Zwölf Kleinen Propheten*[2] (1954), pp. 218 f.

[40] There are different opinions about the role of the angel in Zech 5:8; see Y. Kaufmann, תולדות האמונה הישראלית ד' (1956), p. 257, n. 65/*History of the Religion of Israel IV* (1977), p. 318, n. 65.

[41] Cf. above, p. 165.

[42] Note 12.

to sustain an interpretation as consequential as the one presented here. This objection is not well taken. There is too much certain material in the verse to justify such skepticism. When vs. 13 is read as one sentence—for uncalled-for fragmentation is likewise undue skepticism—and its first half, not just its first quarter, is taken as its protasis, this half[43] combines with the certain elements of the other half[44] to provide ample support for the proposed exposition. As to the literary argument, there is nothing in the literary unit, the vision report, to refute this interpretation. A prophet intercedes with God in view of an impending punishment, and God assents in part; it is a plot of which we should not be suspicious.

The true reason for the rejection of this interpretation lies with a general theory about Isaiah's prophecies and is buttressed by an observation about the redacting of biblical and especially prophetic books. It is the theory that Isaiah did not prophesy—unconditional—salvation;[45] and since vs. 13b contains a prediction of salvation with no condition attached, it is not genuine. The supporting observation is that redactors and early readers provided cheerful or comforting conclusions for biblical books or parts of books that had originally ended with rebuke or gloom; the hopeful ending of Isa 6 is a case in point.

We can quickly dispose of the ancillary observation: it is not applicable. The cognition of the ancient habit of inauthentically appending an encouraging end to a stern text is not that of a symmetrical relation; the mere existence of an encouraging end of a stern text does not justify the inference that this end is an inauthentic appendix.[46]

---

[43] "When there is yet a mere tenth therein and it, too, is about to turn into herbage [or: land] for grazing [or: turn into ruin]—"

[44] "—then its מצבת will be holy growth [זרע, or: plant; cf. 17:(10), 11; Jer 2:21; for Middle Hebrew, see the passages quoted in Ben Yehudah's dictionary, p. 1405, left, bottom] as is the case with an oak or a terebinth which . . . a מצבת . . ."

[45] Authors usually mean unconditional albeit they do not always say so. The condition is Israel's repentance and reform. J. Vollmer, who shares this view, although he does not happen to apply it explicitly to the end of chapter 6, gives expression to his resignation that, in our time, this view is on the defensive and its followers are few; see ZAW 80 (1968), pp. 343 f., nn. 1,5, (6). I think he has little reason for such melancholy.

[46] This is obvious, and it is not likely that anyone will disagree in principle. But the observation about comforting endings of (parts of) biblical books sometimes figures in inductive reasoning so insinuative that the criticized inference seems natural and beyond a reasonable doubt.

The theory proper, strictly conceived, can only be maintained in disregard of the texts. The following passages are generally considered genuine:[47] "I and my children are signs and portents in Israel from the Lord Hosts Who dwells on Mount Zion" (8:18). "What shall one answer the envoys of that nation? 'The Lord has founded Zion, and the afflicted of His people (will) find refuge there'" (14:32). "The Lord says, 'I am laying in Zion a stone for a foundation, an ashlar block ... for a solid foundation'" (28:16). "Pronouncement of the Lord, Whose fire burns in Zion, Whose furnace stands in Jerusalem" (31:9). These passages express the idea, and some emphasize it, of God's close relation to Zion.[48] He does not leave it, as in Ez 10:4, 18 f.; 11:23, intent on giving it over to a destruction and ruin of indefinite duration. Isaiah does not recognize true mobility of God[49]; to him God is defined by Zion.[50] It should be noted, though the opposite has been claimed,[51] that stereotyped phrases are not used in these verses nor is there, with the possible exception of 8:18, a trace of an official lingo; the prophet mints his own expressions and means what he says. Now it would be wholly incongruous with his thought that God would continue to dwell at Zion yet would exchange Israel for another people; the somewhat similar but much more limited plan to make another nation a reliable and lasting instrument of His proved to be ill-fated (Isa 10:5 ff.). The conclusion thus imposes itself that these four passages (8:18; 14:32; 28:16; 31:9) imply the consolation of Israel.

The remnant to be spared in Zion unconditionally is tiny and

[47] A reasonably comprehensive check of critical opinions shows that the genuineness of the first three passages is acknowledged virtually universally (no exceptions noted) and that of the last passage almost so. Further search may well produce additional passages that share the pertinent feature with the quoted onces and which enjoy broad critical consensus.

[48] J. Schreiner, *Sion-Jerusalem, Jahwes Königssitz* ... (1963), pp. 243-270, and also 167–173, deals with the shape that the notion, expressed in the title of the book, takes in Isaiah. The book includes examination of passages which are only tangential to our point and of others whose authenticity is not infrequently contested.

[49] Passages like 29:2 f., 6, which seemingly differ , indeed insist on Yhwh's close topographical relation to Zion.

[50] Compare also G. von Rad (n. 24), pp. 166–179.

[51] See Fohrer, *Jesaja*, a.l

wretched (6:13; 14:32[52]), a shadow of the former magnitude and glory of the nation. An illustration of such greatly reduced form of life, yet assuredly a continuation of life, is 7:21–25.[53] But this shrunken, miserable remnant is conceived as the nucleus for the possible survival of the nation. When conditions become more favorable, it will be the stock from which the tree can grow again; זרע "(seed) growth"[54] has an unmistakable implication.

Cognizance of the Isaianic concept of a small, pitiful remnant, preserved in the land to make a new beginning possible, in no way prejudges the problem of the genuineness of the predictions of a glorious future for Israel, among which the predictions 2:2–5; 9:1–6; and 11:1–9 (ff.) are prominent. Their nature and the exegetical approach that they require are quite different. In order to keep things in perspective, we ought to bear in mind that the word "consolation" as it is applied to 6:13 receives its due connotation from its context: the consolation will not reach many and will not cheer some whom it reaches.

(4) The last problem is the discrepancy between divine charge and prophetic implementation. Stated in a preliminary way: dispensing placebos is the purpose of Isaiah's mission, calling to reform is the essence of the bulk of his known prophecies. Not that he has forgotten the mission. Its theme reappears in 29:10: "The Lord has poured on you a *ruaḥ* of torpor; He has closed your eyes 'II' and muffled your heads 'I'."[55] As was said before,[56] its implementation is by means of prophecies that, painting a rosy future, distract the attention and the energies of the people from the danger and the urgent needs of the present. If we proceed

---

[52] For the latter verse see O. Procksch, *Jesaja I* (1930), p. 207. Zephaniah, in 3:12, probably alludes to it. If so, the above interpretation of Isa 14:32 and perhaps the interpretations of kindred passages of Isaiah have preexilic support.

[53] For vss. 23–25 see N.H. Tur-Sinai 1967 (n. 10), p. 27.

[54] See n. 44. The picture, though not the word זרע, recurs in Job 14:7–9. The small and miserable band of survivors which yet is the nucleus of a new beginning unites both aspects of the biblical concept of the remnant. For these aspects the reader may consult Hasel (n. 33), pp. 239 f., n. 91.

[55] The passage is often assigned to a late stage of Isaiah's activity but for no sufficient reason; see O. Eissfeldt, *Einleitung in das Alte Testament*[2] (1956), p. 380. But it is safe to place it after Uzziah's death.

[56] See above, p. 166.

to ask, which, if any, of the prophecies of record were uttered to induce euphoria within the people, identification proves impossible. The first complication resides in the dispute about the authenticity of (some of) the prophecies of the great salvation and radiant future: A student may be reluctant to base even a side argument of a relatively certain issue, the genuineness of chapter 6, on a relatively uncertain issue, that of chapter 11 and congeners. Or, if he considers these prophecies genuine, he may be unwilling to identify them as the means actually employed by the prophet to dull perceptiveness and prevent repentance. But the main difficulty is that we cannot reasonably assume that the euphoric prophecies have been preserved, whereas a case for the opposite assumption has everything in its favor. It is in the nature of things that those who began the chain of tradition and formed the nucleus of the eventual Book of Isaiah, the prophet himself or his disciples, did not incorporate words that were neither true nor meant to be true.

But if it is difficult to produce a record indicating that Isaiah carried out the injunction of chapter 6—if such a record is extant at all, if indeed there had ever been a record—there is no difficulty in showing what he actually did. Most prophecies which, with some reasonable criticism, can be called Isaianic (their number is large enough to leave a comfortable latitude for disagreement without materially affecting the argument) are not designed to lull the listener into a false sense of security and well-being. Quite the contrary: Even if our observation that in later years Isaiah explicitly called for repentance (31:6) is disparaged as an isolated case, the many castigations and pictures of imminent judgment are uttered with the intention to urge repentance.[57] This, then, is the problem restated: Isaiah is sent to close the gates of repentance yet he holds them open and prompts the people to enter. The answer: After the vision of judgment, Isaiah's extant prophecies were spoken mainly or exclusively in behalf of the remnant to enlarge it and fully secure its survival.[58]

This interpretation may perhaps be viewed with skepticism. Apparently it questions Isaiah's loyalty as a prophet of God in general, and as His emissary to bring His judgment to pass in particular. Is he

[57] See n. 33.
[58] An inkling of this interpretation is found in F. Delitzsch, *Commentar über* . . . *Jesaja*⁴ (1889), p. 131.

double-crossing God?[59] Indeed, the interpretation seems to intensify the contradiction. What first appeared to be a moderate contradiction, an inconsistency, perhaps biographical, perhaps only literary, is now presented as a deliberate counteraction with the prophet substituting his own design for God's yet without proposing to turn in his commission, as Jeremiah did. At this impasse we again look, beyond Isa 6, to 1 Ki 22. We see there that the judgment has been given: Ahab's end at Ramoth-gilead; the mode of its execution determined: seduction to go to battle and win the day; and the executioner appointed: the *ruaḥ* of lie acting through Ahab's prophets. The king's situation seems hopeless but it is not, for there is Micaiah's prophecy. Micaiah tells Ahab and all present what he was shown and what, or who, makes his prophets prophesy. For one moment the curtain of present and future history is pulled aside, and Ahab can see, decide, and be saved, saved even after condemnation. Possible doubt about this interpretation has perhaps been anticipated by the author, for he gives Micaiah one more verse, appended to the vision report, which sums up the sense of the scene in plain words: "Now see how the Lord has put a *ruaḥ* of lie in the mouth of all these prophets of yours because the Lord has decreed ruin upon you" (1 Ki 22:23).[60] The

---

[59] Because Schmidt takes vss. 9 f. seriously, he indeed voices concern, though with restraint (pp. 84–86). He speaks of the "risk" of Isaiah's giving away the divine secret: the people may actually repent. To the implied question "How could the prophet do this?" he proposes two alternative answers. The first, which he greatly favors as commanding the overwhelming probability, is that Isaiah could give away the heavenly secret because there was no earthly chance that the people would believe him. The other answer is the one proposed here, but Schmidt mentions it only as a remote possibility (p. 89). It is the purpose of these pages to show that this answer is not beset with the uncertainty Schmidt thinks it is. But if the undertaking fails to convince the reader, Schmidt's first choice is, to my awareness, the only alternative. It should be noted, however, that this alternative in turn requires certain ancillary assumptions which have their own problems. E.g., the last three words of the chapter are addressed to an audience different from and later than that of the bulk of the report: the disciples of the prophet (thus Schmidt, pp. 84, 88). If so, we would have to assume further that Isaiah reversed the earlier negative sense of vs. 13 by the addition of three words, overturning the original syntax in the process. We would have to, but would we agree to do so?

[60] Some interpretars, not getting the sense of the verse, hold that it is a gloss. Thus E. Würthwein, in *Das ferne und das nahe Wort: Festschr. L. Rost,* ed. F. Maass (1967), p. 250, n. 12, following P. Volz. This judgment is part of his treatment of the narrative, which he cuts up into several components, I think with insufficient reasons.

burden of the story is not the session of the heavenly court but the fact of prophecy, i.e., that a man witnessed the session and tells what he witnessed.[61] With Micaiah's final words Ahab's fate is placed in his own hands for just a few more moments; even in the eleventh hour man still has the freedom of decision.

The prophetic situation in Isaiah is the same in principle but it is more tightly knit. Literarily, this is the consequence of the reduced number of protagonists.[62] In the role of Isaiah there are merged the roles of the *ruaḥ* and of Micaiah. He is to deprive the people of the understanding of their situation, which is the first act of the implementation of their punishment: "Make the mind of the people gross" (vs. 10)—he is ordered to do what the *ruaḥ* of First Kings is ordered to do. But at the same time he is charged to warn them, to announce that he is about to do just this: "Listen attentively, yet there is no chance that you will understand" (vs. 9).[63] The Micaiah story contains no single sentence expressing the warning. The whole vision report is a red alert, but in it the three verses 20—22 stand out, and each verse's "beguiling," three mentions in all, penetrate even a dense mind. Both prophets sound the alarm at the instruction of God (1 Ki 22:19a; Isa 6:9a), Who is playing the game with open cards. In the last hour of the lucidity of mind, when the people are yet in the possession of their faculties, they are told, "Know what these prophecies will do to you." The corollary which everybody can apply to himself is evident: not to be blinded, not to be beguiled. The divine word of Isa 6:9b, like its counterpart of 1 Ki 22:22b, is not an absolute, a "mighty word" that nobody can evade,[64] but a statement intended to keep the options open yet a little longer and make salvation yet possible.

---

[61] Isa 21:1—10 is exemplary. It contains numerous derivatives from roots for seeing (ראה, צפה, חזה) and hearing (שמע, קשב), but at the pivotal points of the report a verb for telling (הגיד) is placed: "Go, post a lookout, let him tell what he sees" (vs. 6), and: "My [people] ... what I have heard from the Lord Hosts ... I have told you" (vs. 10).

[62] See above p. 165.

[63] אל expresses impossibility or great improbability here and in Jer 46:6; Ps 34:6; 121:3; Job 20:17; 40:32.

[64] Jenni, pp. 336 f.; A.F. Key, "The Magical Background of Isa 6:9—13," *JBL* 86 (1967), pp. 198—204. Since normally the word of a prophet is not a "Machtwort, das dynamisch wirkt" (Jenni), the assertion that Isa 6:9 is one ought to be substantiated by an explanation why the norm does not apply here. The explanation is not presented.

It is hard to withstand the lure of "Go ahead and be victorious!" (1 Ki 22:6,12,15) or the fata morgana of future bliss, but it is possible. If one is forewarned that his eyes will be daubed, he can overturn the bucket and spill the daub; if he is told he will be hypnotized, he may be able to resist. Isaiah, far from being unfaithful, is loyal to his Master in all that he tells the people, loyal above suspicion.

The Book of Kings tells of Micaiah that he related his vision to the assembled kings and commoners, and that he capped his testimony with the epitome: You are being led to your undoing (1 Ki 22:23). To these two features of the Kings report only one corresponds in the Isaiah report, publicity, but it is the more important one. In general, Isaiah manifests concern repeatedly and in various ways with the dissemination of his prophecies; see 8:2; 20:3; 30:8.[65] In particular, the report about the throne vision with its crucial verse "Make the mind of this people gross, lest they understand ... " very likely reached the public in his lifetime. Another prophecy, quite similar in one point, says that God has led the people astray by closing their eyes (29:9—12[-14]), and it is assuredly a public address.[66] This latter prophecy is adequately understood and makes its full impact only against the background of chapter 6.[67] It is therefore very likely that the public address 29:9 ff. presupposes public knowledge of 6:9 f.[68]

The epitome of 1 Ki 22:23 has no analogue in Isa 6. At this point the

---

[65] We know of one case where he withholds their propagation (8:16—20). The context suggests that this is a case and these are prophecies of a special kind.

[66] See above, p. 170.

[67] The public character of 29:9 ff. follows from the imperatives in vs. 9 and the 2nd pers. pl. throughout. The relationship between 29:9 ff. and 6:9 f. is further indicated, albeit in a minor way, in that both share the trislegomenon √שׁעע (the third occurrence is 32:3, emended pointing). The "prophets" and "seers" of 29:10 are generally, and rightly, taken as wrong glosses (cf. the masoretic accents).

[68] Schmidt insists most salutarily throughout the last quarter of his study that the charge to make the people obdurate, a constituent of the vision, was, or was made in the course of time, the object of a public proclamation. While he reasons along several lines, different from those followed here, the decisive and ingratiatingly simple step is the first one: He refuses to accept the premise of Jenni, Wildberger, and others, almost axiomatic these days, that Isaiah could not and did not publicly proclaim the content of vss. 9 f. (pp. 79f.). Resolved to take the text by its words, he uncovers in vs. 9, literally understood, a paramount structural and interpretive element of the whole report.

correspondence between the two reports is incomplete—leaving aside possible other reasons—because of the different literary forms. 1 Ki 22:19 ff. is part of a narrative. It is characteristic of a narrative to create with ease, render in the concrete, and arrange in the order of natural occurrence a comparatively large number of constitutive elements. The report of the Book of Isaiah does not share this narrative versatility with the Book of Kings, and this fact may account for the absence of a correlative to the public epitome of Micaiah.

Let us, in conclusion, compare the structures of 1 Ki 22:(2—)19—23 and Isa 6 as distinct from the earlier comparison of language and simple narrative matter.

	1 Kings 22	Isaiah 6
I	Narrative introduction, talk of the kings, first vision (vss. 2—18).	"In the year of King Uzziah's death" (v. 1aα[69]).
II	Statement of the fact and some details of the vision (vs. 19).	Statement of the fact and some details of the vision (vs. 1aβ—4).
III		Purification of the prophet (vss. 5—7).
IV	God's inquiry about an agent (vs. 20).	God's inquiry about an agent (vs. 8a).
V	Volunteering of the agent (vs. 21a).	Volunteering of the agent (vs. 8b).
VI	Confirmation of his agency (vss. 21b—22).	Confirmation of his agency (vss. 9—10).
VII		The agent's pleading (vs. 11a).
VIII		God's limited accession (vss. 11b—13).
IX	Epitome: explicit warning [and implied hope] (vs. 23).	[Implied warning and hope.]

The synopsis shows at a glance the structural near identity of the reports and, at the same time, invites attention to the differences. III:

---

[69] For these words see above, pp. 163 f.

Isaiah has no counterpart in Kings. The *ruaḥ*, a permanent member of the divine council, needs no purification to participate in its deliberations; Isaiah, a son of the unclean people of Israel, does. VII and VIII: The blank in the Kings column stands out. These two elements are the characteristic plus of Isaiah. IX: This item brings out some more similarity (and also some dissimilarity) between the texts. In the Micaiah report the warning is explicit and the urging to use the last chance implicit; in that of Isaiah both are implicit.

The examination, which has led to the tabulation of the structural correspondence, has dispelled the suspicion of Isaiah's disloyalty.[70] Loyalty, however, is not the same as identity of purpose. Isaiah does not efface his personality and disown his intentions. He is commissioned to warn the people at the last moment not to succumb to the clouding of the mind and thereby seal their fate; said affirmatively, he is to warn them to reform themselves. It follows that anyone who does not accept the warning is doomed. Yet Isaiah does not acquiesce in this inference. Asking "How long, O Lord?" (vs. 11a), he strives to secure salvation for a remnant even if its members do not repent.[71] Initially the intentions of God and the prophet differ; at the end God accedes to the prophet, though probably less than he hoped. The chapter closes with the assurance that a regenerative cell will be preserved. It provides no basis for speculations about the outcome of the next critical encounter.

---

[70] See above, pp. 171 f.

[71] It might appear that the question has a different sense: Isaiah asks, "The punishment is decreed and the machinery set in motion; how long will it continue if the nation has a change of heart and repents?" But the text excludes this interpretation. (1) The conditional ("if they repent") is neither stated, nor hinted at nor is there a textual basis for inferring it, and the author cannot rely on the free fantasy of his audience to supply it. (2) In like manner, God's answer does not mention repentance, and this failure is even more grievous. Furthermore, He has just said, "Lest they repent and be healed" (vs. 10), but the desolation of vss. 11—13, progressing at the time of the hypothical repentance, is a situation which cannot be called healthy.

Israelite History
and the Historical Books
of the Old Testament

Modern study of the Bible is coming to grips with the problem of the relation of Israelite history to the historical books of the Old Testament, and it is to the credit of Protestant theologians that they have perceived the problem and addressed themselves to it; for until recently it would seem that no problem existed.

It is noteworthy that the study of Israel's history enjoyed and still frequently enjoys a privileged position among the tools of biblical exegesis. Thus it is that commentators on the historical books of the Old Testament are so fascinated by historical questions as to often neglect in their favor their main business, the elucidation of what the books mean to convey.

Theologians, too, were spell-bound. From the beginning of biblical criticism to the middle of this century they were unperturbed by the results of historical research of the ancient Israelite period despite the fact that these results undermine the foundations of traditional biblical theology. The situation began to change only in the early nineteen fifties. First in Germany, later elsewhere also, biblical scholars faced squarely the contradictions which often present themselves between Israelite history, i.e. the history of ancient Israel as modern research presents it, on the one hand, and biblical history, i.e. the history as told in the Bible, on the other.[1] The modern historian informs us that some events, situations,

---

[1] As in other respects so also in respect to the pair ideality-historicity, classical and biblical studies have undergone similar developments, but biblical studies often with a considerable delay. Reinhardt gives an absorbing description of the effect, first unsettling and eventually destructive, of historical research (including archaeology) and historical thinking on the idealistic construction—the dream image—of classical antiquity. For the

persons, etc. were not, in reality, quite what the Bible tells us, while others have no counterpart whatever in reality. But it must be clear that Christian theology rests both on Israelite history and on the Bible, including, needless to stress, biblical history. It affirms that God chose Israel and made a covenant with it in the expectation that it would live according to the covenant. He tried long and patiently to educate it, to make it His people in truth. This education in progress is, theologically speaking, the history of Israel, Israel's acts constituting its positive or negative answers to God's will. It was a vicissitudinous process and the longer it continued the more disheartening is the record of its failure. When God finally saw that His attempt had come to naught he sent His son, Jesus, to redeem Israel and redeem the world. It should be evident that if Israelite history is removed from the theological edifice of divine redemption coming at the point of man's complete failure, God becomes whimsical, toying with mankind, or even turns into a gnostic deity.

But the Old Testament is no less a foundation of Christian theology than is Israelite history. Moreover, it is Holy Writ, God's word to man, attested by His revelations. And, finally, it is the Scripture of Jesus and his disciples. They read it, understood it, and believed in it unaided by anything comparable to modern analysis and criticism—textual, literary, or historical. They saw in their persons and the events of their times the fulfillment of the predictions of the Old Testament and the culmination of the history it narrates. Thus the Old Testament became the proof text of the New.

---

classics the development began early in the nineteenth century. (K. Reinhardt, "Die klassische Philologie und das Klassische." Published repeatedly, e.g., in his *Vermächtnis der Antike* [1960], pp. 334—360; and in H. O. Burger, ed., *Begriffsbestimmung der Klassik und des Klassischen* [1972], pp. 66—97. The second half of the article is of little interest to our theme.) Good bibliographies of the theological problems are found in J. A. Soggin's articles in *Theologische Zeitschrift* 17 (1961), pp. 385—389, and *Theologische Literaturzeitung* 89 (1964), coll. 721—736. See further J. Bright, *The Authority of the O.T.* (1967), (ch.) III (pp. 110—160; Bright modestly disclaims the pertinence of his exposition to the problem studied here); and G. Wallis, *Geschichte und Überlieferung* (1968), pp. 109—128 (especially pp. 123—128). Very useful surveys and contributions, in English, are those by J. A. Robinson, in *Theology as History* (*New Frontiers in Theology* III), ed. J. A. Robinson ... (1967), pp. 42—62; and G. F. Hasel, "The Problem of History in O. T. Theology," *Andrew University Seminary Studies* 8 (1970), pp. 23—50; also his *Old Testament Theology: Basic Issues in the Current Debate* (1972), pp. 29—47.

Today the number of theologians who see that they can no longer temporize is growing. No longer is it possible to maintain theologically both Israelite history and the Bible. The ways part. Those who give primacy to Israelite history, among them F. Hesse, say: How can a historical faith, that is a faith in God who reveals Himself in His saving acts in history, be based on fiction? Not what the biblical authors say happened matters but what actually happened, that is, historical facts as recovered by sound historical study, standing free of distortion and overgrowth of legend.

On the other side are the biblicists, prominent among them G. von Rad. They say: Whatever we know about the saving acts of God in the history of Israel we know from the Bible, not only as regards the source material contained therein, but also and mainly because it is the record of the religious experience of Israel, and we would not know that these events are His saving acts, צדקות יהוה, had Israel not proclaimed that such they indeed were. When the first Christians recognized the history of Israel as holy history, they recognized it as it was told in the Old Testament—the autobiography of a people testifying in the grip of holy experience that this happened to them.

Attempts have been made, notably by Soggin and Rendtorff, to reconcile these views or develop an intermediary position. Soggin proposes to solve the problem in part by narrowing the area of conflict.[2] He is impressed by the arguments of those contemporary scholars, among whom he mentions W. F. Albright and J. Bright, who give more credence to the stories of Joshua and Judges than was formerly the case, although many scholars today contest such a degree of evidence. The smaller the discrepancy between the events of the premonarchical period (roughly 1225—1025 B.C.) as modern science reconstructs them and what we find in Joshua and Judges, the smaller the theological problem and the less urgent upon the theologian the necessity to choose between the alternative presentations.

Soggin's attempt, in my opinion, solves nothing. Whether in some hitherto unrecognized cases history indeed took the course that Judges delineates is only tangential to our problem. It would be no help at all should we succeed in moving back the frontier of reconstructable objec-

---

[2] *Theologische Zeitschrift* 17 (1961), pp.395—397.

tive history[3] by a century and a half or in adding a few minor points of agreement between Israelite and biblical histories. Even if historians would be able one day to confirm half of the things that the Bible tells about Adoni-bezek (Ju 1:5—7), Cushan-rishathaim (3:8—10), and Shamgar the son of Anat (3:31), they will never be able to confirm the essential events of Mount Sinai as told in the Book of Exodus (chs. 19—20;32—34). This is so because that story does not possess the earmark of historicity, that is to say, the narrative is not made of such stuff as the historian will accept as a source. For this and similar reasons M. Noth begins his *History of Israel* with the settlement of Israel in Palestine. Noth's decision to begin his work there is laudable if only for its timely reminder of the difference between the approach of the modern historian and the view of the Bible that the history, nay the very existence, of Israel has its beginning with Abraham, the exodus from Egypt, and the covenant of Sinai.

Rendtorff's attempt to reconcile the two positions starts from a criticism of the standard treatment of Israelite history.[4] The study of history, he maintains, must not limit itself to political, social, economical, and similar aspects; there is more to history than physical events and material facts. The biblical sources that record the events report at the same time Israel's experience of, and response to, these events. Now the experience and the response were not limited to one point in time, the historic moment when the event occurred, but were thereafter repeated, reshaped, evaluated, and developed. This is tradition. Of its ongoing process successive layers of the Old Testament bear eloquent witness. Tradition itself is part of the history and a legitimate and not to be scanted subject of historical science. The material events and their tradition together form the history of Israel, and in the study of the Old Testament there is, in principle, no room for two different disciplines, the history of Israel and the theology of the Old Testament.

Rendtorff's way, too, fails to lead to the desired end. Israel's tradition as anything done or undergone by man is, to be sure, potentially a subject

[3] "Objective history" in the simple workaday sense of the expression, neither implying absolute accuracy and perfect balance of information nor embellished with the fanciful amplifications of E. H. Carr, *What Is History?* (1962), p. 163.

[4] See particularly his "Geschichte und Überlieferung," *Studien zur Theologie der atl. Überlieferungen* (G. von Rad zum 60. Geburtstag), hrsg. R. Rendtorff ... (1961), pp. 81—94.

of historical study and sufficiently important to warrant the attention of the historian. But for every historian and probably for most theologians there is an essential and qualitative difference between an event and the tradition thereof. In reference to the event, the two aspects relate to one another as history and historical reflection or history and posthistory, and anyone interested, for whatever reason, in the former can disregard the latter. True, the significance of a historical phenomenon is often recognized by its sequences or consequences, i.e., its posthistory, but the significance is not bestowed by the latter upon the former; the consequences are indicators and not generators.

Moreover, the events or situations of the past that gave, or may have given, rise to tradition are often vaguely and with great difficulty recovered; we frequently do not know whether they took place at all.[5] Their nature and even factuality are the subject of learned disputes, but the subsequent tradition is not, in as much as it is a matter of record, written on the pages of the Bible. For the interpretation of that record it makes no difference whether one assumes or denies historical ascertainability of the primary event. Two scholars, one affirming, one denying the historicity of event E, may offer indistinguishable interpretations of a tradition relating to that event, except that one author adds (if he is so inclined), "And this tradition has sprung from event E," and the other does not. The inclusion of a statement of historicity in the interpretation of a given tradition or its deletion from another does not in itself change the interpretations. To use an analogy: The primary event is to the study of tradition what the Ding an sich is to natural science or to epistemology. The work of a physicist, including the formation of theories, is unaffected by his acceptance or rejection of this concept, and the inquiry of a philosopher even in the realm of transcendental idealism remains similarly uninfluenced by whatever his view about this noumenon may be.

It follows that of the two parts of tradition commonly regarded as constitutive, the primary event with the report of those who witnessed it[6]

[5] Rendtorff is alert to this circumstance. He mentions a whole class of traditions that have no primary event behind them, the etiological traditions (see ibid., p. 89, n. 20. An etiology explains something in the present—a landmark, a name, a custom—fictitiously as the result of a past event).

[6] As a matter of convenience, I follow Rendtorff (ibid., p. 89) in including the primary event in the tradition. Actually, the event is not part of the tradition.

and the later narrative, only the second is a reliable historical source. What is always available and certain is not the primary event nor the contemporary report but the subsequent tradition, i.e., a formulation in which the authors purpose to recapture and reexperience the event, retelling it, professing and proclaiming its truth. To put it differently: Reporting events of the past is the quintessence of tradition, but tradition, as a rule, is a historical source for the time reporting, not for the time reported. This analysis shows that that which is valid in Rendtorff's position is quite similar to von Rad's approach. This comports well with Rendtorff's accentuation of the material: His exposition embraces both the primary event and its tradition throughout the generations, but the emphasis is placed on the tradition.

To summarize these observations: The prominence that Rendtorff accords to tradition as the medium in which Israel expresses its self-understanding as the people of God and its conception of God's acts in history makes clear his affinity to von Rad's view.[7] Similarly, the eagerness of Soggin, in a theological context, to expand the area of critically established historical events discloses how attracted he is by the position of Hesse. This comes as no surprise. For not only have the attempts separately failed to reconcile the views of the historicists and the biblicists, but it is the only to be expected result that an analysis of the attempts should polarize them around the two basic views. The views preempt the field and constitute true antinomies, and no dialectics can bring the opposites into accord.

This brief exposition hopes to highlight the significance of the theological discussion, a significance that transcends theology. Theology is the agent that throws the problem "history and the book" into sharp relief, and all should be thankful for this service. The study of history and the study of literature may use the same material, viz., Scripture, but other than that they have nothing in common. To anyone interested in Israelite history, be his reason theological or otherwise, the Bible is a source among others, and he so uses it. True, it is the main source of Israelite history, but this is chiefly due to the paucity of extrabiblical

---

[7] "Wie sollen wir, wenn wir heute das Handeln Gottes zu erkennen suchen, feststellen, wo er gehandelt hat, wenn die Deutung Israels uns dabei nicht als Leitfaden dienen darf?" (idem, p. 90).

sources. On the other hand, anyone who reads the Bible without such extraneous motives reads it as he would read any work of literature because he is interested in its meaning. The study of history and the study of literature are two different disciplines with different aims and different methods. Both form, to be sure, part of the nexus in which all scholarly disciplines are interconnected. To the historian, however, history is the center, and this places all the others in ancillary positions of greater or lesser importance; while, similarly, the students of literature selects and ranges certain disciplines around his field of activity. If the literature is the Bible, these are, among others, studies of geography, history, folklore, religion. Disciplines as they relate to other disciplines can be characterized in terms of their central or subsidiary roles as assigned to them by the scholar. The scholar is free in making the assignment, but once it is made, he is committed to keep the discipline of his choice central and all the others subsidiary. Any vacillating on his part strains the web of disciplines to the breaking point, if not beyond; uncertainty will then prevail as to what are the main questions, which answers are given to which questions, and by which methods are the answers obtained.

Applied to the study of Scripture, I understand this to mean: The biblical scholar must undertake to answer primary questions—what is the material content of a given literary unit, what is its purpose, and by what means is the content presented and the purpose expressed? To these primary questions other considerations are sometimes added: Literary prehistory; diverging purposes of a large literary unit and those of the smaller units, its parts[8]; Sitz im Leben, and the like. Nonliterary questions are at best subsidiary and they are admissible only to the extent that they are useful to answer the literary questions. The questions of historicity is no exception to the foregoing. The author of the Book of Judges, for example, told of an event or a sequence of events which he assumed occurred. The object of the study of Judges, in contradistinction to

---

[8] For example, it is commonly held that certain narratives of Genesis are of local or tribal origin and that some of them had an etiological past while others had served particular social, cultic, or political ends. As the narratives later became part of the literary whole, those particular functions or intents receded or disappeared altogether, and other purposes, those of Genesis or the Pentateuch, took their place.

the study of the premonarchical period, is the description of the events as
the author assumed them to have happened and the consequences of this
assumption; the correctness of the assumption is not at issue, only the intention of the author which rests on the assumption.

The danger of indulging in questions of historicity in the sense just
discussed is that the interpreter is prone to misinterpret the intention of
the Bible by virtue of his subjective selectivity in putting this question to
some historical texts and not to others. He asks it, for instance, in regard
to the Syro-Ephraimite war (734 B. C.; 2 Ki 16:5) but not the flood or the
ark of Noah.[9] The reason for this differentiation is that, in his eyes, the
war is or may be history while the flood and the ark are not. Such differentiation runs counter to the intention of the Bible—how then can the
interpreter hope to understand the intention of his text if he and the text
are at cross-purposes? For in the large unit Genesis to Kings there is, as
the Bible understands it, no division of parts into facts and fiction; the
waters of Noah are no less real than the waters of Shiloah.[10] The legitimate approach for the interpreter of the Bible is not to sit in the historian's chair and sort out fact from fiction but to read the whole either as
history or as legend; which way he chooses is his personal decision and
not a topic for public debate. The public is interested in the ability of the
interpreter to withstand the temptation of historicizing and to confine
himself to presenting the message of the book. Yet note how few modern
commentators on Samuel fail to tell their readers[11] how factual the narratives of the second half of Second Samuel (ch. 11—20) are, how historical,
and therefore, implicitly, how good. Is this the language, are these the
categories of exegesis?

[9] Pace M.E.L. Mallowan, *Iraq* 26 (1964), pp. 62—82. Cf. also H. J. Lenzen, *Baghdader
Mitteilungen* 3 (1964), pp. 52—64; R. L. *Raikes, Iraq* 28 (1966), pp. 52—63.

[10] H. Cancik, *Mythische und historische Wahrheit* (Stuttgarter Bibelstudien 48, 1970),
p.93, thinks otherwise, but the facts he presents in note 6, the space of which—to be sure
—is limited, in support of his opinion indicate only that the differences between the two
ages (three ages, if we accept his structuring) are fundamental to the mind of the modern
reader. He does not show that the facts were significant to the ancients as well, and there
is not the slightest indication in the texts that they were indeed.

[11] L. Delekat is an exception. His judgment of these narratives is the opposite of the
common one (in *Das ferne und das nahe Wort; Festschrift L. Rost*, ed. F. Maass [1967],
pp. 26—36, especially p. 29). Cf. also E. Würthwein, *Die Erzählung von der Thronfolge
Davids—theologische oder politische Geschichtsschreibung?* (Theologische Studien 115,
1974).

These observations should not be construed to mean that the interpreter of biblical history has no use for the achievements of the study of Israelite history. Quite the contrary! He has a genuine interest in them for he requires information about the social, economic, cultural, and relgious background of his texts. Which means that the history which is ancillary to biblical interpretation is, for the most part, generalizing history; this holds true for the earlier books of the Old Testament and for many of the later ones. One does not find it easy, for example, to overestimate the contribution of recent historical research for the understanding of the stories of the patriarchs; consider such themes as the wanderings of Abraham or the Abraham-Sarah-Hagar triangle. What he does find himself able to dispense with is the question of the historicity of the persons or the personalities of the patriarchs themselves.

So much for the primary concern of the biblical scholar. On a secondary level, however, as we review the relation of biblical history to Israelite history, we may ask whether there may be profit to the study of the historical books of the Bible with a view to individualizing history as well. Can the reader or commentator of these books make use of what the modern historian tells about particular circumstances, special events, specific individuals? Without losing sight of the judgment that there is no profit to exegesis except in that which enhances the understanding of literature, that is its content, form and intention, I propose an affirmative answer to this question. For at least three reasons—there may be more—the reader of the Bible, particularly of the historical books, should concern himself, albeit secondarily, with the individualizing history of Israel.

(1) The picture of Israelite history that the modern historian draws may serve the biblical reader as a foil for the picture the Bible presents. By this juxtaposition he may discern how biblical history diverges from Israelite history. These divergencies betray the nature of biblical composition and often reveal its intentions. Surely there is no absolute preference for either picture; both are legitimate, but the reader of the Bible is not concerned with the bare facts of objective history but with what the Bible makes of them. The question, "What does the Bible make of its historical raw material?"[12] is analogous to the question, "What does the Bible make of its literary raw material?" E.g., What does Genesis make of

---

[12] The complicating possibility that the material did not reach the Bible in its pristine raw stage need not be considered here.

the contemporary myths of creation? What does Proverbs make of Egyptian wisdom? The pattern is: What does the Bible make of x, y, or z? The interest of the commentator in x, y or z (e.g., ancient religions, wandering motifs, or history), the indirect objects of the interrogative sentence, is aroused by his expectation that they will shed light on "the Bible," the subject of the sentence, through the elucidation of its predicate "does make."

(2) Knowledge of Israelite history enables the student of the Bible to distinguish between fact and fiction. Although in regard to this point I have stressed earlier the danger of irrelevance and, worse, of seduction from the purpose of biblical study, I would observe that these dangers may be neutralized by a determinedly philological approach. Knowing whether a story is fact or fiction makes a difference for its understanding. The difference relates to the possibility of the author's involvement, the nature of such involvement, and our reading of the story in the light of this involvement. The author of a factual story or his source may have been close to the event; indeed, the audience may have been close as well. Any or all of them may well have been engaged as witnesses or even participants; or the circumstances of their lives were so similar to those in the narrative as to raise the likelihood of a similar denouement; or, having experienced the consequences of the narrated event, narrator and/or audience may have been caught up in the desire to reinforce or counteract these consequences. Such attachement, identification, and reaction cannot but leave a stamp of immediacy on the narrative, which the interpreter neglects at his peril. It is true that the author of Genesis 3 was intensely interested in his subject because the outcome of that event determined his life and his world, yet is is equally true that any possible identification with the various elements of the myth is at a distant remove, fragmented and strained. Missing in the mythological narrative are the ingredients of immediate social, political, and partisan involvements. The author of the story of the foundation of kingship in Israel, whether he was contemporary with the content of his story or not, could argue in his private or public life with the protagonists of the positions to which he lent voice and could even try to alter the configuration he had inherited. With whom, by contrast, could the author of Genesis 3 argue and what should he change?

(3) Also the third reason, like the preceding ones, is literary. The writ-

ing of history is literary composition with a given material, the facts as they are known to the author. The requisite adherence to them imposes severe limitations. Now a piece of writing which, fulfilling this requirement, recreates the past and is at the same time well told possesses an esthetic quality which is denied to a work free of this obligation. I refer to an observation of the penomenology of the creative act that, within certain limits and with other things being equal, the greater the difficulties and the more severe the limitations the greater the work. The grandeur of the first movement of Beethoven's Fifth Symphony can be attributed in part to the imposition of a stringent limitation, the four-tone motif, present in virtually every one of the more than four hundred bars up to the coda. The limitation of biblical historiography, unlike that of Beethoven's symphony which is freely conceived, lies in the material, and only the strictness with which the author adheres to the facts is a matter of his free choice. The story of the succession to the throne of David (2 Sam 11—20; 1 Ki 1—2) is here cited once again for demonstration. Historians and commentators alike assert that these chapters are written with intimate knowledge of, and faithful adherence to, the events.[13] As was noted above,[14] such faithfulness does, in itself, not represent a literary value. This value lies in the beauty of the language, the vividness of the narration, the clarity of the composition, and the power and conviction of the idea, ever concealed and ever present. But it is appreciably heightened when, as is the case here, ideality, the work of literature, is transformed reality and the correspondence of the two is detailed and accurate. Once again, the study of individualizing history, establishing particular situations and events, contributes to a better understanding of the historical books; it permits an insight into the nature of this literature and reveals an achievement which would otherwise have escaped us.

The tension between Israelite history and biblical history is genuine and irreducible in biblical theology. In biblical philology it can be fully resolved, but only if misconceptions of the role of Israelite history for the study of the Bible are corrected and the student maintains a clear picture of his proper task.

[13] But see n. 11.
[14] P. 184.

Common Sense and Hypothesis
in Old Testament Study

The study of the Old Testament in modern times is marked by a progressing reduction of the influence of dogma, tradition, legend, and concern of the authority of Church or Synagogue and by a concomitant increasing emphasis on common-sense arguments. Looking back over a history of almost two centuries it would seem that biblical scholars have reason to take pride in biblical philology's having reached the status of a science. It is the burden of this paper to question the extent to which this notion is justified.

Arguments based on common sense as such have little or no place in the sciences, the humanities included. (For the convenience of argument I subsume philology under science.) And this failure to achieve place is due to this: that common sense does not assess the available evidence on which its conclusions are or should be properly based. The case for common sense is further weakened by its tendency to engage in a search for apparently plausible "first principles" whose disclosure may be used to account for so-called "facts" or postulate the very existence of such "facts".[1]

An examination of the procedures of Old Testament philology will reveal that this branch of learning all too often does not submit its cognitive claims to the challenge of such evidence as exists or might theoretically exist. This tendency is especially to be remarked in provinces to which I shall direct attention here, higher criticism and, to a lesser degree, history

---

[1] This definition-by-description of common sense follows E. Nagel, *The Structure of Science*, 1961, pp. 12f. Different but not incompatable statements are those of E. E. Harris, *Hypothesis and Perception*, 1970, pp. (296–298), 299; and K.R. Popper, *Objective Knowledge*, 1972, pp.33f.,60, and elsewhere.

of text.[2] Questions typical in these areas are: 'Is a given segment of a book genuine?' 'Is it unified or composite?' 'Did the original author utilize existing material?' 'What reconstruction of the prehistory of a text receives support from its ancient witnesses?'

Biblical scholarship has commonly answered such questions by having implicit recourse to "first principles" possessing prima facie plausibility, principles such as putative universal characteristics of such phenomena as the writing of books, the behavior of authors, or the operation of literary influences. It is presupposed that authors do this and do not that; that books have not a variety of fates but only fates a, b, or c, whereas d, e, and f are not options granted by philology. In like vein, it may not be allowed that several parts of a work by one author may use different names for the same person; that he may freely project different aspects of religion; further, that the descendants of an official text, themselves official, may appear multicolored as did Laban's flock before Jacob set up his regulative rods. That scholars do not ordinarily state these principles explicitly does not affect the ubiquitous use of such principles.

The place of the common-sense notion in a reasoned argument is a matter of no little importance, which prompts a brief digression. A reasoned argument, the primary example of which, in science, is an explanation broadly speaking, has two main parts: one, the premises and two, the conclusion. Among the premises one distinguishes universal statements or propositions and particular statements. The former may range from loose generalizations to lawlike formulations or hypotheses; the latter are the data, namely the object under investigation and pertinent information about it.[3] To concretize with an example from Hebrew palaeography. I wish to establish the age of a manuscript. Universal

---

[2] Attention to other provinces of Old Testament study will probably reveal that the statement applies to a wider area than is treated here. It should be clear, however, that the extensions of its applicability must stop short of studies which stand in ancillary relation to Old Testament philology, e.g., history of Israel, geography of Palestine, Hebrew linguistics.

[3] A notable exposition of the subject is that of C. G. Hempel and P. Oppenheim, "Studies of the Logic of Explanation" *Philosophy of Science* 15 (1948), pp. 135—175; several times republished, e.g., (with some changes and an addition) in C. G. Hempel, *Aspects of Scientific Explanation and Other Essays . . .*, 1965, pp. 245—295. In note 7 (p. 251 [1965]), the authors disclaim novelty for their approach and refer to predecessors.

statement: Hebrew script after 400 A.D. consistently uses the final letters kaf, mem, etc. Particular statement: The manuscript under investigation has no final letters. Conclusion: The manuscript is earlier than 400 A.D.[4]

Turning now to the question of the place and the function of a common-sense notion in an argument one observes that, whereas in our illustration the universal proposition is either true or subject to refutation, the common-sense notion is featured in this role of a universal proposition with this crucial difference: for all its seeming plausibility its truth is far from corroborated, and there are no criteria for putting it to a test.

The failure of Old Testament philology to probe its universal premises, so far stated in a general way, is reinforced by a special circumstance. Let such a premise be a hypothesis about the behavior of authors. Realistically speaking the Old Testament critic develops this hypothesis in the course of his work with a limited class of objects, say the Old Testament narratives, and he formulates it with a view to the totality of this class. Now it is obvious that the data which serve as material for the framing of a hypothesis cannot be employed for testing this hypothesis. For the hypothesis will be so formulated and the data so presented that the hypothesis and the data will not contradict each other. Contradictions thus ruled out, it goes without saying that the need for testing will never be asserted. This is a radical weakness of modern Old Testament research.

Scholars engaged or interested in the areas of study to which this paper invites attention, if they would remedy the situation will find that they must go outside the biblical field for part of their scholarly endeavor. And this not in order to broaden their horizon nor to learn new tricks but rather to perform work abroad that cannot be performed at home. Indeed, it is likely that they will have to travel to distant shores. For while the biblical scholar may understandably be attracted to the early litera-

---

[4] This proposition does not rest only on the absence of contrary evidence ('All ravens are black,' for no nonblack raven has ever been seen); it receives considerable support from the testimony of the talmudic insistence (e.g., jMegilla 1:9 [71d]; bShabbat 104a) upon the obligatory use of these letters. There are various traditions about the age of this prescription, but the third century A.D. seems to be a reasonable terminus post. For the subject consult N. H. Tur-Sinai, *Hlšwn whspr* I (1954), pp.4—5(ff.); and N. Avigad in *Scripta Hierosolymitana* 4 (1958), pp. 64, 66, 70, 72f.

ture of ancient Greece, especially Homer and Homeric philology, he will find that, external though these be to the Old Testament, they are not far enough afield. The Old Testament and Homer have several features in common as have Old Testament and Homeric studies. During the past two hundred years the two disciplines have gone through similar phases. The similarity of the objects of study and of methods employed and results achieved are, to be sure, enlightening and have proved useful to biblical scholarship; the writings of Dornseiff, to mention only one author, are impressive textimony.[5] But essentially, Homer is not the text with which the Old Testament scholar can successfully check his methods and explanations because, in crucial aspects, Homer and the Bible are too similar. Explanations of Homeric phenomena and hypotheses about them are marked by a comparable lack, or very low degree, of internal testability. The kinds of things which are uncertain in the Bible are often uncertain also in Homer. A biblicist who attempts to answer critical questions in biblical philology by invoking Homeric philology risks interpreting *ignotum per ignotum*.

There is no hope for progress unless he breaks out of these charmed circles and reaches bases of testable facts. These he will discover in modern literature. It is in and about modern works that he will find sufficient information for checking arguments put forth in Old Testament philology mainly by testing their universal premises. The information consists of drafts, autographs, and the like, documented biographies of authors and their friends, and so on. It is simply a matter of extant information, the happy accident of available sources.

In the following section a number of examples from literature and music will be deployed. With one exception, which is from the ancient Near East, they are from late-eighteenth-century Germany. The purpose of the presentation is to test the quality of hypotheses current in Old Testament scholarship and to cast an occasional glance at the conclusions derived from the hypotheses and the manner of derivation.

The *Magic Flute* of Mozart and his librettist Schikaneder features

[5] F. Dornseiff, *Antike und Alter Orient*, 1959.

two camps, the powers of good and the powers of evil, the former represented by the Queen of Night and her retinue, the latter by Sarastro and his. This holds for the first third of the work. With the beginning of the first finale a volte-face takes place: The Queen of the Night now represents the evil principle and Sarastro the good one. No reason is given for the change, no attempt made to harmonize the parts. Scholars have had a field-day with this matter.[6] The very existence of the break and the consequent contradiction have been denied or explained away; alternatively, the break has been acknowledged but justified in terms of a putative profound symbolism; others have responded to the esthetic problem by picturing a pitiable Mozart, a great musician helpless in the clutches of an inferior librettist.[7]

We need not dwell on these speculations. What we need to do is to note the universal premise common to criticisms of Mozart and the Old Testament: Imperfections, such as contradictions, just do not occur in a work of art produced by a single creator. The modern biblical critic seeing the explanations offered by Mozart critics would likely be reminded of exegetical essays that were in vogue in his own field in centuries past but are renounced today, and properly so. He does not explain away or harmonize or resort to mystification. He stipulates several independent strands in a text which as a whole is not compatible with his propositions. Now this approach of the biblicist presents the one answer which is not available to the Mozart philologian. For the latter the background of the *Magic Flute* and its composition are illumined by the bright light of documented history; flight into the shelter of source conjecture is the one avenue barred to him.

---

[6] "Toujours inexpliqué" [T. de Wyzewa and] G. de Saint-Foix, *W. A. Mozart; sa vie musicale* ... V [1946], p. 220).

[7] A rich bibliography of the *Magic Flute* between 1911 and 1962 is contained in L. von Köchel, *Chronologisch-thematisches Verzeichnis sämtlicher Tonwerke W. A. Mozarts* in the 6th ed. by F. Giegling a.o., 1964, pp. 713f. Comments on the above problem will be found in many of its items. Later literature is listed in the annual Mozart bibliography of the subsequent volumes of the *Mozart-Jahrbuch*. F. Klingenbeck, *Die Zauberflöte*, 1966, discusses the theme on pp.70—92. Examples of contrived profundity or mystification are the writings of E. Schmitz, in *Festschrift Max Schneider*, ed. W. Vetter, 1955, p.210; and, a more intelligent and refined specimen, J. Chailley, *Mozart-Jahrbuch 1967*, 1968, pp.100—110.

We now turn from opera with its literary ingredient to literature proper. The first example has its focus on a modern author's comment on one of his own works, a comment made against the background of hypotheses which had been proposed about ancient literature. In a letter drafted to Schiller and dated July 7, 1796, Goethe writes about his novel in progress *Wilhelm Meister*: "I myself scarcely believe that one will find in the book a unity other than that of steadiness in progress (der fortschreitenden Stetigkeit), but we shall see; and since it is the work of so many years ... I am in this—if one may compare the little with the great—both Homer and Homerid at one and the same time". Goethe is commenting on the unsatisfactory integration of *Wilhelm Meister*. Such a shortcoming, detected in the Homeric epics by the then nascent criticism of Homer, would—Goethe implies—be charged to Homerid meddling with the pristine original.[8] This is double-edged criticism on the part of Goethe: explicit criticism of his own novel and implicit criticism of the studies of Friedrich August Wolf, the father of modern Homer criticism in Germany. Goethe means to convey that lack of integration in a work of literature is an esthetic phenomenon, which cannot be interpreted as a clue to the prehistory of that literature. This point he substantiates by reference to his own work.

This example is not given with the intention of invoking Goethe as an ultimate authority for the evaluation of the critical philology of Homer and, by extention, of the Bible. But the issue of testing hypotheses about ancient literature by means of exemplars from modern literature looms behind this epistolary passage of his, and this author is as well qualified as any to offer such critical comments.

The next example features another aspect of premises and their operation in the study of literature. Its subject matter is the forerunner of *Urfaust* as discussed in Goethe philology. *Urfaust* is the conventional name for that version of *Faust* that Goethe brought to Weimar when he settled there in 1775; it was the only *Faust* known, and at that only to a small circle of friends, before the publication in 1790 of the next version, *Faust; a Fragment*. Not meant for publication and never published during its author's lifetime, *Urfaust* was discovered in 1877, half a century

---

[8] The Homerids are the post-Homeric rhapsodists.

after his death. Now in the opinion of a number of scholars, the very title *Urfaust* is a misnomer. For they hold that *"Urfaust"* was itself preceded by one or more yet earlier if rather incomplete versions of the work; this hypothesis they flesh out with a partial description of that proto-*Urfaust*. For its reconstruction they employ elements and produce results which, in essence and up to a point, resemble those appearing in Old Testament higher criticism: prose versus poetry and various types of poetry versus one another; uncertainty as regards the identity and image of personae; apparently gratuitous duplications; and the unsettled question regarding the focus of the drama, its aim and conclusion. The constituents of the argument comprise both facts and constructs which, properly formulated and organized, are said to lead to the hypothesis of proto-*Urfaust*.[9]

The invitation to compare the criticism of the Old Testament and of *Faust* is obvious. In respect to the Old Testament the examination of a class of features of a text, a part of the Old Textament, results in one or the other of several hypotheses: the text is a fabric woven from different recognizable strands; the text represents a main constituent complemented by a number of additions; or, in the case of certain narratives, the text is a recast of an ancient Hebrew epic. In respect now to *Urfaust*, its examination, supplemented by an examination of other *Faust* versions, culminates in the hypothetical onetime existence of a vaguely describably earlier stage of the text, and this text like the extant ones is the work of the one author.

For reasons similar to those which obtained in the case of the *Magic Flute*, the student of *Faust* explains a type of features in a way markedly different from that of the student of the Old Textament. The rich number of particular premises available to *Faust* research, i.e., the known facts about *Faust* and its sources and Goethe and his time, precludes the type of answers yielded in Old Testament research. Biblical research has at its

---

[9] A detailed (313 pages) overview of *Urfaust* research is given by V. Nollendorfs, *Der Streit um den Urfaust*, 1967. (Out of the great number of passages which highlight different sides of the problem I mention pp. 83f., 103, 136–140,220.) After Nollendorfs there appeared a book which deserves listing: H. Reich, *Die Entstehung der ersten fünf Szenen des Goethischen 'Urfaust'*, 1968. For first acquaintance with the problem I suggest E. Staiger, *Goethe* I, 1952, "Urfaust" (pp. 204–244, especially the first half of the chapter).

disposal, beyond the texts themselves and whatever little information can be culled from them, only a very small number of particular premises. Therefore the possibility here of a rather wide variety of explanations and answers, a possibility uncommon in many other branches of philology. (That not all of these possibilities are realized in Old Testament study is more a matter of trends and fashions in scholarship than of logical requirements or exclusions.) Given this state of the science, the question as to the worth of these explanations becomes all but rhetorical. To put it differently: The failure to test universal statements together with the paucity of particular statements is the reason for the common-sense pre-scientific nature of part of Old Testament scholarship.

Our next example, Friedrich Hölderlin's poem "Brot und Wein", will be instructive for yet another reason. This elegy exists in three authentic versions. In any single one, the incongruities, while present, are not overwhelming. But when we compare all three versions (all written shortly after 1800), we are faced with a difference, which is momentous. The earliest version, called "Der Weingott", and the last version both build up to a culmination in a reference to Dionysus, which is as unambiguous as it is impactful. In the climax of the second version, however, Christ, unmistakable for all his not being so named, takes the place of Dionysus. His appearance is anticipated and reinforced in the poem's new title "Bread and Wine", a likely allusion to the Last Supper.[10] The incongruity inhering in the poem is compounded in the third version, where Christ has all but disappeared; at best, only faint traces are left.

Now Hölderlin was unquestionably not frivolous as artist or thinker. He did not toy with the divine, nor were the names of the Greek gods for him arbitrary symbols, capriciously chosen. To the extent that I understand him, I may own that I know of no writer of postclassical times who was so piously drawn to the Greek gods as he. And as regards Jesus Christ, let us note that Hölderlin repeatedly strove to integrate him into what is essentially a Greek pantheon; this, too, is piety, and here, too, he is altogether serious.

Imagine now the reaction of scholars should there come to light an ancient duplicate of a biblical text with Baal appearing where now we

---

[10]The change from "Der Weingott" to "Brod und Wein" is made in a correction of the autograph of the second version; see F. Beissner in the large Stuttgart edition II 2, p. 592.

have Yhwh. Our received text would by unanimous pronouncement be declared to be an Israelite adaptation of a Canaanite original. But we need not appeal to imagination when, in fact, a biblical text, Psalm 29, has been[11] and is, with mounting frequency, being identified as such in the absence of that imaginary duplicate or any other textual evidence deserving this name.

Interpreters of Hölderlin are at pain to understand both the thrust and the complex of ideas in "Bread and Wine" and in his other Christ poems.[12] Their proposals, while often less than convincing, represent serious philological efforts, generally more sober than the Papageno-like stabs by some musicologists in the murk of the *Magic Flute* problem. The interpreter of the Old Testament might well view Hölderlin philology with wistful envy, not only its material basis, that is to say, its particular premises (texts based on autographs and some authentic editions as well as biographical information) but also the general sobriety of its speculations—for speculations they are. When he then looks again at his own discipline, he cannot be oblivious to the facility of its stipulation of universal premises and the consequent eventuation of assorted assumptions fulfilling these stipulations.

The final illustration is a group of texts from the ancient Near East. It will bring us close in place and time to the provenience of biblical literature, whose study is the subject of our discussion. A prefatory word: Given our very limited knowledge of the lives of authors and of the earliest histories of their works in that region and era, we can hardly expect to find ancient Near Eastern literary works with which we might test other and unrelated works of that civilization, be it in regard to matters of higher criticism or to the issue of complexes of ideas. In respect, however, to the history of the Old Testament text the conditions for comparison must be seen more favorable. Therefore, for the examination of Frank M. Cross's hypothesis about early biblical text types, which follows, Near Eastern texts may be utilized.

---

[11] Since 1936: H. L. Ginsberg, *Ktby 'wgryt*, pp. 129–131.

[12] The following studies are significant for the problem at hand (disregarding general interpretations of the poem and essays on the so-called Christ hymns): Primarily F. Beissner, *Hölderlins Götter*, 1969, pp. 26–36; then P. Böckmann, "Friedrich Hölderlin: Brod und Wein ...," in B. Wiese, ed., *Die deutsche Lyrik* I, 1959, pp. 394–413.

Cross arranges pre-Christian texts of the Old Testament in a stem-matological fashion. This he does by assigning three different text types, respectively, to three countries. Two of these types he assigns by index fossils to Egypt and Palestine, respectively.[13] The third he places in Babylonia on the strength of the following argument: Egypt and Palestine have been preempted, and the possibility that different "textual traditions . . . can exist side by side in the same . . . locality for centuries" must be "brusquely" rejected.[14] I think Cross is overly assertive in his claim for this as a principle of textual history. The prima facie plausibility which he discerns for the rejection of the centuries-long common domicile of different textual traditions may be refuted by any number of instances to the contrary in the case of ancient Near Eastern texts. I cite but a few examples.

(1) Text 1 of Shalmaneser I (1274–1254) in Weidner's publication. It has quite a number of variant readings other than simple matters of phonetics and morphology.[15] All manuscripts of this text come from the temple of the god Ashur in the city of Assur.

(2) The eleventh tablet of the Epic of Gilgamesh. This features variants of the kind found in the Shalmaneser I text.[16] Virtually all of the manuscripts are from Assurbanipal's library in Nineveh, seventh century.

(3) The Phoenician inscriptions from Karatepe. For this eighth-century monumental text G. D. Young's conclusions in regard to its variants[17] are in full agreement with those advanced in this paper.

(4) The Hittite Laws. Almost all known texts are imperial copies, probably thirteenth century, of originals of some four centuries earlier; all come from the capital Hattusas. Here, too, the variants conform to the types of variants in the previously mentioned specimens.[18]

---

[13] The merit of the placements is not assessed here. They are accepted for the sake of argument.

[14] F. M. Cross, *HTR* 57 (1964), pp. 297–299.

[15] The variants are from [E. Ebeling . . .] E. F. Weidner, *Die Inschriften der alt-assyrischen Könige*, 1926: p. 112, vars. e, o, u, x; p. 116, var. l'; p. 120, vars. l, a';p. 122, vars. m, s; p. 124, vars. b, w, f'; p. 126, var. a.

[16] The list is from R. C. Thompson, *The Epic of Gilgamesh*, 1930: p. 62, vars. 7,32f., 36, 37; p. 63, vars. 1, 12; p.65, vars. 8, 26; p. 66, vars. 12–13.

[17] G. D. Young, *OS* 8 (1950), pp. 291–299.

[18] As a sampling there follows an incomplete listing of variants from §§ 41–46 of the first tablet; text KBo VI 4 (whose sections are conventionally Roman-numbered), which

The variants in these examples are approximately of the order of the variants in the Pentateuch and Samuel that are featured in Cross's hypothesis. The texts in which they appear are official documents—one of them, Gilgamesh, is even characterized as canonical. This text as well as the text of the Hittite Laws own a history of centuries' duration. The Assur and Karatepe texts are equally pertinent in spite of their lack of prehistory; for they did not evolve gradually from popular, divergent, uncontrolled material, but were, from the moment of their composition, official in every respect—for all this no one apparently was concerned about a uniform version.

In summation, this is another case of a universal lawlike statement refuted by testing. My purpose for citing it, however, is not to single out its author for criticism. This case, in common with all the others, is typical of an ambience in which such statements with their ramifications well-nigh represent the norm, an ambience from whose influence no one is immune.

At this juncture we must anticipate an objection as to the validity of the analogical illustrations which we have adduced.[19] All of our illustra-

---

has more variants, is not included in the overview. Reference is according to Friedrich's main text (KBo VI 3:II), which applies also to the editions of F. Imparati, *Le leggi ittite*, 1964, and R. Haase, *Die Fragmente der hethitischen Gesetze*, 1968. (For easier identification I have added the numbers of the footnotes of J. Friedrich, *Die hethitschen Gesetze*, 1959).

On the age of one text containing these section (Friedrich's text A) see H. G. Güterbock, *JCS* 16 (1962), p. 17. § 41:47 (n. 36) *danzi/pianzi* "one takes/one gives" (a difference of the order "to wind up/to wind down" [as, a campaign]). § 42:49 (n. 5) *nu Ú-UL sarnikzi/sarnikzil* [NU.GÁL] "*he does not make restitution/there is no restitution.*" § 43:52 (n. 14) GUD-ŠU/GUD.ḪI.A "(his) ox/oxen." § 44b:56 (n. 34) a pair of somewhat extended variants. § 46:59 (nn. 43 f.) A.Š[À.ḪI.A *sa]ḫḫana*/A.ŠÀ.ḪI.A-*an/saḫḫanas* A.ŠÀ.ḪI.A "field(s) and fief/a field/a field of fief." § 46:59, 60 (nn. 46, 49) *takkussi/takku* "if him/if."

[19] Our listing of various literary incongruities which may not be utilized for higher criticism is far from comprehensive; attentive readers of modern literature will find that they can extend it considerably. Long ago E. Stemplinger, *Studien zur vergleichenden Literaturgeschichte* 7 (1907), pp. 194–203, assembled material of this kind (not included here), but not all his examples are impressive. See also Dornseiff (n. 5), p. 5. Professor M. Dahood has reminded me kindly that *The New Yorker*, a weekly well-known to American

tions, with the exception of the last, appear to be open to the objection that examples from Western civilization are not appropriate for, and have no bearing on, the interpretation of ancient Near Eastern phenomena. More specifically, one might quarrel with the analogy of literary inconsistencies in modern Western works, which may be a relatively rare phenomenon, for the critical analysis of the Old Testament, where this phenomenon is frequent. The employment of this analogy may appear as an attempt to disprove a hypothesis formulated for one area by applying it to another area for which it was not intended and for which it is irrelevant; this is to say, that it was formulated for an area which features a large number of occurrences, occurrences which it—presumably—explains, while the latter area features a small number of similar occurrences, mere exceptions, which it admittedly fails to explain. To state it differently: The criticism is that undue significance is accorded to exceptions which, at that, are extraneous. Such criticism would be cogent but for the following considerations.

First, in regard to the quantitative element in this criticism. I readily agree that inconsistencies are more frequent in the Old Testament than in modern literature. The question is "How much more?" Erroneous ideas about true proportions abound, that is, precision beyond the rudimentary comparatives "more" and "less", and in particular as regards relative frequencies of occurrences. And scholars are not unsusceptible to such aberrance. One example: The rarity of the assimilation of the Hebrew consonant nun in the preposition *min* before the article (*e.g., mehabbayit*) is stressed in Bauer-Leander and supported demonstratively by the citation of just three instances. Sperber counters this assumption of impressionistic scholarship, listing ninety instances.[20]

Further, where the elements to be quantified are stylistic or structural inconsistencies, divergent religious modalities, traces of foreign influence, or similar literary imponderables, the very count will depend crucially upon the precision of the analysis of the text and the judgmental acumen

---

readers, regularly carries a collection of writers' foibles: short quotations, many from current newspapers, which it accompanies with its own caustic comments. The individual entries are normally nonliterary, but they may alert the reader to what happens in literature.

[20] A. Sperber, *JBL* 62 (1943), pp. 140–143.

of the quantifier with specific reference to the range and order of his literary criteria for the imponderables. The determining factors will depend
on the setting of the threshold for the admission or exlusion of individual
phenomena; hence, widely differing results may be expected.

Again, the dubiety of the quantification of criteria presents a problem
to literary research in general. But the problem is considerably sharpened
in biblical philology. The Old Testament is the more diligently researched
as to literary tensions and inconsistencies, differing religious outlooks
within narrow literary confines, varying stylistic features, and other
potential material for higher criticism. The reason for this is clear: the
researcher's labors are rewarded with the discovery of elements making
for impressive hypotheses about the origin and growth of the literature.
In the case of modern literature, the reward for those who engage in such
enterprise is, generally speaking, substantially less. The smaller or the
less likely the reward, the less awareness of these imponderables and the
less energetic the search for them. It is an old and unphilological story:
the hope for reward creates proof texts.

These three points taken together render far less formidable the quantitative aspect of the objection to the use of modern examples for the
study of ancient literature. But the objection in its essential aspect is
altogether without merit for the following reasons.

One. In what is probably the majority of cases, the critical analysis of
Old Testament texts takes its departure from what may broadly be called
literary faults and incongruities: unmotivated changes of names, contradictions, repetitions, and the like.[21] Now the proportionately few occur-

---

[21] A remark on these faults and incongruities is in order. There are contradictions in
the Old Testament which are so obvious and of such substance that they require the
assumption that the texts featuring them are composite or glossed. A celebrated case is Ex
6:3 (God speaking to Moses): "I appeared to Abraham, Isaac, and Jacob as El Shaddai,
but I did not make Myself be known to them by My name Yhwh." This statement, dia-
metrically opposed to several passages in Genesis, e.g., 15:2,6,7,8, plays, as a consequence,
an important role in the analysis of the Pentateuch and its critical resolution into literary
strands for which an earlier independent existence is posited.

Since the present study does not deal with the documentary theory, i.e., the analysis
and literary prehistory of biblical texts, I constrain myself to brevity in the following
comments. Incongruities as striking and significant as the contradiction just cited are
often paraded to justify and indeed demonstrate the necessity for critical operations on the
Bible. What requires stress is how rare these incongruities are relative to the totality of

rences of inconsistencies in modern Western texts must be seen greatly to outweigh the proportionately many in the ancient Near East, for standards of consistency (like other features of rationalism) are the property of the heirs of Aristotle's Poetics to a degree far beyond that characterizing the heirs of other cultures. Therefore it is that an argument based on even a few cases of violation of these standards in the West is potent, and even a few Western cases may supply legitimate controls for the testing of universal propositions of Old Testament study.

Two. Any standard brought to bear on Old Testament literature for the purpose of higher criticism is a Western standard; no such standard is formulated in the Old Testament itself and none can be derived from it (as opposed to some noncritical philological standards which can; for instance, standards of poetical parallelism). If this be granted, works of modern Western literature may not be deemed unsuitable for the critical assessment of ancient Israelite literature; especially if, for considerations discussed before, quantitative proportions must be heavily weighted in favor of Western literature. Unless we are prepared to propose the frivolous notion that only Western authors are privileged to disregard Western

operations performed. It is a regrettable fact that critical hypotheses in Old Testament studies are not, or not in the main, built upon faults of so high an order as the contradiction between Ex 6:3 and the Genesis passages; most of the faults which are assigned roles in Old Testament analysis are of a low critical order. A high-order fault very properly alerts the scholar to possible complications in the prehistory of a text, but the specific solution of the problem will be determined by the many more numerous incongruities of a low order; the latter are, for the most part, the bricks and mortar of critical theories in biblical science. The student of the Old Testament who is predisposed to accord critical significance to literary incongruities would do well to arm himself with this consciousness: In criticial arguments the particular premises—the antecedents—which predominantly determine the nature of theories derive, for the most part, from the inconspicuous incongruities of a low order, this merely by virtue of the relative mass of these incongruities, and not from the impressive ones of a high order. He would further do well to remember that the number of low-order incongruities that figure in biblical criticism is as large as it is precisely because standards of purported literary incongruities are so lax. When the critical method admits in evidence for the reconstruction of a unit's prehistory minuscle irregularities of grammar, style, logic of narrative plot, religious beliefs, or, to name yet another example, correspondence between literary description and historical reality, the high number of irregularities at the disposal of the critic will inevitably result in a high number of possible reconstructions. Again inevitably, this will eventuate in a low quality of the resulting theories of prehistory.

standards, we shall be constrained to accept that the literary standards applied to the Old Testament by modern research for the purpose of higher criticism—standards which are generally not so applied in the criticism of modern Western literature—are unreasonably stringent.

Here the reader might take issue with the recommendation following from the preceding paragraphs to relax critical standards for certain kinds of exegesis and rethink the critical approach of Old Textament philology. He might be concerned lest such rethinking impair the ability of the exegete to understand his literature. Such concern, however, would not be well founded. If it is true that the prevailing standards of Old Testament scholarship are too stringent, operations shaped and directed by them are likely to be deformed and misdirected. Therefore, the standards are to be relinquished; no impairment to the understanding can possibly follow from the relinquishment of inappropriate standards. This simple logical cognition is complemented by a philological consideration. To look at the text one is studying with an anticipation of finding perfection is unhelpful when it is not misleading. The philologist ought not to maximize for his text an expectation of consistency and unflawed esthetics.

The concluding remarks, I confess, represent more my personal stance than philosophy of philology. I am aware that I may be criticized for counselling underinterpretation. My response: underinterpretation, while bad, is a shade better than overinterpretation. Overinterpretation breeds a host of untestable hypotheses; like the hoped-for nuclear fusion reactor it produces its own fuel. Yet facile hypotheses (in the biblicists' jargon, "bold hypotheses") are more a hindrance than a furtherance of Old Testament science.

Rigor is a requisite ingredient of Old Testament philology as of all science. Rigor, however, may not be posited as existing in the object under investigation but should be recognized as an ideal to be realized in the operations, the methods and, foremost, the epistemological foundations of science. As wrong as it is to expect the authors studied to be always rigorous, so wrong is it to permit the scholar ever to be less than rigorous. Adherence to this principle is indispensible if we are to raise Old Testament philology above the level of common-sense reasoning and set it on what Kant called *den sicheren Gang einer Wissenschaft*.[22]

---

[22] *Die Kritik der reinen Vernunft*, 2nd ed., preface.

Bibliographical Information

"The Meaning of the Book of Job." *Hebrew Union College Annual (HUCA)* 37. Cincinnati, 1966, pp. 73–106.

"The Basic Meaning of the Biblical Sabbath." *Zeitschrift für die alttestamentliche Wissenschaft* 84. Berlin, W. de Gruyter, 1972, pp. 447–459.

"Hagar and the Birth of Ishmael." Unpublished.

"The Biblical Account of the Foundation of the Monarchy in Israel." *Tarbiz* 36. Jerusalem, Magnes, 1966/67, pp. 99–109 (Hebrew).

"The Steadfast House." *HUCA* 34 (1963), pp. 71–82, and *Biblica* 46. Roma, Pontificium Institutum Biblicum, 1965, pp. 353–356.

"Yhwh Ṣeba'ot." HUCA 36 (1965), pp. 49–58.

"God and the Gods in Assembly." *HUCA* 40–41 (1969–1970), pp. 123–137.

"The Death of the Sons of Eli." *The Journal of Bible and Religion* 32. [Missoula,] American Academy of Religion, 1964, pp. 355–358.

"The Throne Vision of Isaiah." זר לגבורות (Z. Shazar Jubilee Volume). Jerusalem, Kiryat Sefer, 1972/73, pp. 161–172 (Hebrew).

"Israelite History and the Historical Books of the Old Testament." Unpublished.

"Common Sense and Hypothesis in Old Testament Study." *Congress Volume Edinburgh 1974 (Vetus Testamentum*, Supplement 28). Leiden, E.J. Brill, 1975, pp. 217–230.

Index

Biblical References

Authors and Subjects